IMAGES
of America

LaRue County

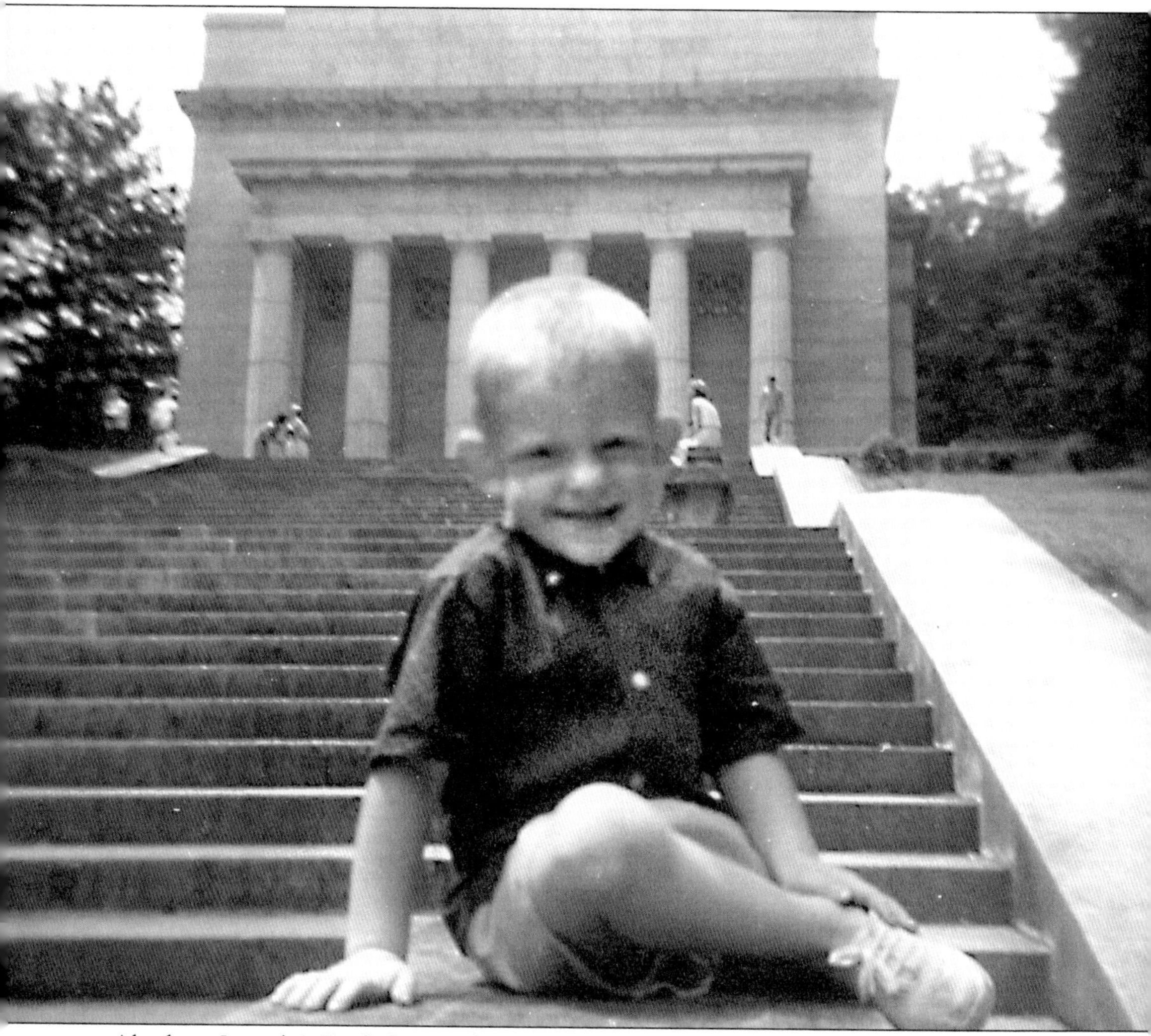

Abraham Lincoln's Birthplace and Picnic Area generates around 200,000 visitors a year from around the world. This photograph was taken of Jesse Douglas Fields in 1965 at Abraham Lincoln's Birthplace, located in Hodgenville, Kentucky. Jesse is the son of Raymond and Elizabeth Priddy Fields. Behind Jesse, are the 56 steps leading up to the Memorial Building. Each step represents one year for Lincoln's life. Inside the memorial, there are 16 columns, which represent Lincoln as our 16th president of the United States. For more information on Abraham Lincoln and LaRue County, go to www.laruecountychamber.org. (Courtesy Patricia Fields Hornback.)

ON THE COVER: This picture of a baptism was taken in the 1890s. The gentleman standing next to the preacher is Will Reynolds. The young boy in the baptism line next to the woman is Doran Bowling. Although it is unclear just where in LaRue County this photograph was taken, it was a very big celebration for this community. The photograph can be seen in full on page 112. (Courtesy Darlene Routt Bryan.)

IMAGES
of America

LaRue County

Rhonda Hornback Nichols

ARCADIA
PUBLISHING

ISBN 978-0-7385-4408-3

Published by Arcadia Publishing
Charleston SC, Chicago IL, Portsmouth NH, San Francisco CA

Printed in the United States of America

Library of Congress Catalog Card Number: 2006936569

For all general information contact Arcadia Publishing at:
Telephone 843-853-2070
Fax 843-853-0044
E-mail sales@arcadiapublishing.com
For customer service and orders:
Toll-Free 1-888-313-2665

Visit us on the Internet at www.arcadiapublishing.com

I dedicate my first book in memory of my father, Marion Lee Hornback. My father was born and raised in LaRue County, where he lived his whole life. My father taught me to be strong and independent, how to drive tractors, and to work together as a family on our farm. He had a special gift for farming; although he worked long, hard hours, he truly enjoyed being a steward of the land. I have always been very proud to be a Hornback and of my country upbringing. I never truly understood how much my father sacrificed for our family until he was ripped from our lives on June 4, 1996. I started out writing this book in hopes of sharing my father with you and the area in which I grew up, called LaRue County.

Contents

ACKNOWLEDGMENTS

First and foremost, I would like to thank my Heavenly Father, for without Him, I would be nothing. He opened so many doors for this country girl from LaRue County. I deeply appreciate Kendra Allen from Arcadia Publishing for believing in me and assisting any way she could. She was a godsend to me. A special thanks goes to Arcadia Publishing and everyone involved for allowing me to share a part of LaRue County with the world. I have a deep appreciation for those who have paved the way in genealogical and research work. Thanks to my father and mother for inspiring me to write this book. Sincere thanks to my husband, Bill; my children, Victoria and Alexander; my mother, Patricia; and my brother, Stephen, for helping me stay sane, their valuable input, words of encouragement, and all of the running we did to get this book together. I deeply thank all of those wonderful people who invited me into their homes to share in their private collections of photographs, sharing their personal stories, for without you, I could not have written this book. Thanks to Darlene Routt Bryan for the wonderful image for the cover of the book, chosen by Arcadia Publishing. I would like to thank Mary Kathryn Puckett, Beatrice Gibson, Alva Martin Tharp, June Routt, Darlene Rout Bryan, Linda Routt Daniels, and Patricia Hornback for entrusting me to use whatever photographs I wanted. A special thanks to all my photograph contributors. Thanks to Beatrice Hornback Gibson for supplying me with information on Mount Tabor Baptist Church in Buffalo, Kentucky, and Pat "Cookie" and Bobbie Walsh for supplying information on Oak Hill Baptist Church. Thanks to Shirley Lucas, department manager from the Elizabethtown, Kentucky, Wal-Mart Photo Lab for assisting me with my photographs. A special thanks goes to our UPS driver, Mickey Underwood, for delivering all of my Arcadia articles with a smile and enthusiasm. Thank you, reader, for purchasing a copy of my first book. If I have left anyone out, I am truly sorry, but please know that I thank you from the bottom of my heart.

INTRODUCTION

The Bluegrass State of Kentucky gained its statehood in 1792, becoming the 15th state admitted to the Union. On June 20, 1792, five commissioners—John Allen, Henry Lee, John Edwards, Robert Todd, and Thomas Kennedy—chose a location for the state's capital. They choose Frankfort, named for a German city, Frankfurt. Kentucky is greatly known for its fine racehorses, burley tobacco, and whiskey. The rolling hills and highly fertile fields produce many agriculture items such as corn, soybeans, wheat, fruit, hogs, cattle, and dairy products. The state is famous for people such as boxer Muhammad Ali; country music singers such as Crystal Gayle, Loretta Lynn, Wynona Judd, Naomi Judd, and Bill Monroe; actors Johnny Depp, Ashley Judd, and George Clooney; all were born here in Kentucky. Kentucky Derby Horse Racing officially opened in 1875 at Churchill Downs in Louisville, Kentucky.

Kentucky has 120 counties that make up 39,728 square miles in land area. One of these counties is LaRue County, established in 1843. Immigrants came from New York, North Carolina, South Carolina, Pennsylvania, and Virginia to establish new territories throughout the state. In 1780, a group of pioneers explored land around the Nolynn River. Robert Hodgen, one of these settlers, built a mill along the Nolynn River in 1788. In 1818, Sarah Hodgen petitioned the courts to have this settlement named after her husband. The town was named Hodgenville. LaRue County is most famously known as the birthplace of our 16th president, Abraham Lincoln. Lincoln Days is held every second Saturday in October in Hodgenville. There are many historical facts and stories written on Kentucky, LaRue County, and Pres. Abraham Lincoln, all of which make up the history of LaRue County. But there are many other unsung heroes that we may never know who contributed and sacrificed to make LaRue County what it is today. These were our grandfathers and grandmothers, great-great-aunts and -uncles, and friends and neighbors who built our early churches and schools and who now fill our cemeteries. These early settlers laid the foundation for us to build upon and strengthen this land

I can recall hearing stories of my ancestors growing up in the horse and buggy days. Dresses were made from feed sacks with printed patterns on them, and white feed sacks were bleached, and undergarments were made from those. When farmers would head into town for sacks of grain, he would ask his wife which pattern she would prefer to finish her dress or curtains she would be working on. Children's clothing was all hand-sewn or inherited hand-me-down clothes from older siblings or cousins. Before running water and bathrooms, water could be carried from a creek or a hand-dug well. Bathrooms were little buildings at the back of the house called outhouses. Babies were often born at home without the comforts of a hospital with the doctor or midwife. Children walked to school and were taught how to read and write in a one-room school building filled with children of all ages. A wood stove would keep children warm in the wintertime. Houses and barns were built with timber wood cut right off of the land on which the family lived. All the meat, eggs, milk, butter, and soap could be made supplied from home. Sometimes the only two products people would need from the local merchant would be flour and sugar. Women canned everything from meats to fruits and vegetables right out of their own garden. When hogs were killed, no part of the hog was left unused. Fresh chickens, turkeys, and eggs supplied families with fresh meat. Tobacco leaves were rolled to make cigarettes or chewing tobacco. Moonshine stills were run throughout the countryside. Neighbors would get together and help each other with crops or raise barns together. Women would walk throughout the neighborhood to bring chicken soup, breads, or desserts when friends and relatives were sick. In small, close-knit communities, families often were intertwined; two sisters of one family may very well marry neighbor brothers. One family may have as many as 10 to 15 children. Large families were very important in the 1800s and early 1900s—more hands to work on the farm. In the Oak Hill community, it has been said that you either are a Hornback or married one. Some have told me, "We didn't know we were poor back then, it was just a way of life." Although this way of life no doubt could be very difficult, those were some of the best times had. I hope you enjoy this book. For some, it may be a reminder of good times had and others a new insight. I welcome any photographs or stories to be used in later books.

Rhonda Hornback Nichols
2328 Oak Hill Road
Sonora, Kentucky 42776
nichols994@aol.com

One

Humble Beginnings

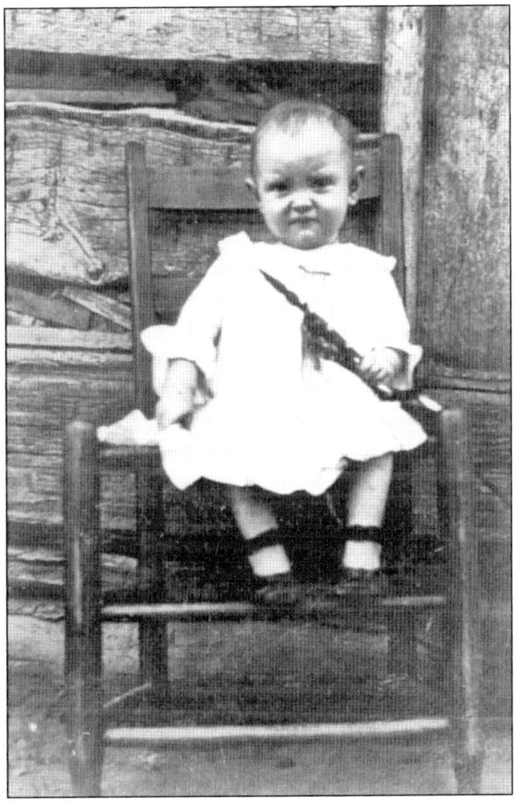

Alma Ruth Quinn poses in a straight-back chair with an American flag held tightly in her little hand in June 1919. World War I had just ended, and it provided a newfound sense of patriotism. With so many deaths or absences from the local men gone off to war, women were forced into the workforce in great numbers. At the same time, industries needed to replace workers who left to fight in the war. These circumstances laid the difficult path for voting rights for women. (Courtesy Darlene Routt Bryan.)

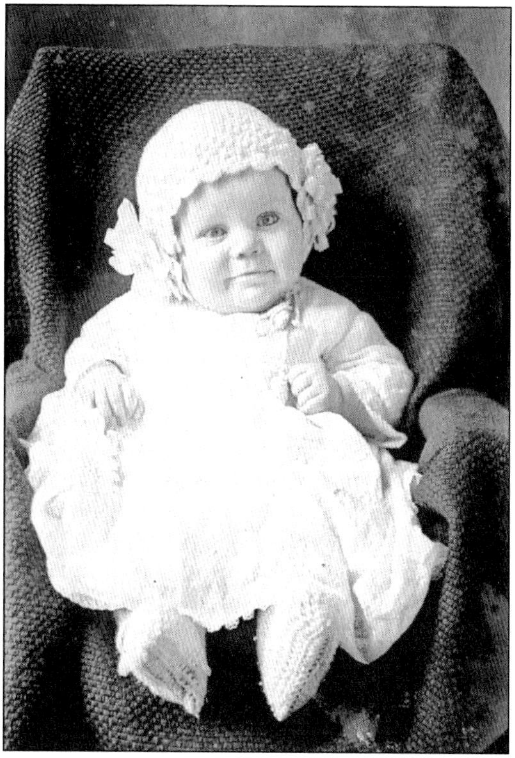

Irene Hudgins was six months and three days old when this photograph was taken in 1922. Grandmothers, mothers, and aunts crocheted baby blankets, bonnets, and booties for newborns as heirlooms to be passed down from generation to generation. There was a variety of patterns used in creating these gifts. (Courtesy Darlene Routt Bryan.)

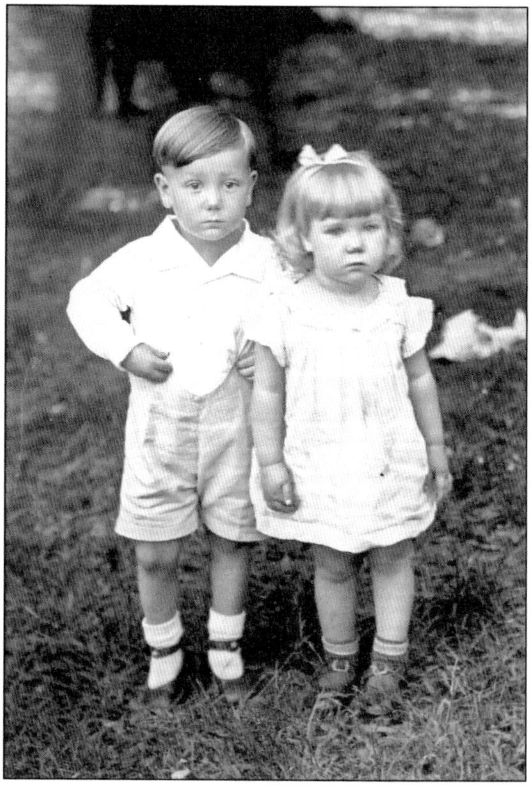

Donald Lee Puckett (three-and-a-half years old) and his sister, Helen Jane Puckett (two years old), was photographed at a county fair in Munfordville, Kentucky, on October 1, 1932. County fairs were important to small communities because they gave farmers a chance to show their prized heifers and pigs. The ladies could show off pickles, jams, and jellies or their favorite recipes. The children looked forward to the sounds and smells of baked goods in the air along with carnival rides. It was a day to get all dressed up and socialize with other members in the community. (Courtesy Donald Puckett.)

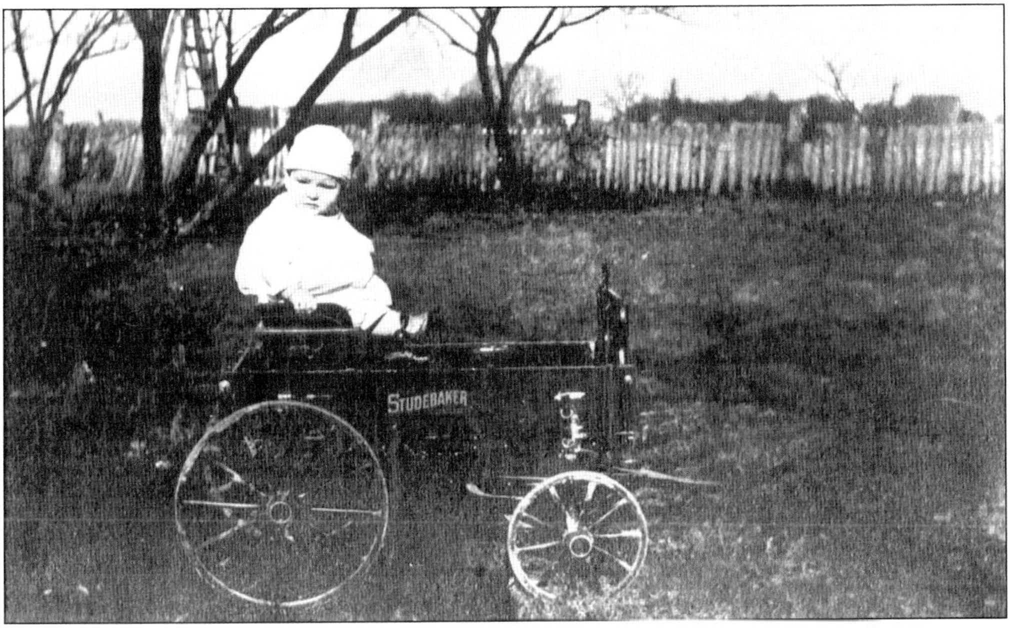

Arleigh Monroe Gibson, born October 15, 1917, in Buffalo, Kentucky, is posed in this miniature Studebaker farm wagon in front of an orchard. Note the ladder in the midst of the trees. H&C Studebaker Brothers ran a blacksmith shop in 1852. Studebaker was the only manufacturer of horse-drawn wagons to successfully switch to gasoline-powered automobiles. (Courtesy Beatrice Hornback Gibson.)

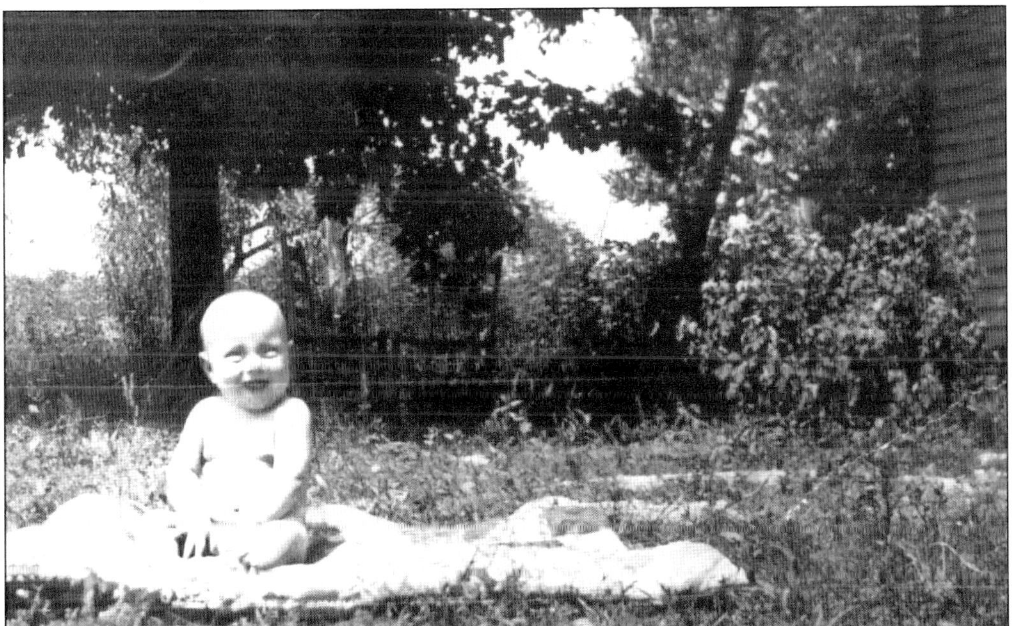

Alva Martin Tharp, a local dairy farmer and oral historian, was born December 5, 1919, in Sonora, Kentucky. Tharp has farmed and worked on farm machinery his whole life. He still lives in the house where he grew up. He has known several generations of local families and has been an excellent source of anecdotes and information to the author. (Courtesy Alva Martin Tharp.)

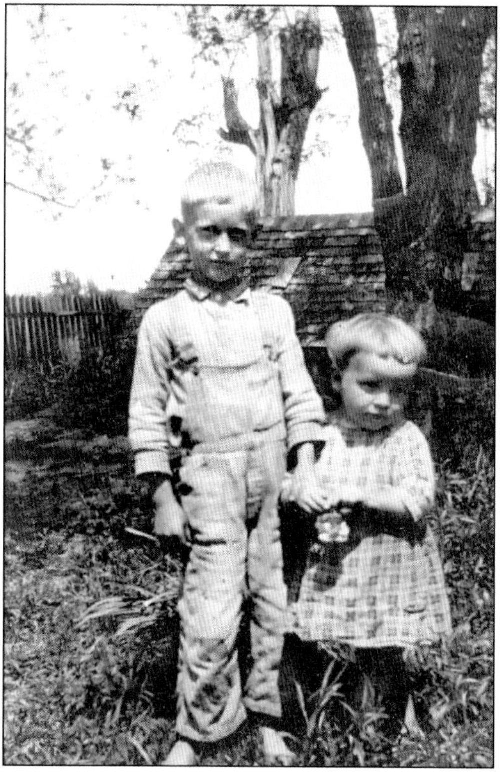

Claude and Lura Tharp, two of the children of Christopher Columbus and Sallie M. Hornback Tharp, were born in Hodgenville, Kentucky. Claude, born April 4, 1912, and Lura, born August 21, 1916, lived in LaRue County until the death of their father in 1933. After this, they moved to Champaign, Illinois, to live with their sister, Lena Tharp Routt. Claude married Christine Kathryn Reifsteck on November 3, 1934, and had three children. He farmed and later had his own construction business. As a small child, Lura was stricken with polio. She later married Clifford Robert Lorenz on September 8, 1945, and the couple had a daughter, Joan Lorenz Waldbusser. They ran a bait shop out of their garage. (Courtesy Joan Lorenz Waldbusser.)

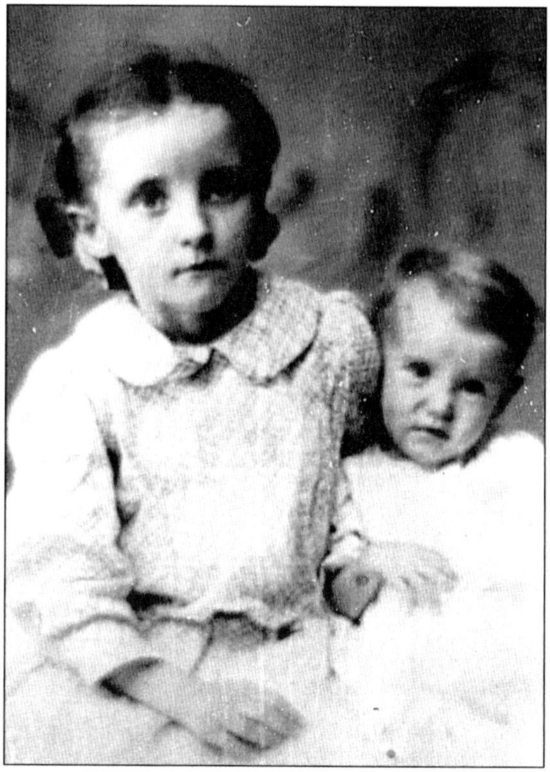

Sisters Lena (left) and Blanche Tharp are photographed together. Blanche Tharp later died in childhood. Before the use of vaccines in the United States, childhood diseases often claimed the lives of many children. In 1796, the United States was licensed to use the smallpox vaccine, although it didn't become widespread until 1900. Measles and diphtheria were common diseases in the 1920s, and the United States was licensed in 1963 to use these vaccines. (Courtesy Joan Lorenz Waldbusser.)

In the 19th century, photography developed into commercial use. This professional photograph was taken around 1904 of Edmond Routt, the son of Samuel and Mary Jane Reasor Routt. In 1884, George Eastman from New York developed a dry gel on paper or film. In 1888, George produced his Kodak camera, which went on sale with the slogan "you push the button, we do the rest." (Courtesy Darlene Routt Bryan.)

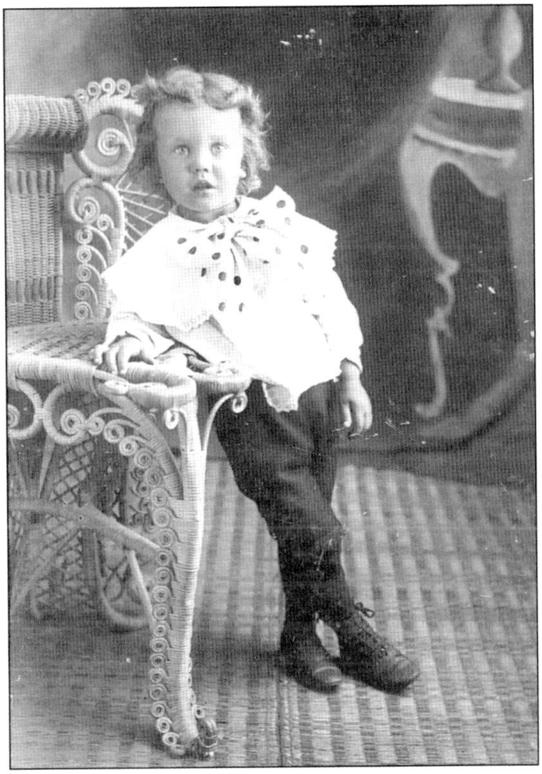

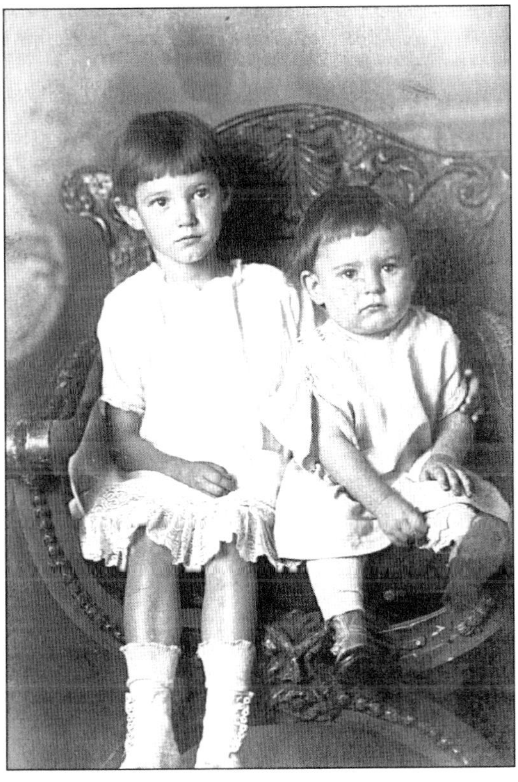

Louise and Walter Angel, pictured, were the children of Charles and Irene Hornback Angel. Charles Angel worked for the Louisville and Nashville Railroad Company as a car repairman. Although Charles and Irene were from LaRue County, business with the railroad would lead them to Florida to raise their children. (Courtesy Beatrice Hornback Gibson.)

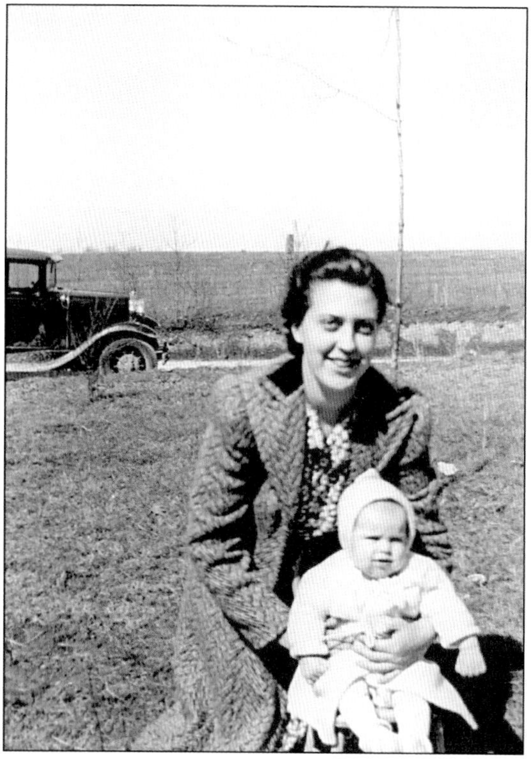

Juanita Hornback poses with her son, Marion Lee Hornback, in her front yard in Sonora, Kentucky. Marion was born October 21, 1942, while his father, Steve, was away serving in the army. Juanita was the daughter of Elzie and Jo Robinson Hornback. (Courtesy Patricia Fields Hornback.)

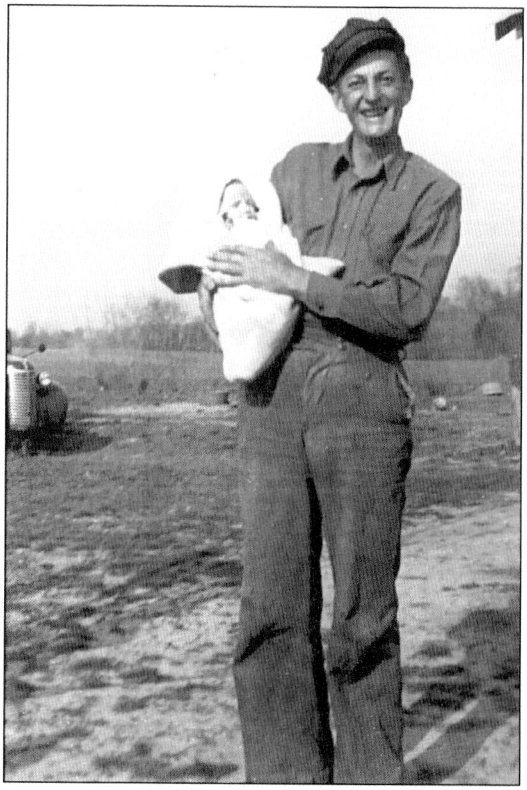

David Underwood proudly holds Darlene Routt. David was a neighbor and good friend to the Routts. He was a farmer and lived in Hodgenville. Darlene Routt, now a retired nurse, married Billy Bryan and lives in Sonora. (Courtesy Darlene Routt Bryan.)

William Leslie Hornback Jr. is photographed in this baby buggy with his doll. This photograph was taken around 1922. Decades later, the doll was discovered with some items left under a stairwell; Patricia Hornback rescued the doll and had it restored. William is the son of William Leslie and Maude Pearl Jackson Hornback. William Hornback Jr. went on to become an FBI agent. (Courtesy Patricia Fields Hornback.)

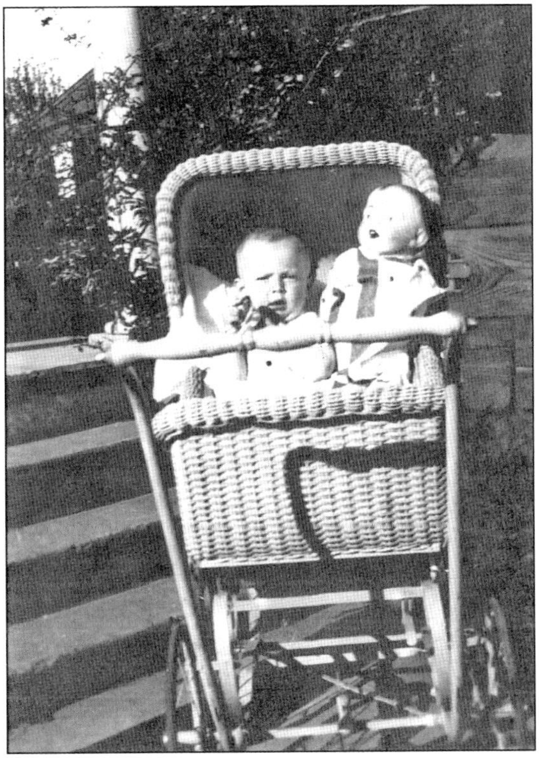

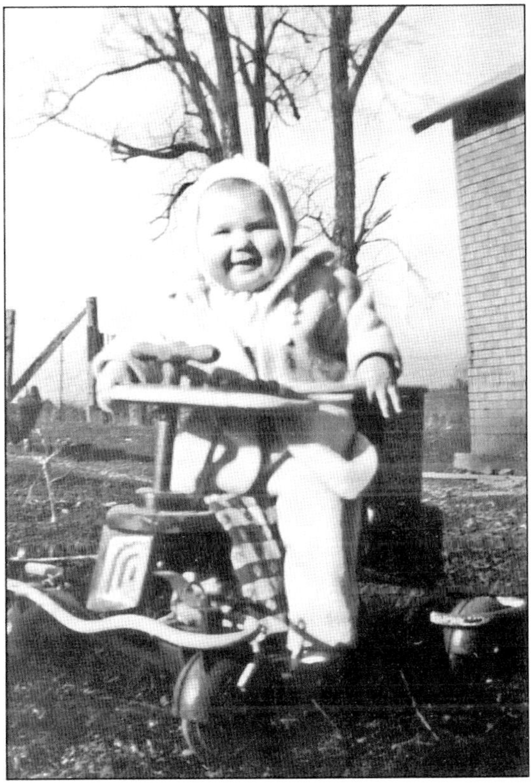

Martha Priddy smiles at the photographer and seems pretty content just sitting around on her toy scooter. Martha, the daughter of Josie Routt Priddy, was born around 1945. (Courtesy Darlene Routt Bryan and Linda Routt Daniels.)

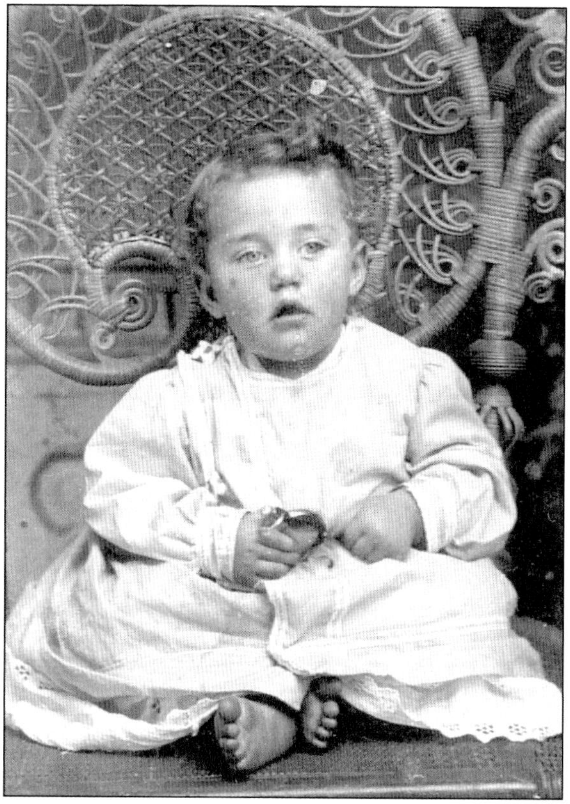

Virgil Allen Wheeler was born March 11, 1909, in Buffalo, Kentucky. Virgil lived in LaRue County the first seven years of his life. The family later would move to Illinois, where he died in April 1978. (Courtesy Pat Wheeler Lassonde.)

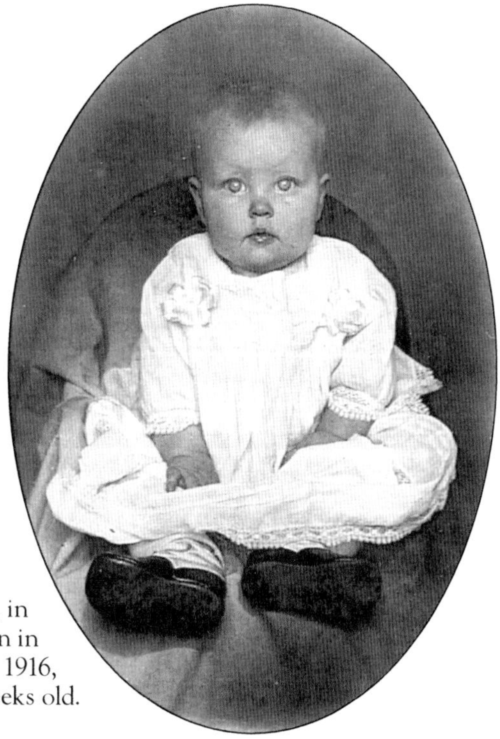

David Green Wheeler was born January 24, 1916, in Hodgenville, Kentucky. Although David was born in LaRue County, his parents moved to Illinois in 1916, traveling by covered wagon, when he was six weeks old. (Courtesy Pat Wheeler Lassonde.)

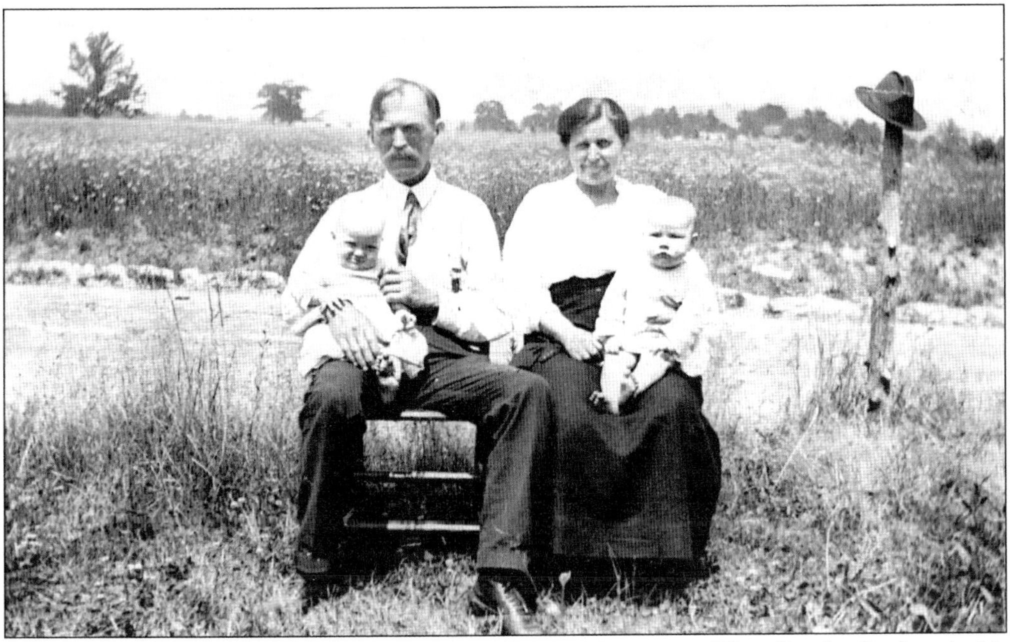

Ira Harry Puckett holds his daughter, Virginia Mae. Margurette Ellen Renfro Puckett holds Virginia's twin, Catherine. The Renfros lived on their farm in Upton, LaRue County. Ira Puckett was born August 8, 1872. Margurette Renfro Puckett was born November 3, 1876. Note the hat hanging on the corner post next to the cornfield. (Courtesy Kathy Hensley Cooke.)

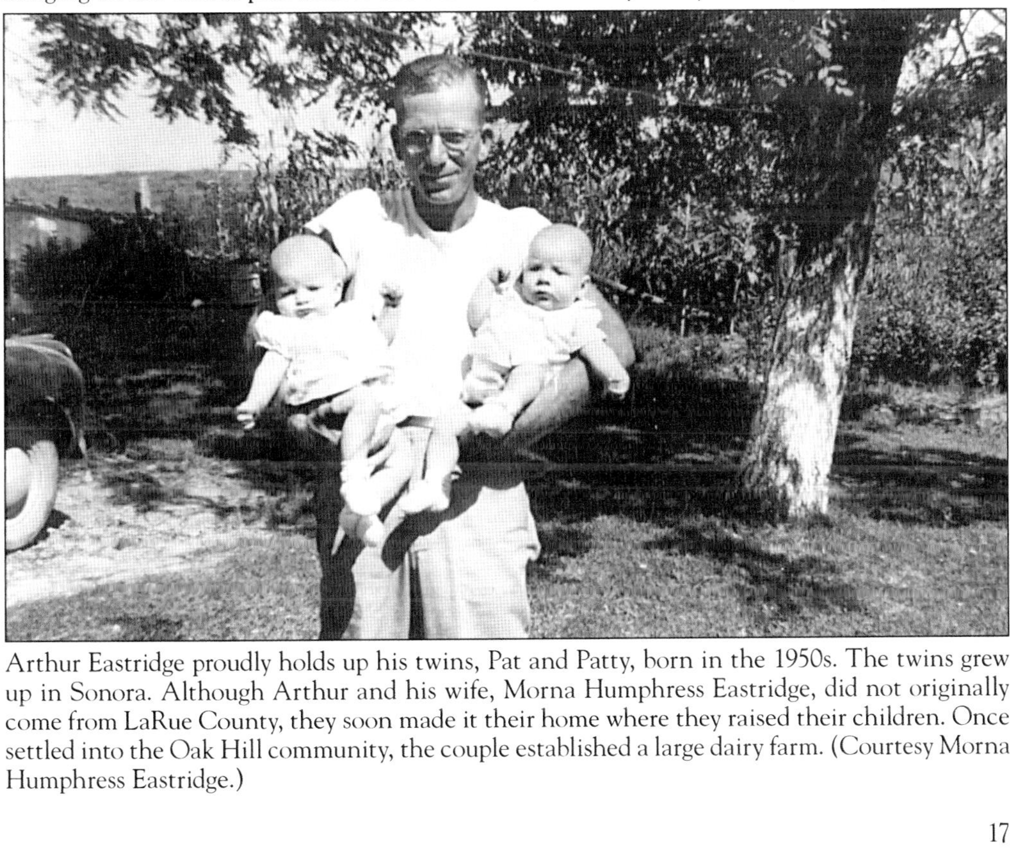

Arthur Eastridge proudly holds up his twins, Pat and Patty, born in the 1950s. The twins grew up in Sonora. Although Arthur and his wife, Morna Humphress Eastridge, did not originally come from LaRue County, they soon made it their home where they raised their children. Once settled into the Oak Hill community, the couple established a large dairy farm. (Courtesy Morna Humphress Eastridge.)

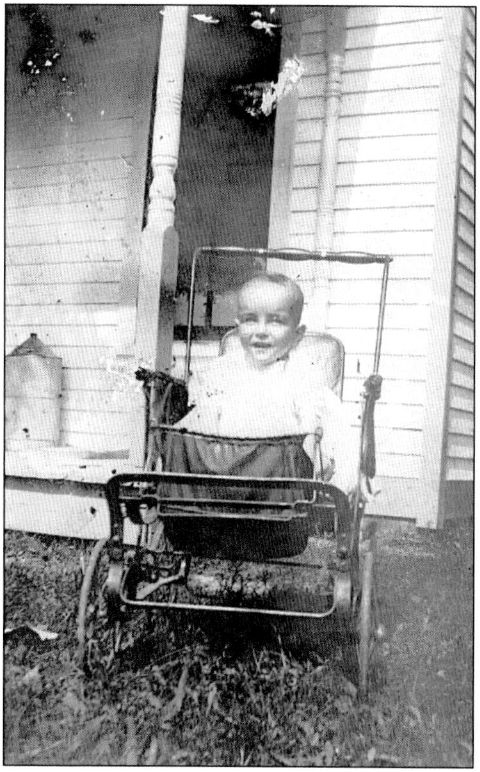

Charles "June" Routt Jr. is photographed in his stroller. June, as he likes to be called, was born in June 1920. He lives in the same farmhouse his parents started out in a century ago. June is famous for his mules, and he has a room full of trophies and ribbons he has won at the LaRue County Fair. (Courtesy Darlene Routt Bryan.)

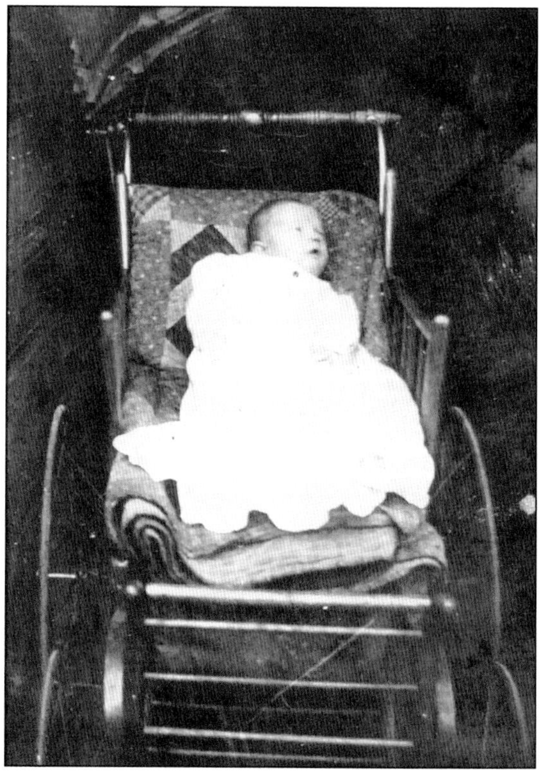

Katherine Hornback was born in 1921 and did not live to see her adult years because of complications of diabetes. She was the daughter of John Wesley and Ella Lee Wheeler Hornback. This photograph was in the private collection of Steve and Juanita Hornback. (Courtesy Shirley Hornback Miller.)

Curt Philpott and Dorothy Hornback are pictured while they were courting. A short time later, the couple was married and raised two daughters, Anna Mae and Mary Catherine, in Upton, Kentucky. Dorothy is the daughter of Elzie Curtis and Jo Robinson Hornback and now resides in Bloomfield, Kentucky. (Courtesy Beatrice Hornback Gibson.)

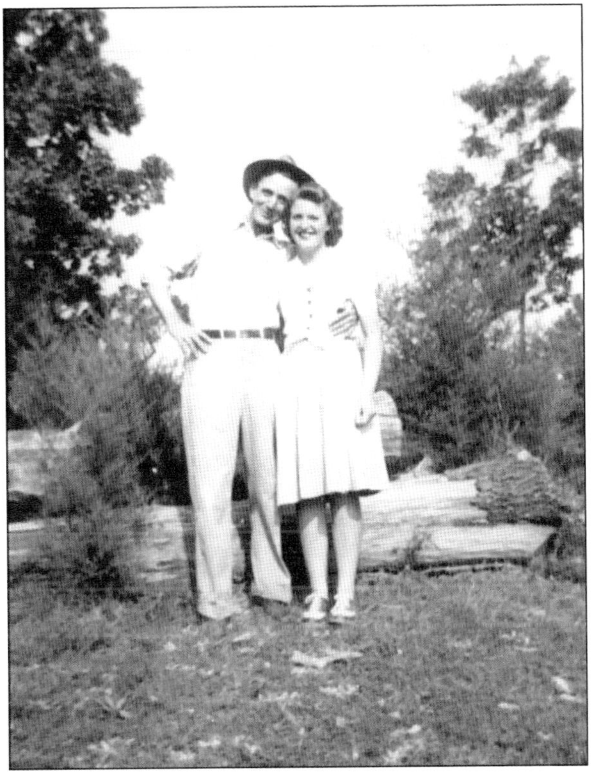

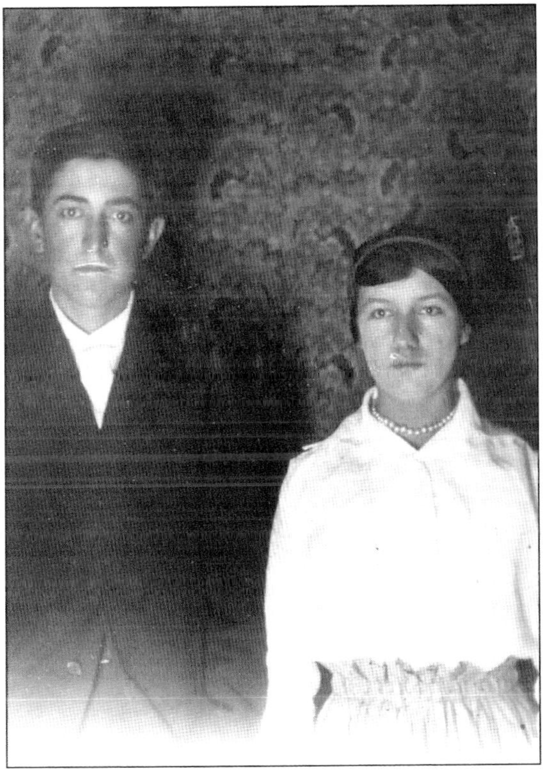

Elzie Curtis Hornback and Annie Pennington were cousins who lived in the Oak Hill community in Sonora, Kentucky. Elzie Hornback was the son of William Leslie and Maude Pearl Jackson. Annie Pennington was the daughter of James and Martha Hornback Pennington and was born c. 1900. (Courtesy Mary Kathryn Pennington Puckett.)

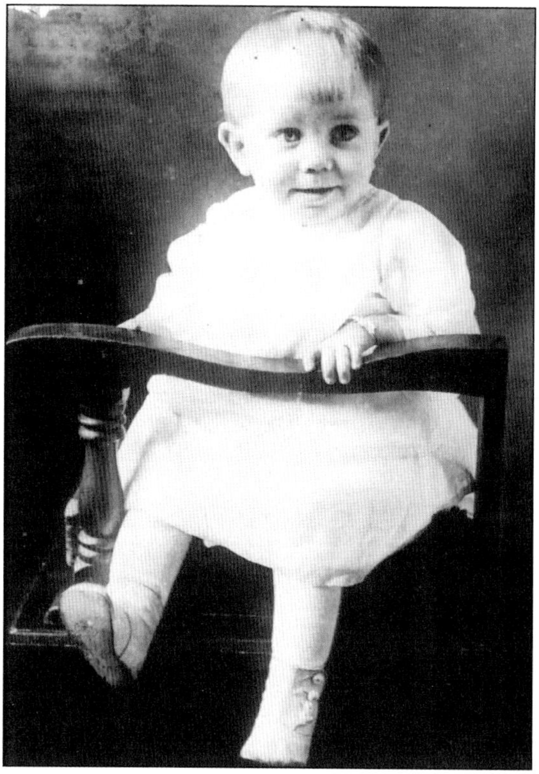

Irene Hudgins, the daughter of Bowlin and Pearlie Mae Routt Hudgins, sits on the side of this sitting stool. Her button-up shoes show that she is ready for walking. The hard, solid bottom of the shoe provides a firm foundation and prepares the child to take her first steps. (Courtesy Darlene Routt Bryan and Linda Routt Daniels.)

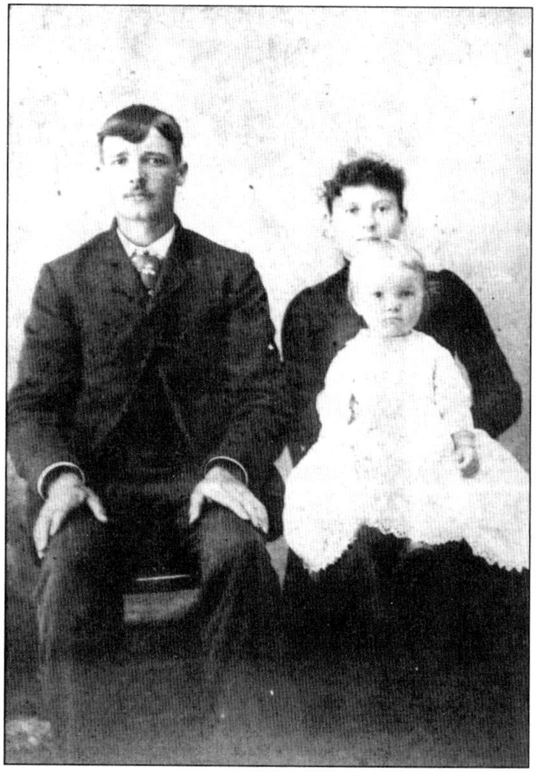

Henry B. Jackson and Minnie Belle Jackson pose with a baby, believed to be Mary Ethel Jackson. Henry Jackson was born December 23, 1869. Minnie Bell Jackson was born November 26, 1871, and died January 18, 1900. They were lifelong residents of LaRue County. (Courtesy William Leslie Hornback Jr.)

Dorothy Routt poses in her beautiful wedding gown with an elegant bouquet of anthurium lilies. There is an old poem on how the color of your wedding gown influences your future: "Married in white, you'll have chosen all right. Married in grey, you'll go far away. Married in black, you'll wish yourself back. Married in red, you'll wish yourself dead. Married in blue, you'll always be true. Married in pearl, you'll live in a whirl. Married in green, ashamed to be seen. Married in yellow, ashamed of the fellow. Married in brown, you'll live out of town. Married in pink, your dreams will sink." (Courtesy Darlene Routt Bryan and Linda Routt Daniels.)

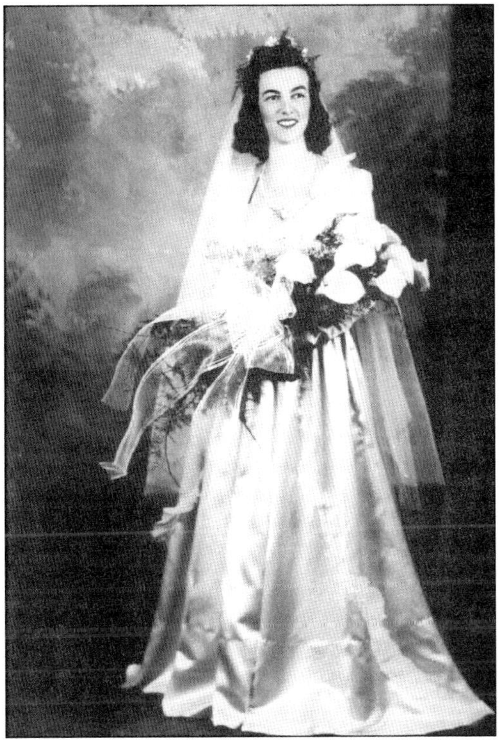

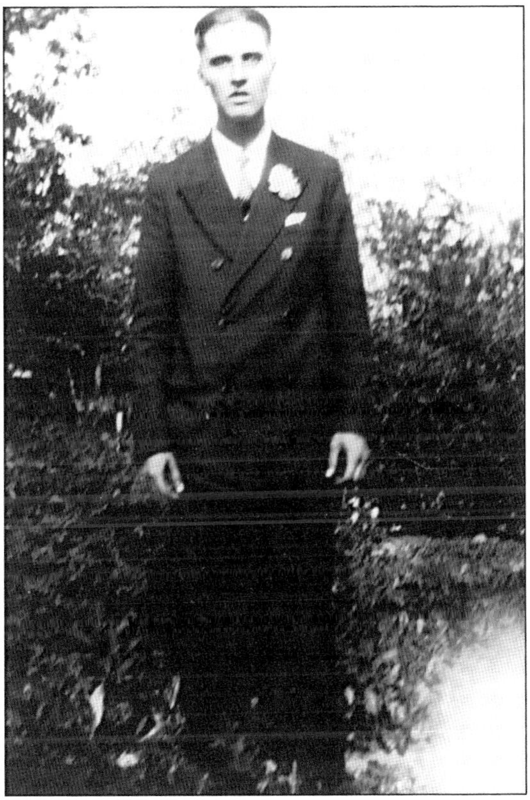

Herman Hornback stands looking solemn on his wedding day. Herman married Bertha Richardson. Herman was the son of John Wesley and Ella Lee Wheeler Hornback. (Courtesy Patricia Fields Hornback.)

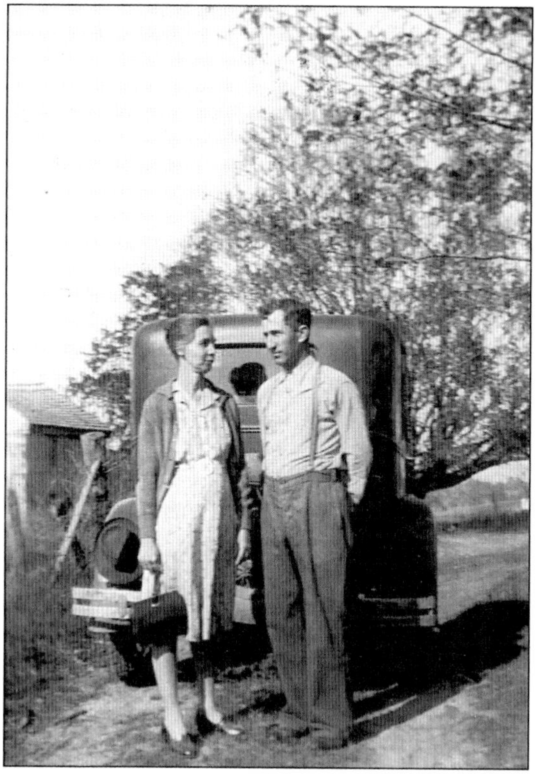

Nannie Hodges Hornback and Ollie Hornback were photographed in the 1920s standing behind their car. They lived in Sonora where Ollie had served as a caretaker of Oak Hill Baptist Church. The church later bought land from Nannie and Ollie for the parsonage. The couple raised two children in the community, Wilburn and Beatrice. (Courtesy Beatrice Hornback Gibson.)

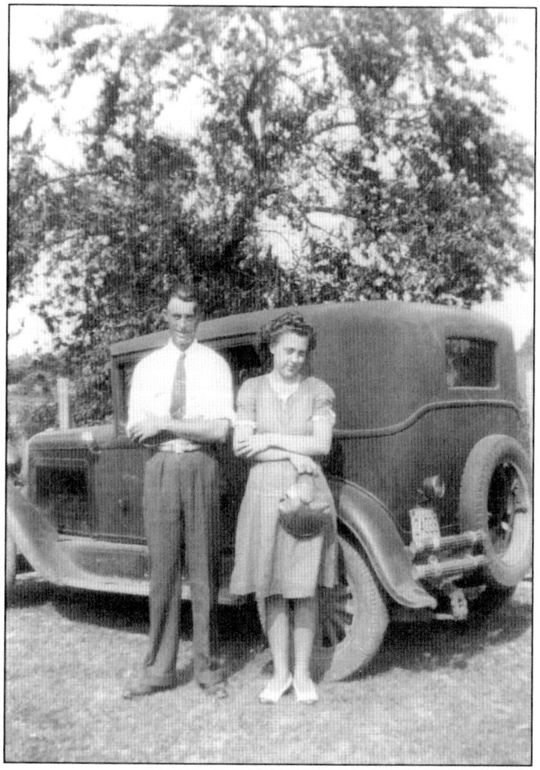

Steve and Juanita Hornback pose behind their car on their wedding day, November 22, 1941. Rev. John S. Roscoe performed the ceremony with Elzie Hornback and Raymond Cobb as witnesses. A celebration for the couple was held at Elzie and Jo Hornback's house. Steve and Juanita started their new life together in Sonora, where they farmed and raised five children. Juanita lost her life on October 23, 1963, in a house fire. Alva Martin Tharp was the first to respond to the fire. He was a neighbor across the field and saw the smoke rolling in the sky. (Courtesy Patricia Fields Hornback.)

William Thomas Hines worked as a logger. He was born January 26, 1879, and died April 27, 1913, as a result of a logging accident in the woods. He was taken to Dr. Smith's Sanitarium where an operation was performed in the attempt to save his life. He died around 11:00 that night. His wife, Myrtle Sue Hines, was born October 5, 1876, and died January 16, 1931. The couple was married in LaRue County on July 11, 1899, and resided in the Leafdale area. He left behind his wife and five children. (Courtesy Jay Wheeler.)

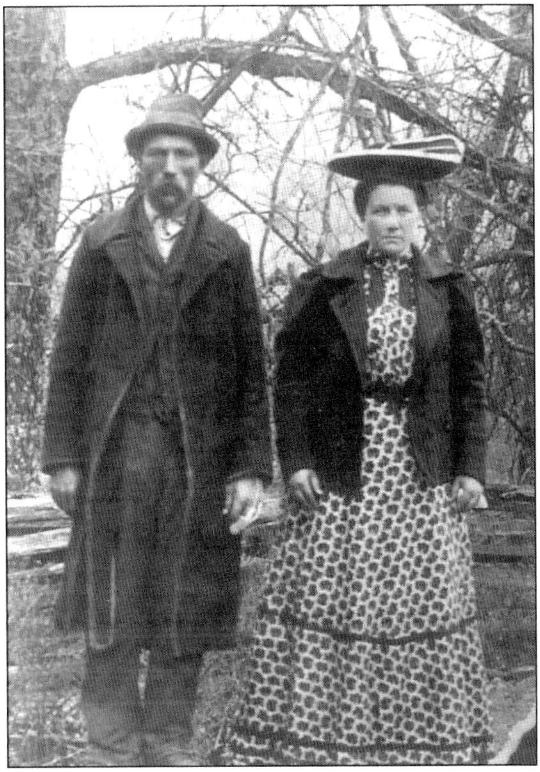

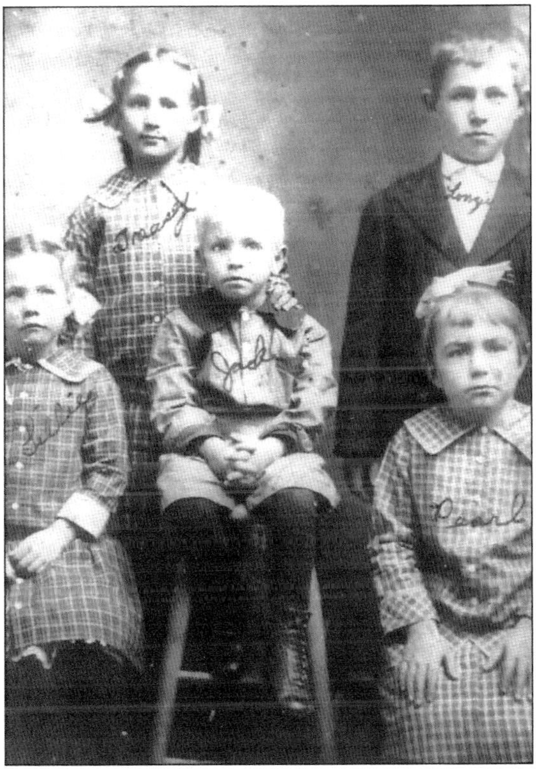

William and Myrtle Hines's children are pictured from left to right: (first row) Lillie, born October 1, 1909; Ernest Jackson "Jack," born April 4, 1911; and Pearl Edna, born October 4, 1908; (second row) Treasey, born January 9, 1907; and Lonzie Logan, born July 18, 1905. Because of financial difficulties, Myrtle Hines could no longer care for her children after the death of William. The children were placed in the Glendale Home. This picture was taken the day they left in their new outfits. Myrtle later remarried David Sidebottom. (Courtesy Jay Wheeler.)

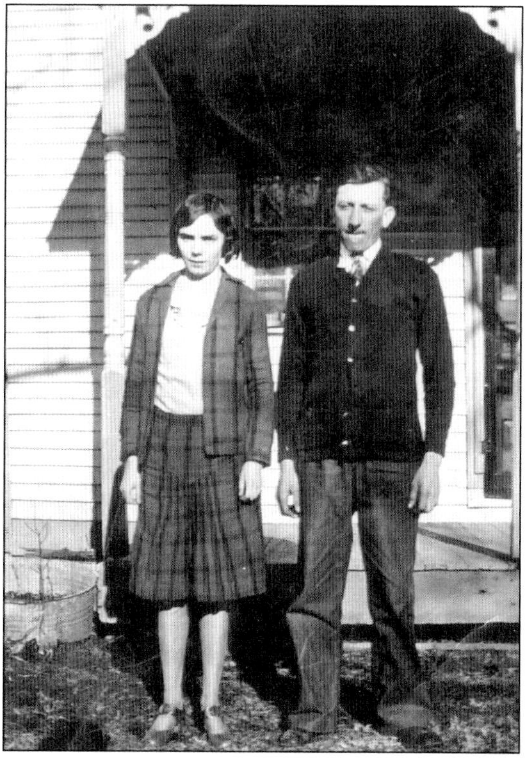

Thelma and Virgil Pennington resided in the Oak Hill community, where Virgil, known as "Penny," served as a deacon and custodian for many years at Oak Hill Baptist Church. Thelma Dye Pennington taught Sunday school and Bible study. This photograph was taken February 19, 1931. (Courtesy Mary Kathryn Pennington Puckett.)

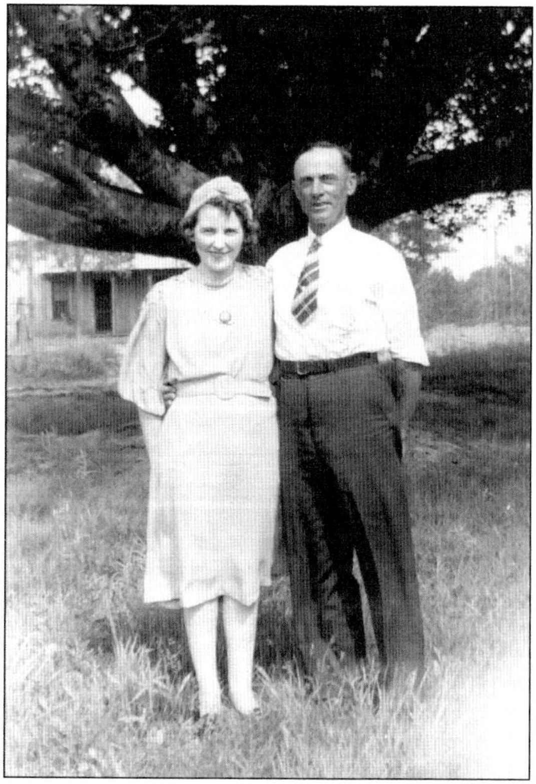

Solon Hornback and his unidentified wife are pictured in front of Ollie and Nannie Hornback's house. Solon lived in the Oak Hill community in Sonora. (Courtesy Beatrice Hornback Gibson.)

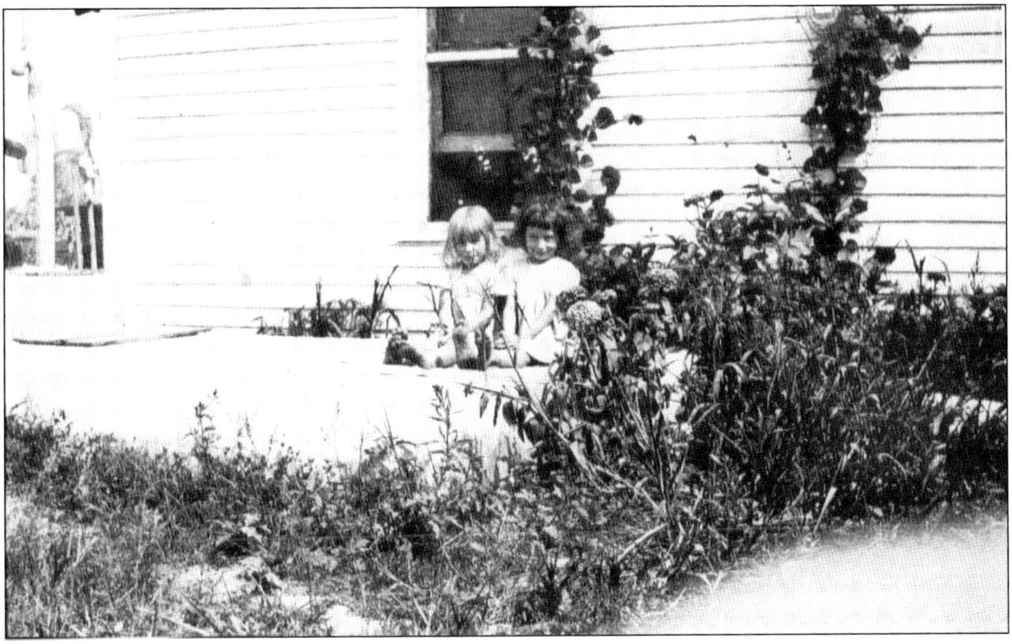

Mary Kathryn and Yvonne Pennington pose at Ed Wheeler's store at Maxine, LaRue County. This photograph was taken August 23, 1940. Country stores played an important role in small communities as a source of socializing. Farmers could purchase supplies, trade crop news, get weather reports, and sell produce. Country stores often sold seed, fertilizer, tools, fresh eggs, candies, and so forth. (Courtesy Mary Kathryn Pennington Puckett.)

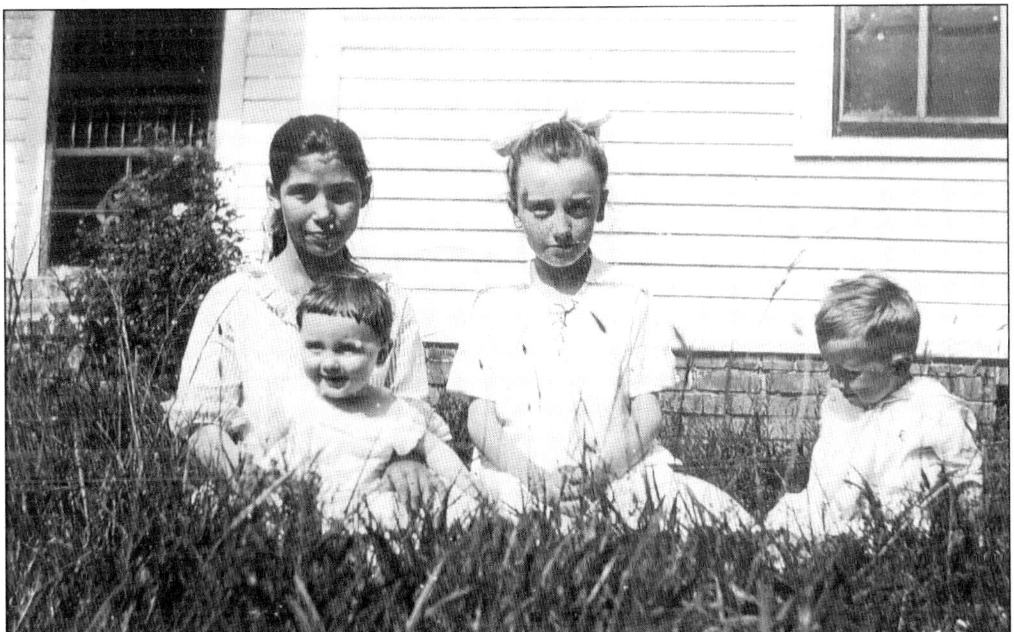

Josie, Maude, Susan, and Brown Routt are pictured in this 1922 photograph. Maude, Susan, and Brown were the children of Lee and Crouch Adams Routt. Josie was a first cousin of the other children. (Courtesy Darlene Routt Bryan and Linda Routt Daniels.)

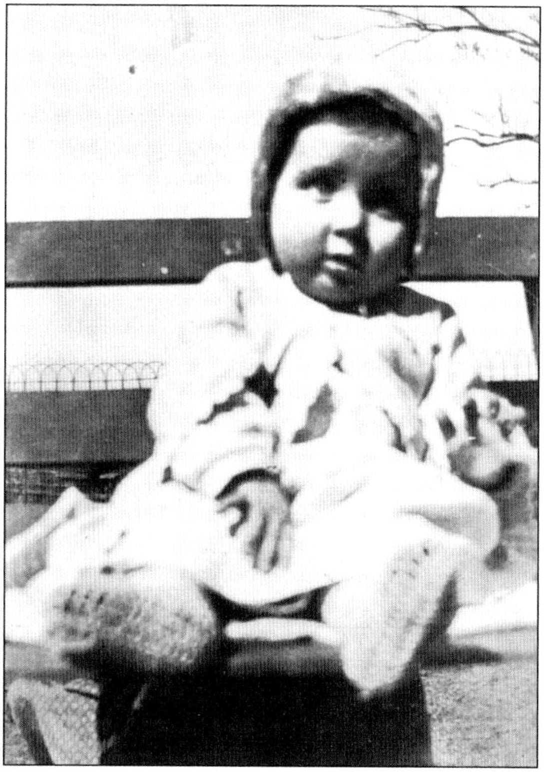

Maude Routt, born in 1920, sits on this bench as the photographer captures her innocent little face. Maude attended Barren Run Baptist Church, where she worked in the church. In her later years, she loved to play Scrabble and was very good with definitions of words. (Courtesy Darlene Routt Bryan and Linda Routt Daniels.)

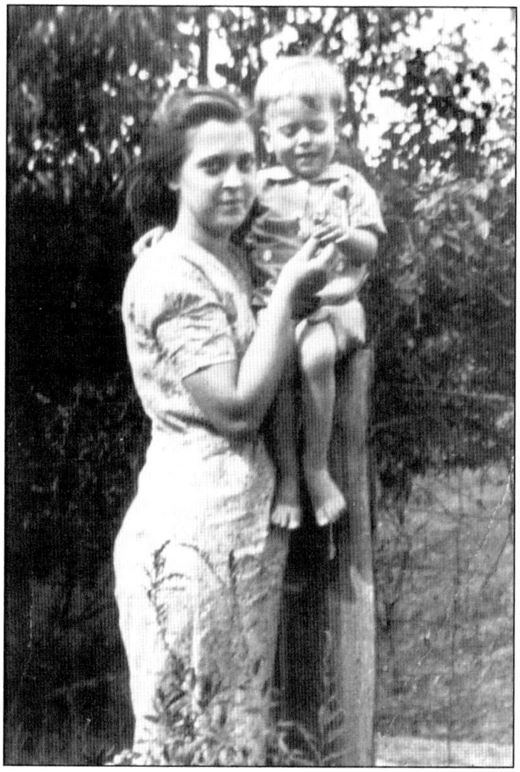

Juanita Hornback stands with her little brother, Charles, in this tender moment between big sister and little brother. Juanita and Charles are the children of Elzie and Jo Robinson Hornback. This photograph was taken in 1939. (Courtesy Patricia Fields Hornback.)

Stephen Ray Hornback hugs his poodle, Mickey. Stephen is the son of Marion and Patricia Fields Hornback and attended Magnolia Elementary School. He graduated from LaRue County High School. Mickey loved to ride in a pickup truck, on the tractor, or in the hay wagon and loved going sleigh riding with Stephen. Mickey would round cattle and once wrestled with a groundhog. He was fearless. (Courtesy Rhonda Hornback Nichols.)

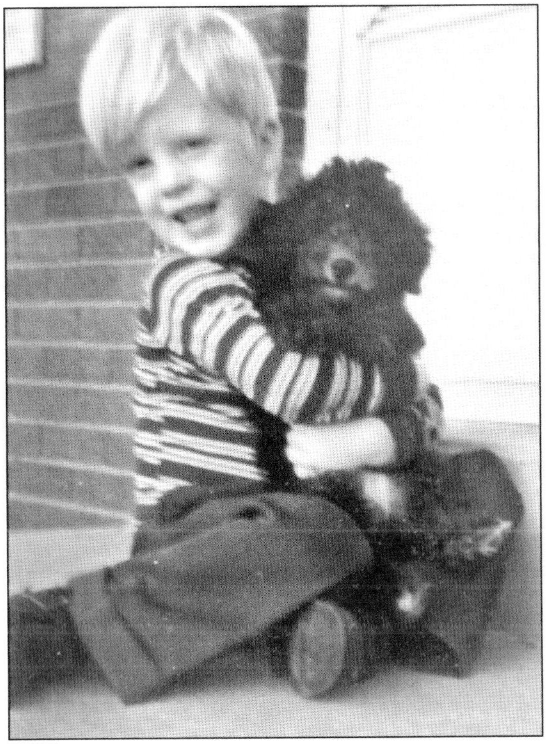

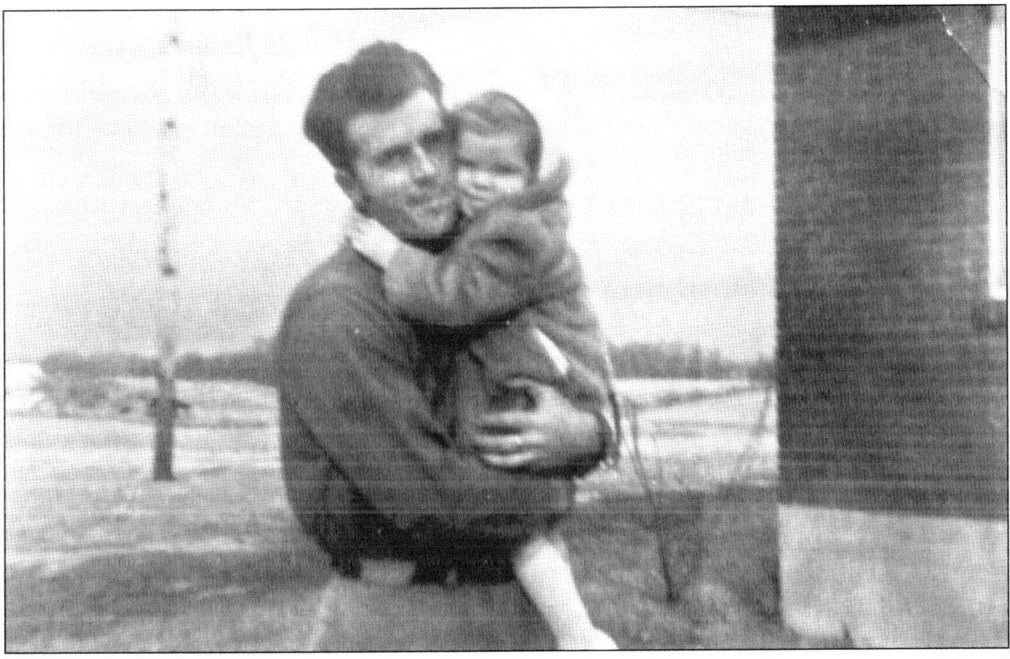

Marion and his daughter, Rhonda Hornback, the author, share a tender moment as "Mom," Patricia, snaps their picture. This new brick home stands where once stood what was called the "Old Tone Routt Place." Alva Martin Tharp recalls having played music at a "music party" in which neighbors would get together and play their musical instruments. Alva Martin Tharp played the guitar, and Tone Routt played the fiddle. (Courtesy Rhonda Hornback Nichols.)

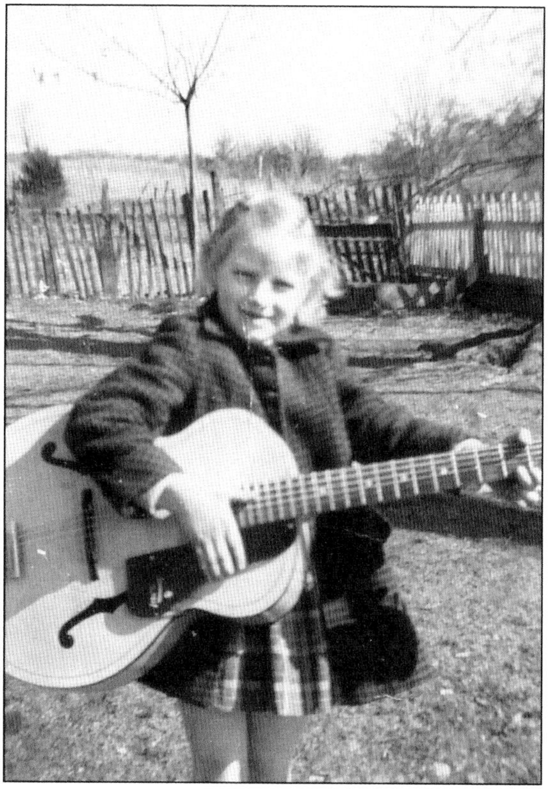

Patricia Ann Fields is the daughter of Raymond and Elizabeth Priddy Fields. Although she was born in Hart County on March 11, 1949, she and her family moved to LaRue County during her elementary school years in 1959. Patricia attended Magnolia Elementary School and LaRue County High School. Patricia and her brother, Raymond Fields, sang an arrangement by the history teacher, Mrs. Haney, at the dedication of the new LaRue County Public Library in the early 1960s. They sang two songs, one of which was "Dixie Land." (Courtesy Patricia Fields Hornback.)

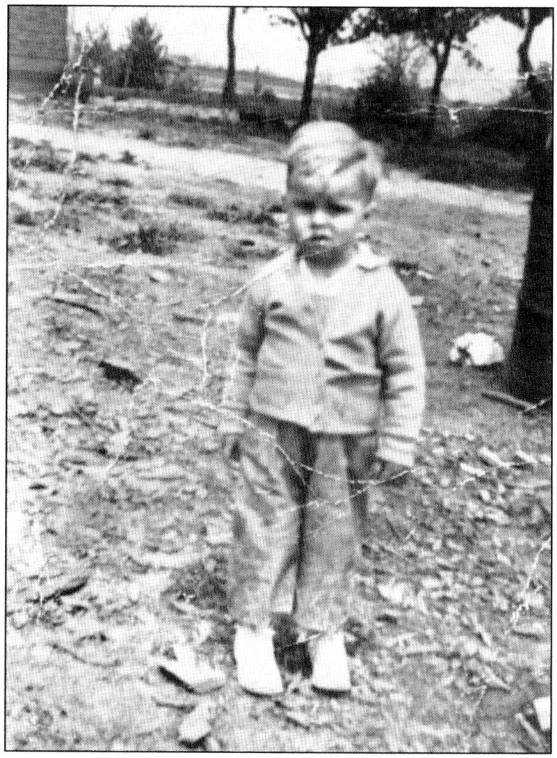

Marion Lee Hornback was born in LaRue County on October 21, 1942, the son of Steve and Juanita Hornback. A born farmer, Marion raised purebred Simmental beef cattle, burley tobacco, alfalfa, corn, wheat, pigs, and dairy cows. He ran for sheriff in the mid-1980s. He also started his own construction business in the early 1970s. Marion built the Agrico building, which is now called Crop Production, in Hodgenville. (Courtesy Patricia Fields Hornback.)

Patricia Fields and Marion Hornback were married on November 18, 1967, at Pleasant Hill Baptist Church in Upton, Kentucky. Marion was a member of Oak Hill Baptist Church of Sonora, where Patricia later joined. They were married by Rev. Edmond "Sonny" Fields, who got his license just so he could marry the two. (Courtesy Patricia Fields Hornback.)

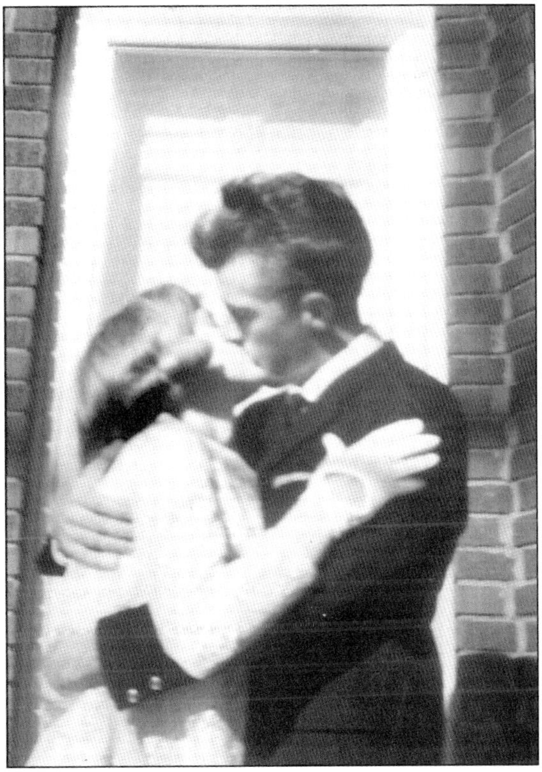

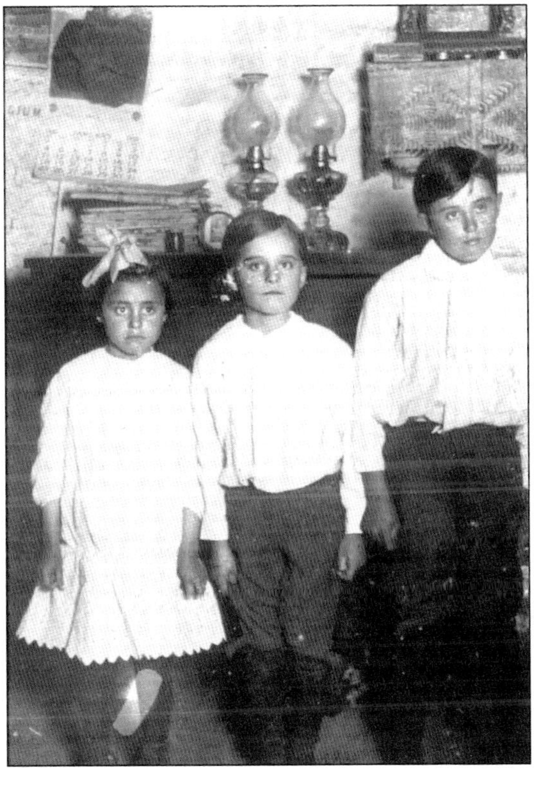

Pictured from left to right, Blanch, Herman, and Steve Hornback were the children of John Wesley and Ella Lee Wheeler Hornback. John and Ella were married in 1909. The couple raised their family in the Oak Hill community in Sonora. The children would walk through the woods to the Oak Hill School building. This photograph was taken January 1920. (Courtesy Patricia Fields Hornback.)

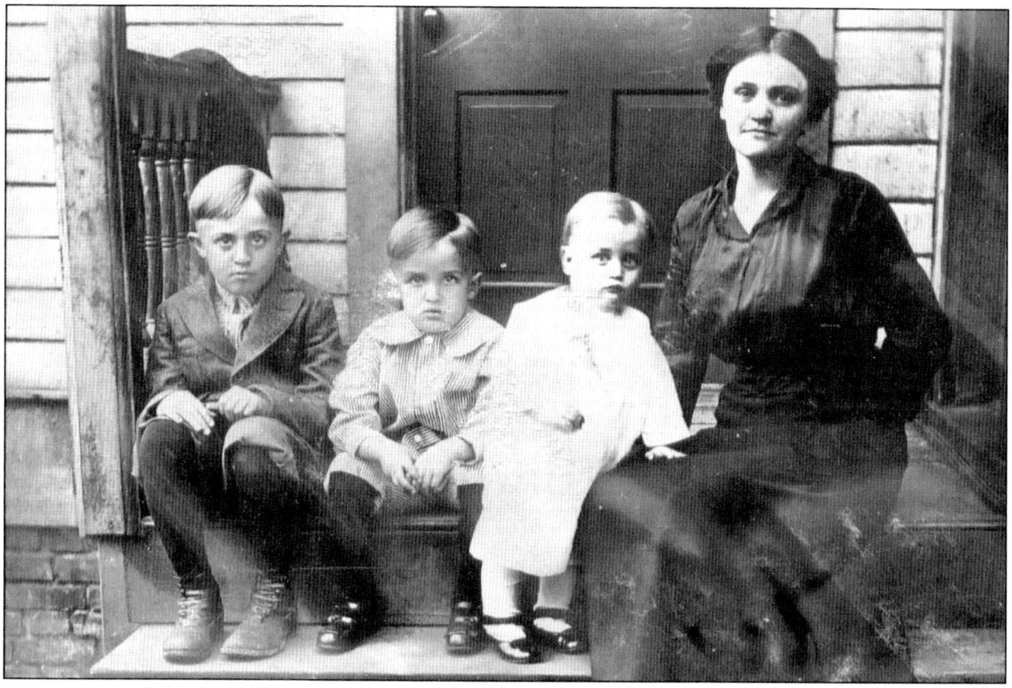

From left to right, Ryar, Raymond, and Edward sit on the front steps with their mother, Allie Arnett. Allie Edith Routt Arnett was born February 12, 1890, and died June 3, 1960, the daughter of Perde Routt. She married Granville Arnett, born March 12, 1884, and died January 1968 in New Haven, Kentucky. This photograph was taken in the early 1920s. (Courtesy Shirley Hornback Miller.)

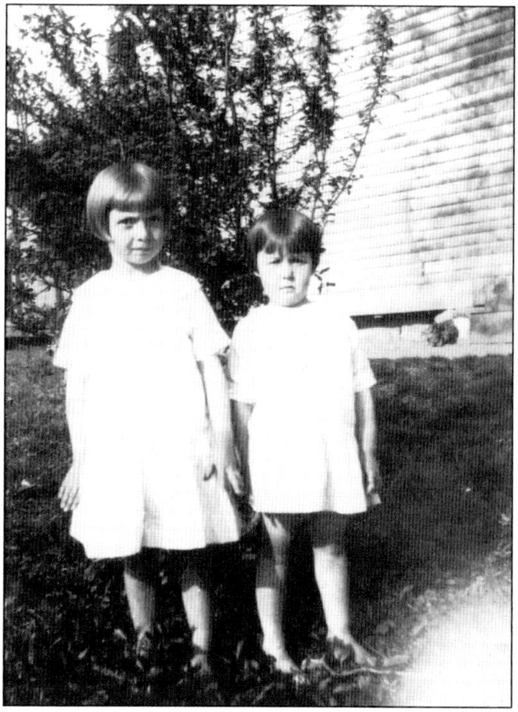

Beatrice Hornback (left) and Mildrid Williams stand in the backyard to have their picture made. The girls were early childhood friends who attended Oak Hill School. The photograph was taken in 1925. (Courtesy Beatrice Hornback Gibson.)

Two

FAMILY TIES

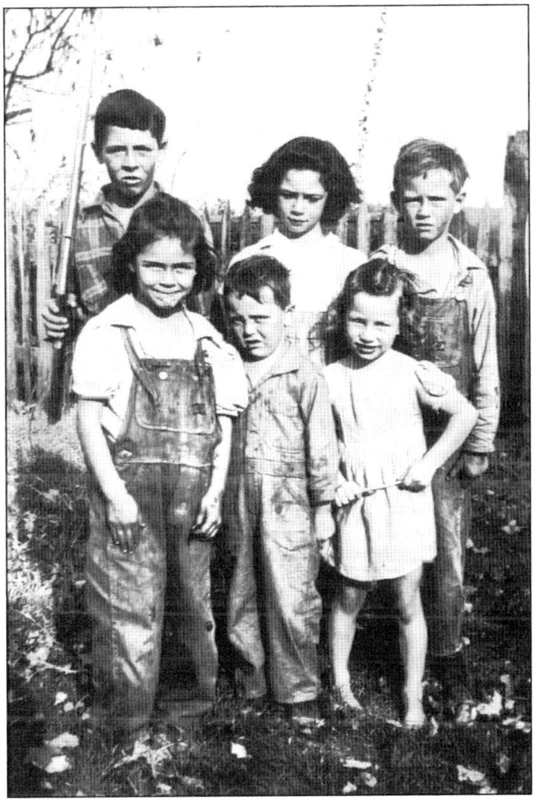

This 1945 photograph of Routt cousins shows, from left to right, (first row) Thelma, Junie, and Darlene; (second row) Norman, Mary Evelyn, and James. Growing up in the same community and attending the same school, these cousins were also the best of friends. The Routts grew up in the Barren Run area of Sonora. Note Norman with the BB gun. (Courtesy Darlene Routt Bryan.)

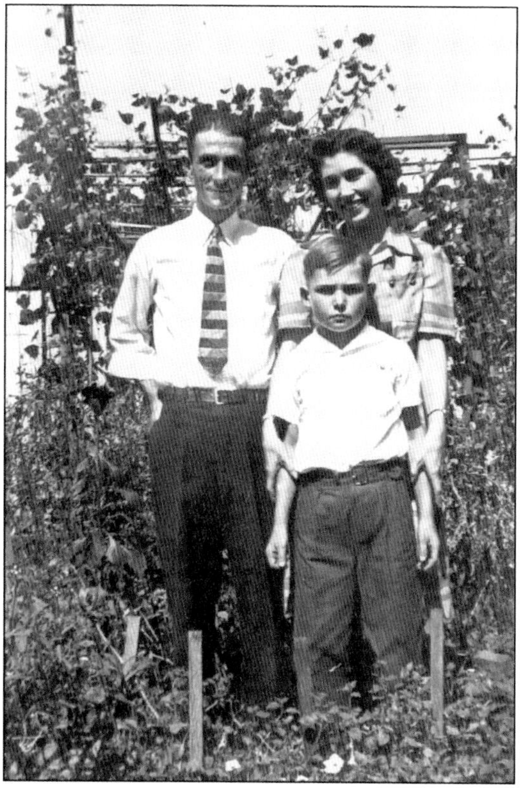

Garnett Priddy, Josie Routt Tucker Priddy, and her son, Walter Lee Tucker, stand in front of their house. Garnett was born December 14, 1911, and died January 12, 2001. This photograph was taken in September 1941. (Courtesy Darlene Routt Bryan.)

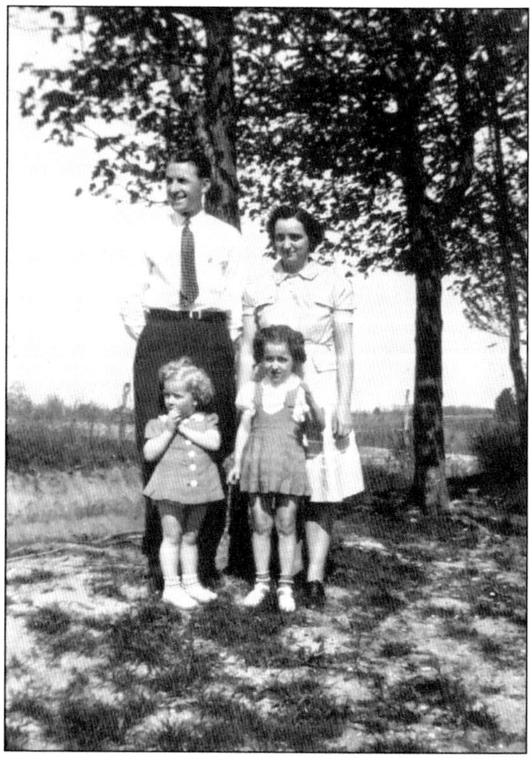

Rev. Jesse and Alma Milby Hornback along with their two daughters, Verna Dean and Dixie, stand together on a sunny day in the 1940s. Rev. Jesse T. Hornback was ordained to preach December 12, 1953, at Oak Hill Baptist Church. His first pastorate was Friendship Baptist No. 2 at Hodgenville. (Courtesy Beatrice Hornback Gibson.)

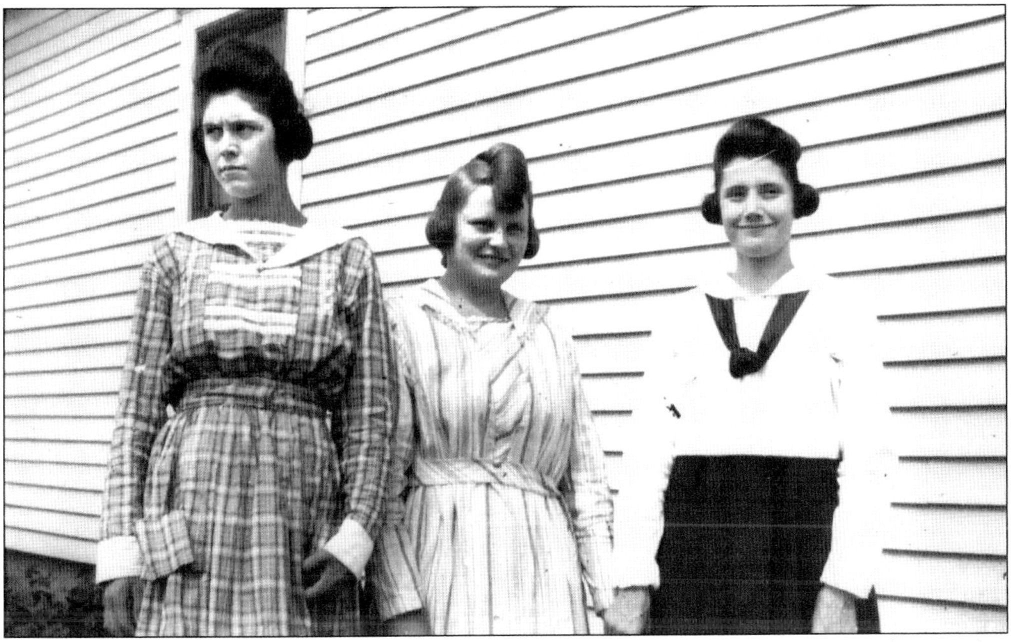

Ola Routt (left), Nettie Hazle (middle), and Ruby Routt pose alongside of the Routt home. This photograph was taken in the summer of July 1919. Note the different hairstyles. A lot of the hairstyles in the 1900s were fashioned from England. (Courtesy Darlene Routt Bryan.)

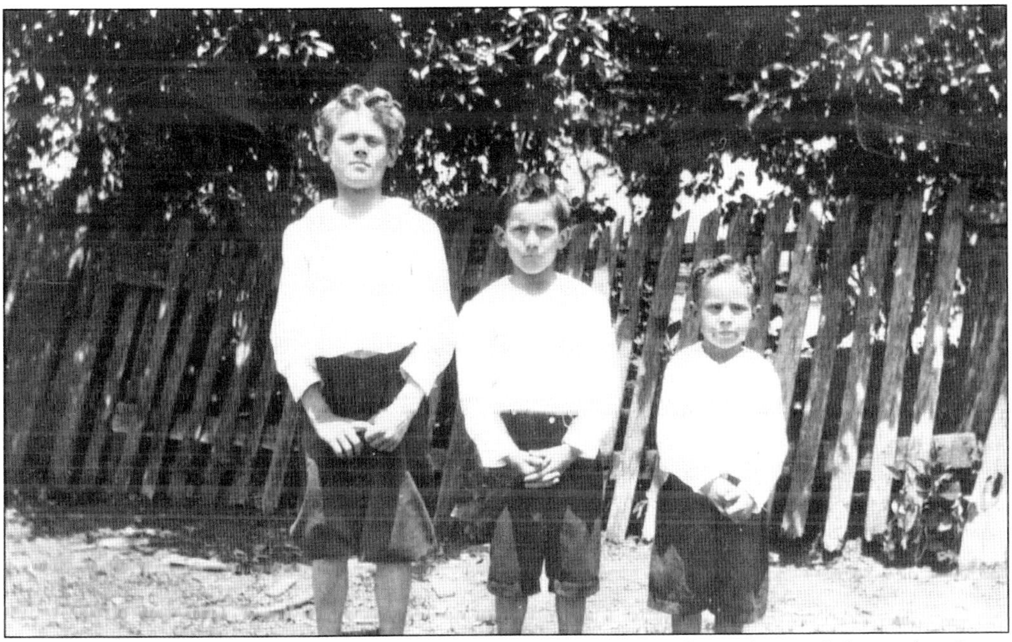

Eston, Opal, and John W. Routt Jr. are pictured from left to right in front of this picket fence in 1918. Before World War I, pants were worn at the knee but generally with stockings. After World War I, shorts were just above the knee with knee-length socks leaving the knees bare; buttons were often sewn at the bottom of the pants for enclosures. In 1924, the BF Goodrich Company registered the "zipper," although it wouldn't be used for a number of years except on shoes. (Courtesy Darlene Routt Bryan and Linda Routt Daniels.)

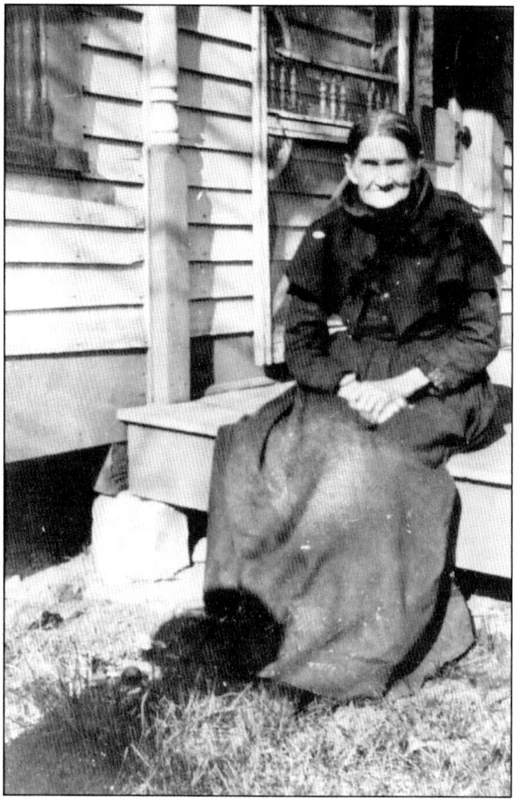

Margaret Catherine Yates Walsh was born November 24, 1835, and died August 12, 1920. Her father was William Yates, who came to the area from Virginia. She married Adgar Walsh, born February 6, 1824, and died April 28, 1905. They were residents of Upton, Kentucky, in LaRue County. (Courtesy Kathy Hensley Cooke.)

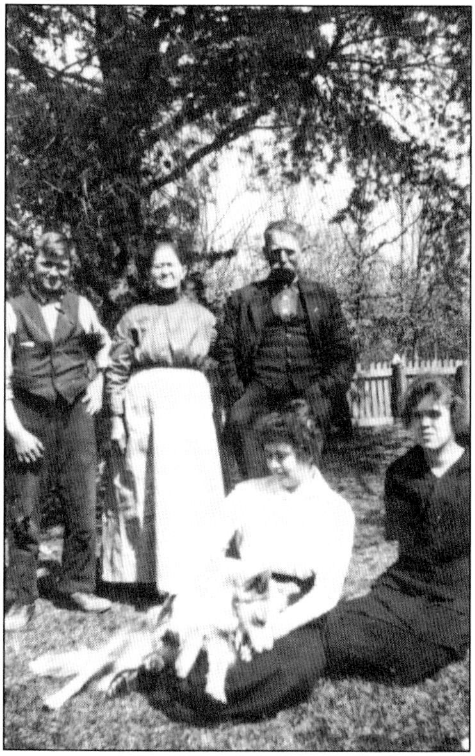

The Renfro family is pictured lived in Upton, Kentucky. Standing from left to right are Arvin Edward Renfro, Malvina "Vina" Walsh Renfro, and Fielding Asberry Renfro. Fielding was born April 14, 1855, and died May 22, 1929, in LaRue County. Fielding Renfro's daughters sit on the ground with their dog. Both girls grew up to be schoolteachers. (Courtesy Kathy Hensley Cooke.)

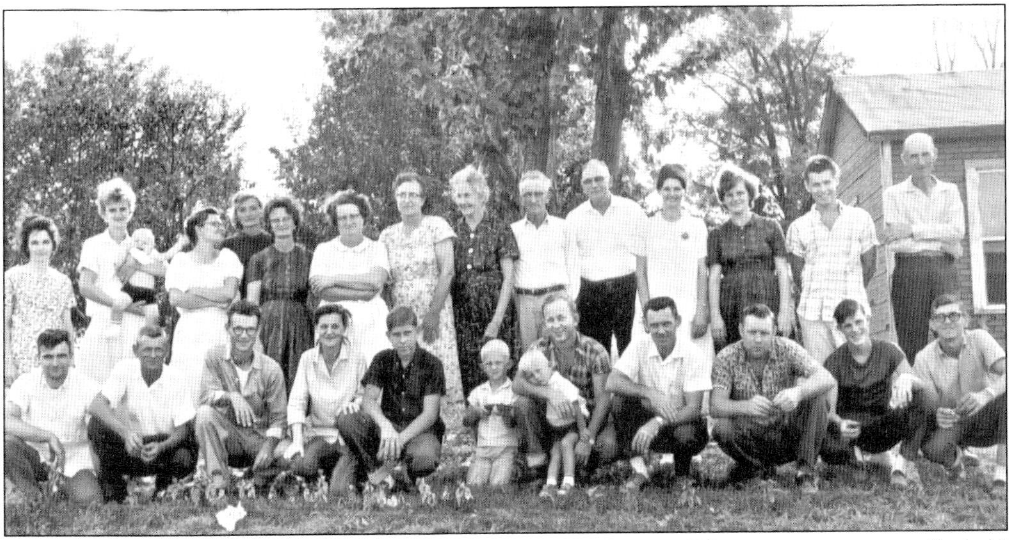

This Fields-Priddy reunion was held in August 1964 in Sonora. The reunions are usually held around Raymond Fields's birthday in August. Pictured from left to right are (first row) Frank Nall, Pete Yates, Hester Priddy, Odessa Priddy, Charles Richard "C. R." Fields, Ronnie Shuffett, Elroy Shuffett holding Junie, unidentified, Raymond Fields, Raymond "Junie" Fields Jr., and Larry Marcum; (second row) Ann Hornback Nall, May Fern Goodman holding unidentified, Elinor Priddy White, unidentified, Beatrice Goodman, Hazle Yates, Isabell Yates Flowers, Eva Leasor Hornback, Albert Hornback, Herman Flowers, Geneva Shuffett, Elizabeth Fields, Donnie Fields, and Mac Goodman. (Courtesy Patricia Fields Hornback.)

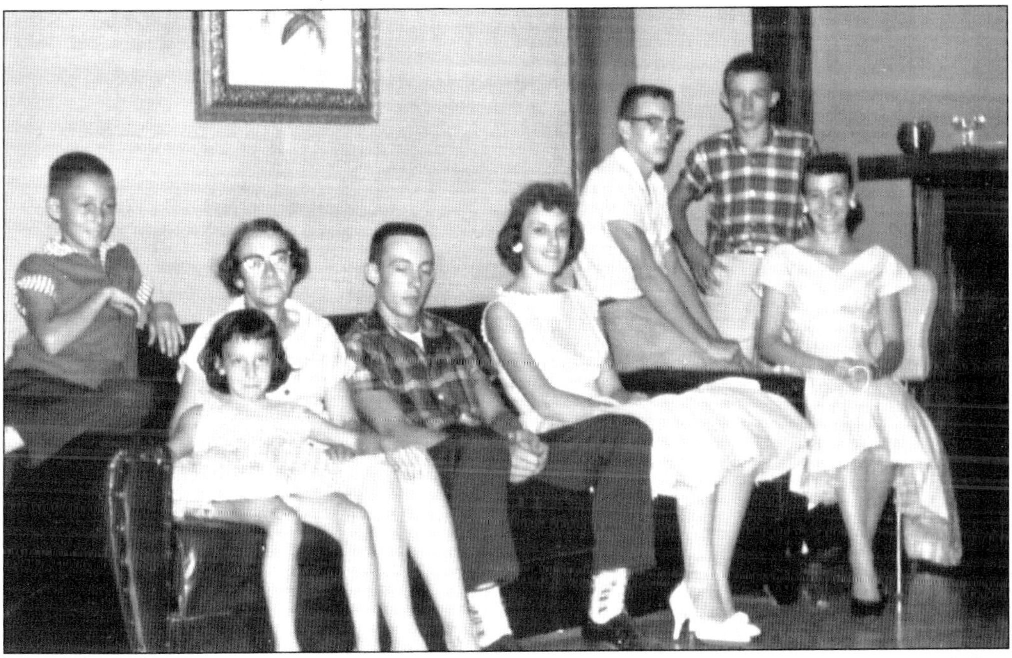

Photographed in September 1959 are, from left to right, Jerry Bland, Judy Bland in Ella Bland's lap, David Bland, ? Bland, Jack Bland, Billy Bland, and Barbara Bland. Ella worked as a housekeeper for Mrs. Highbaugh in Sonora and later retired from Elizabethtown Community College as a custodian. (Courtesy Nancy Pennington McCubbins.)

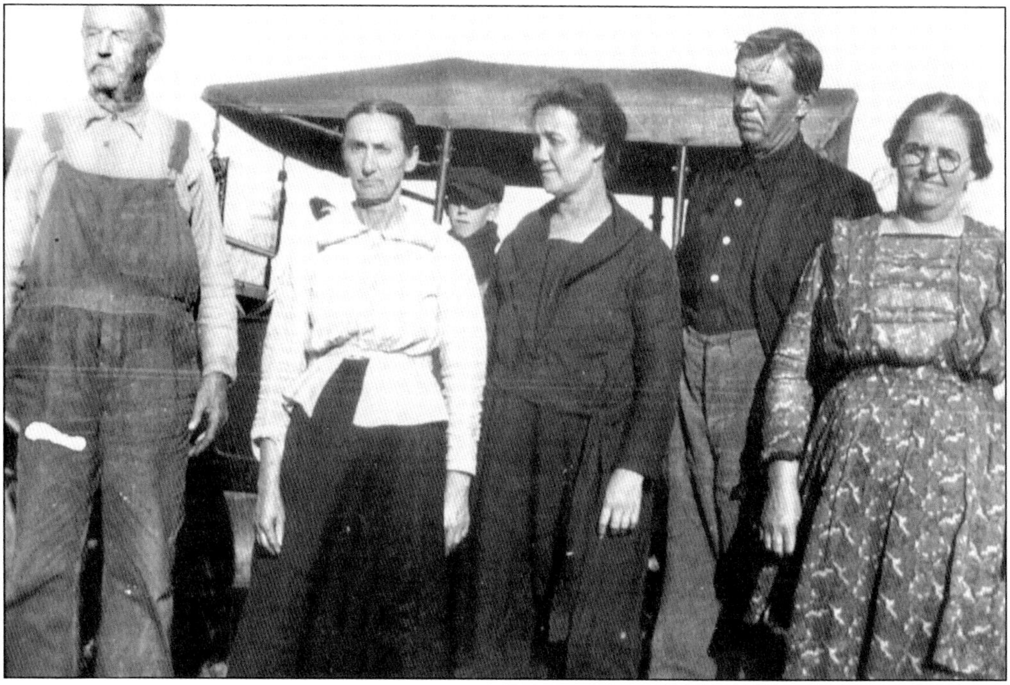

From left to right, Sam Taylor, Melvina Hornback Taylor, Marie Routt, Ed Taylor, and Mary Elizabeth Taylor were photographed in the early 1920s. Bernice Routt is seated in the car. Melvina Hornback Taylor was born in 1865 and died in 1940. (Courtesy Beatrice Hornback Gibson.)

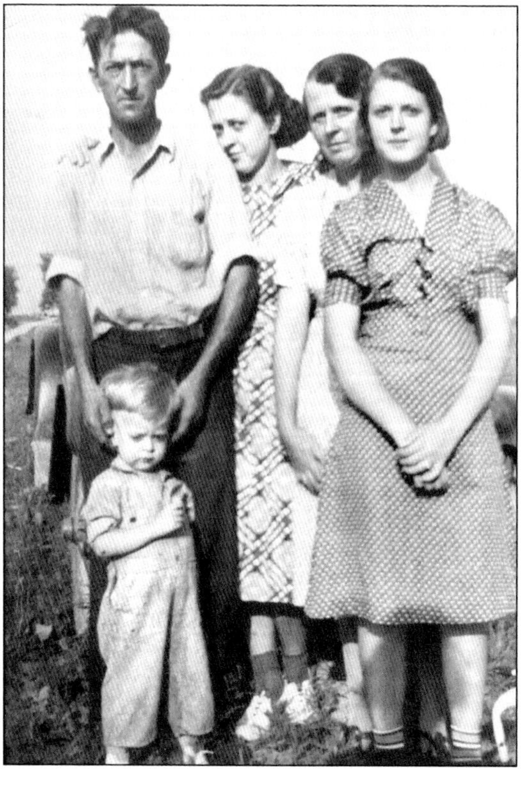

Elzie Hornback with son Charles, Juanita Hornback, Dorothy Hornback, and Jo Robinson Hornback stand in front of their automobile in 1942. Elzie and Jo also had two other children, Delma Lee and Eula Mae, who died in their childhood. It was said six-year-old Delma and three-year-old Eula Mae had ingested poison berries. The two were buried at Oak Hill Cemetery in the early 1930s. (Courtesy Patricia Fields Hornback.)

This photograph was taken around 1920 of Tom and Martha Highbaugh with their daughter, Marie. Marie Highbaugh was born March 28, 1918, and later married Fred Dennison. (Courtesy Darlene Routt Bryan.)

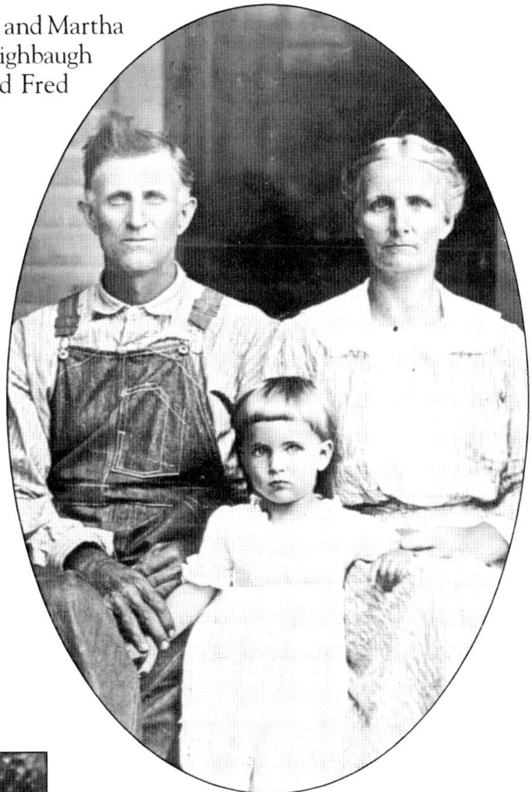

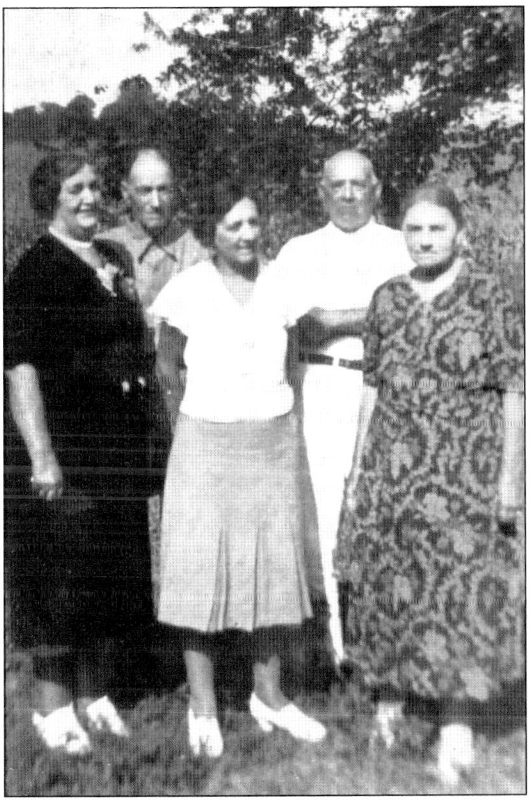

From left to right, Lilly, Jim, Adie, Robert, and Molly Abell stand at the old homestead on Oak Hill Road. The farm is called the "Old Jim Abell" place. (Courtesy Alva Martin Tharp.)

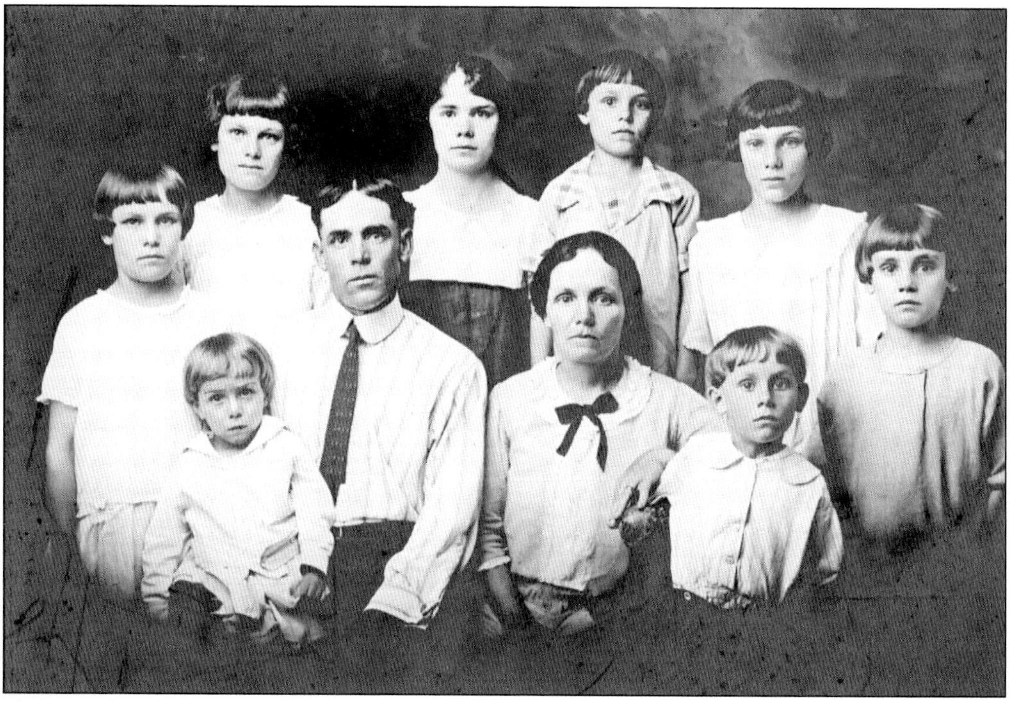

Photographed here are parents Walter and Katie Jones Dye and their children, pictured clockwise from Bertrand in Walter's lap, Ethel, Mason, Zara Mae, Thelma, Geneva, Mary, Ruby, and Floyd. (Courtesy Mary Kathryn Pennington Puckett.)

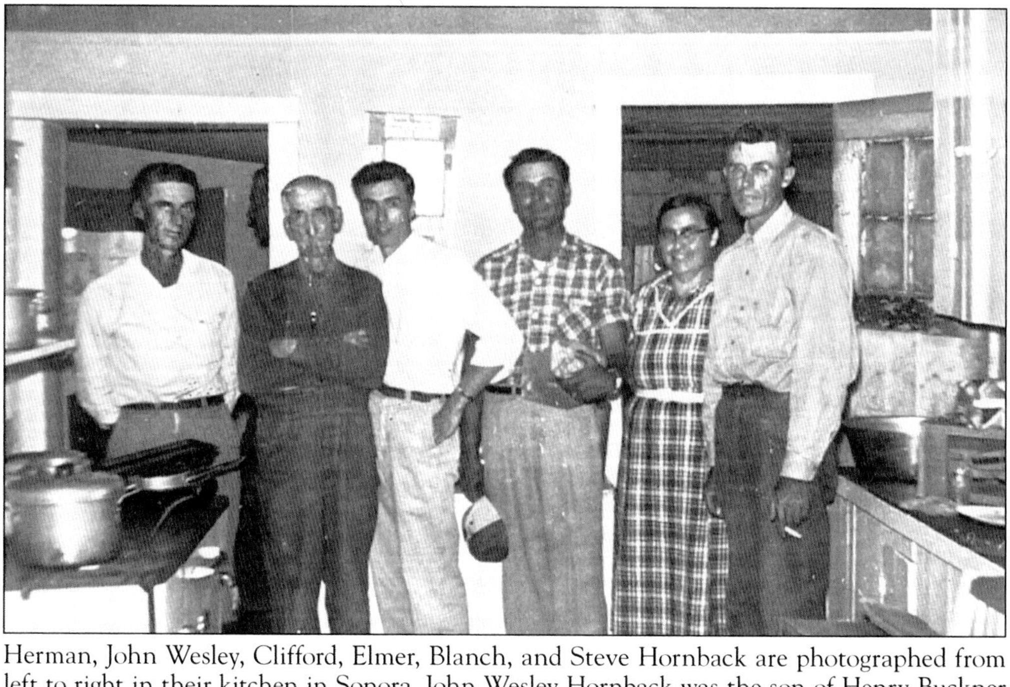

Herman, John Wesley, Clifford, Elmer, Blanch, and Steve Hornback are photographed from left to right in their kitchen in Sonora. John Wesley Hornback was the son of Henry Buckner and Martha Jane Hornback. This photograph was taken in the mid-1950s. (Courtesy Patricia Fields Hornback.)

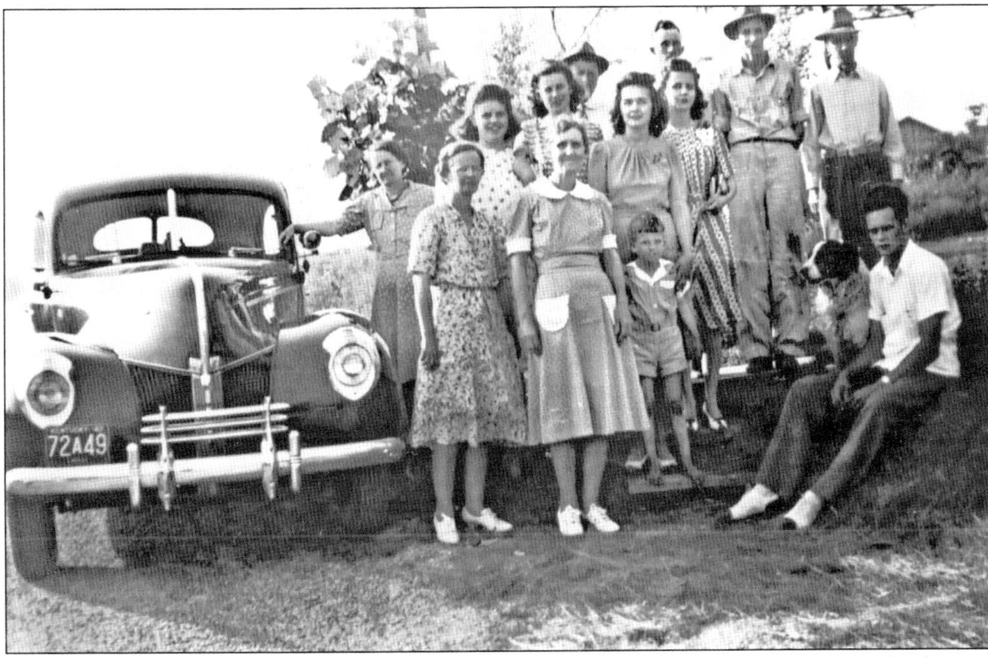

The Gibson family from Buffalo, Kentucky, stands on this bank side in the 1930s. Charles and Lillie Gibson raised their family in the Mount Tabor area. Their three boys would serve during the war in 1942. (Courtesy Beatrice Hornback Gibson.)

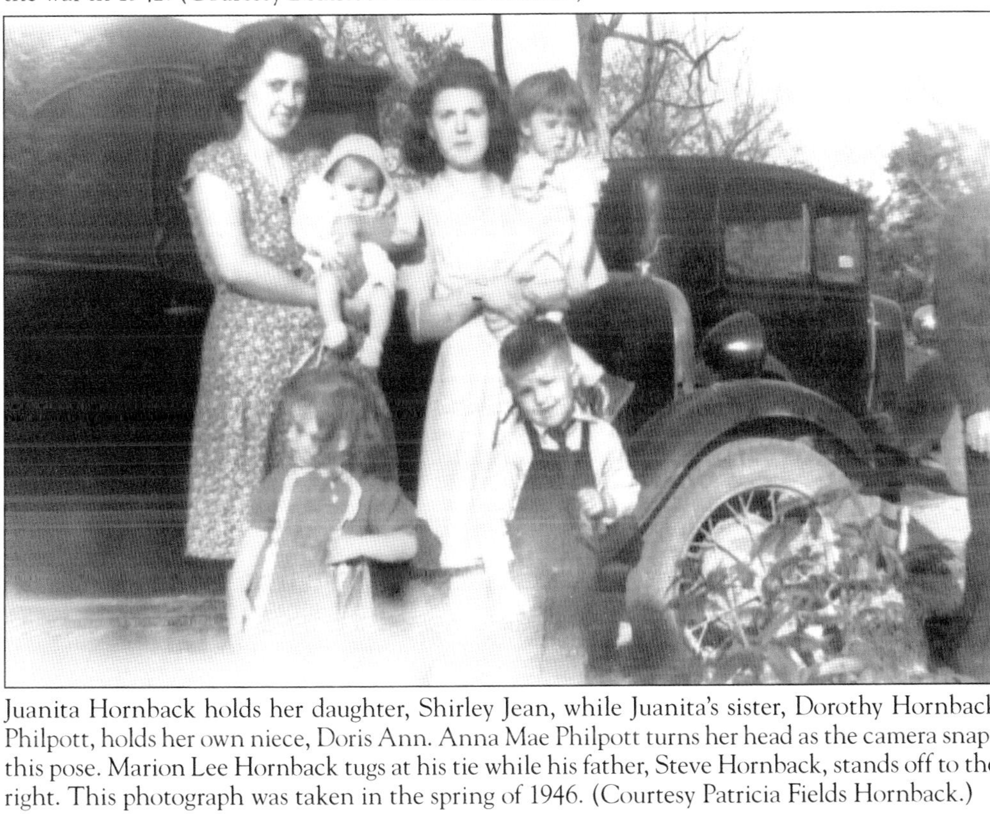

Juanita Hornback holds her daughter, Shirley Jean, while Juanita's sister, Dorothy Hornback Philpott, holds her own niece, Doris Ann. Anna Mae Philpott turns her head as the camera snaps this pose. Marion Lee Hornback tugs at his tie while his father, Steve Hornback, stands off to the right. This photograph was taken in the spring of 1946. (Courtesy Patricia Fields Hornback.)

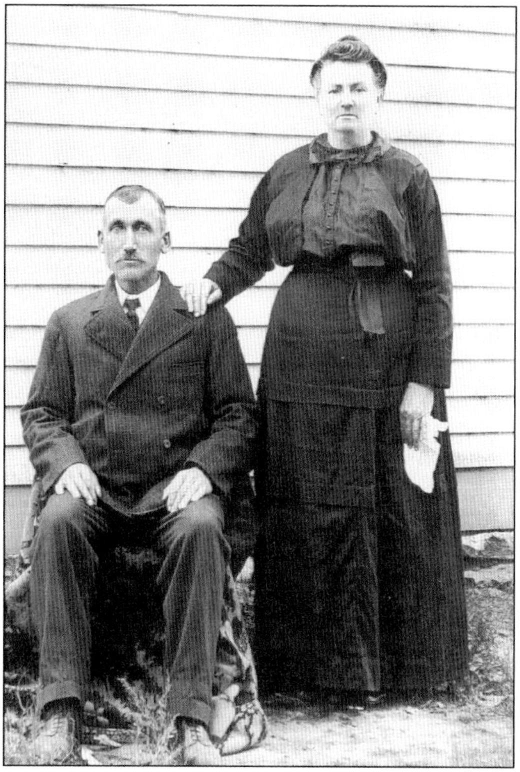

Malcolm and Artimicia Routt stand by their house in the early 1900s in the Barren Run area. Malcolm was the son of William Harrison and Gabriella Brashears Routt. Malcolm and Artimicia both were born in 1860. (Courtesy Darlene Routt Bryan and Linda Daniels Routt.)

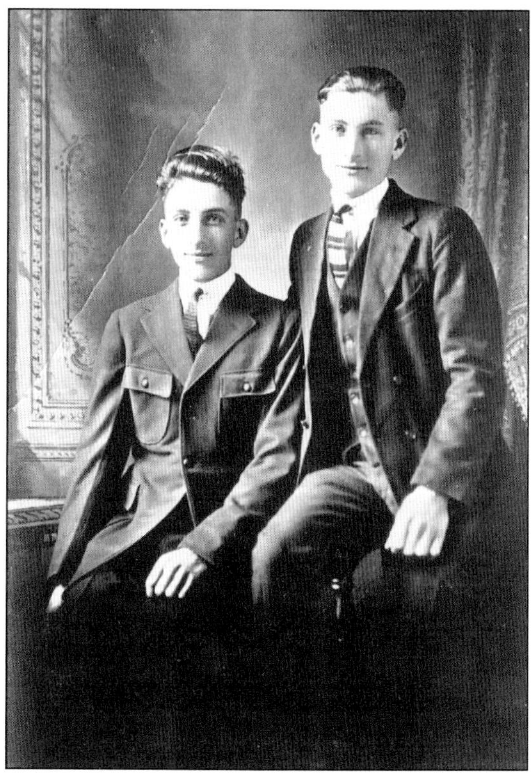

Omer (left) and Homer Routt, twin sons of David Cotton and Mary Francis Tucker Routt, were born in 1902. The back of the photograph states the boys were 21 years old. Christopher Columbus Tharp's daughters married the twin brothers. (Courtesy Darlene Routt Bryan.)

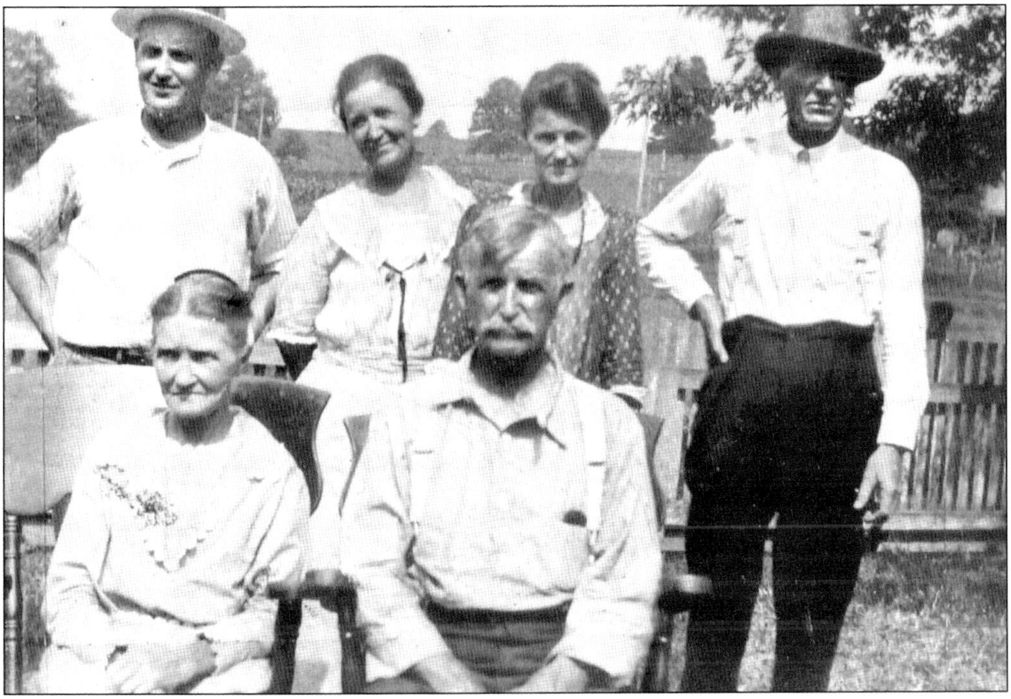

Lydia Ann Brooks sits beside her husband, David Brooks, with their blended family. Lydia had remarried after her first husband, Elijah Jackson, passed away. In the second row are, from left to right, David and Lydia's children, Jesse and Lillie Brooks; and Mary Ann and Henry Birk Jackson, Lydia and Elijah Jackson's children. (Courtesy William Leslie Hornback Jr.)

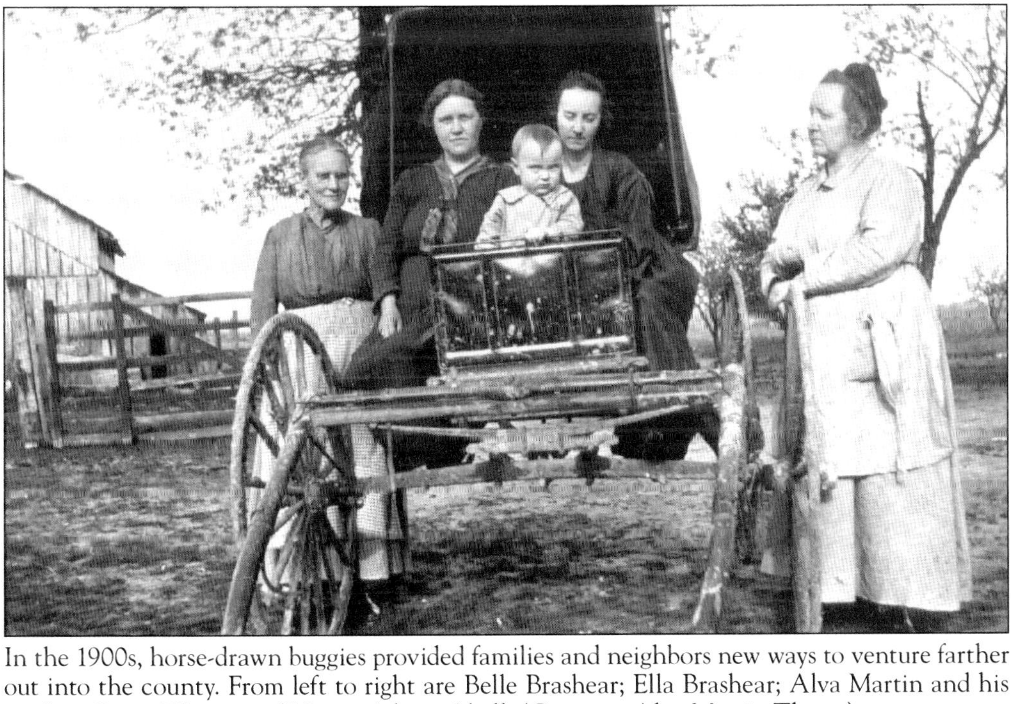

In the 1900s, horse-drawn buggies provided families and neighbors new ways to venture farther out into the county. From left to right are Belle Brashear; Ella Brashear; Alva Martin and his mother, Susan Tharp; and Hessie Adams Abell. (Courtesy Alva Martin Tharp.)

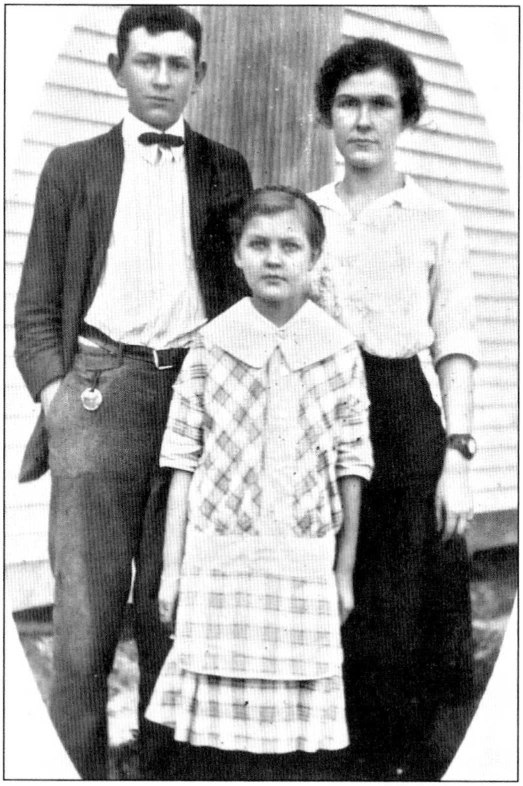

Harvey and Mattie Ward stand by their store with Mattie's daughter, Mary Willia Ward. The Wards purchased the little country store in the Maxine area from Gus Rock. The store provided supplies to neighbors in the surrounding areas of Tanner, Oak Hill, Barren Run, and Maxine. (Courtesy Mary Kathryn Pennington Puckett.)

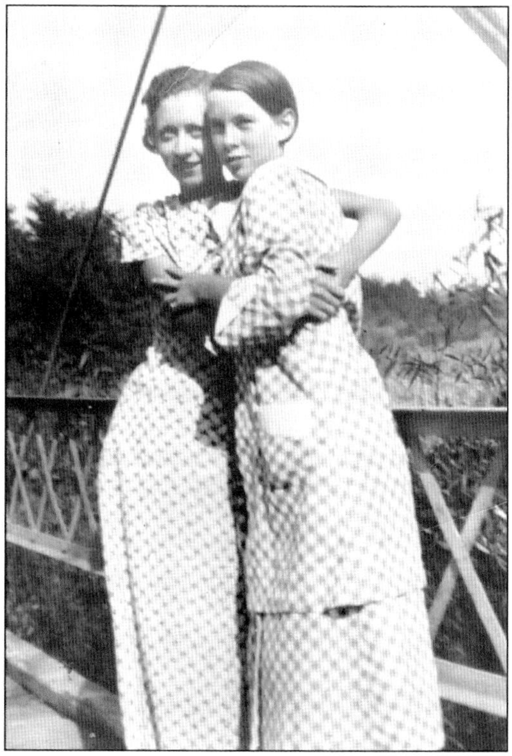

Mather's Mill Bridge is located on Highway 84 between Sonora and Hodgenville. Bessie Bowling (right) and Florene Mather pose on this bridge together in 1930. Bessie was only 14 at the time. (Courtesy Darlene Routt Bryan.)

From left to right, Gusty Rock, Blanche Routt, Josie Routt, and Mildred Routt pose together. In the 1920s and 1930s, these flapper dresses were very popular. Blanche holds a large ceramic cat possibly won at the county fair. (Courtesy Charles "June" Routt.)

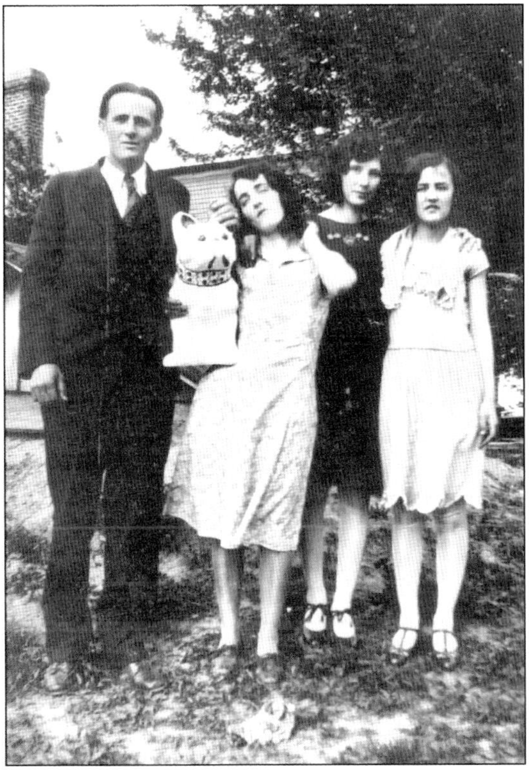

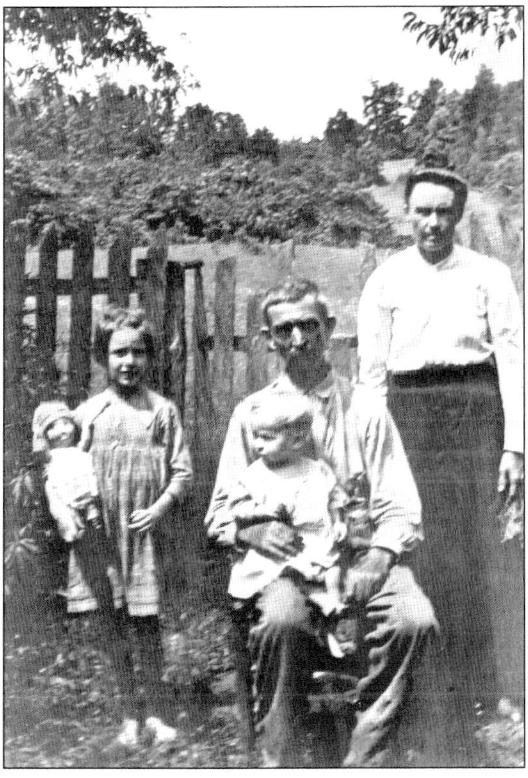

Benjamin Thomas and Martha "Mattie" Wheeler Hornback spent the day with their grandchildren. The girl is unidentified while the boy is thought to be William Leslie Hornback Jr. Benjamin remarried after his first wife, Ida T. Hornback, died. (Courtesy Patricia Fields Hornback.)

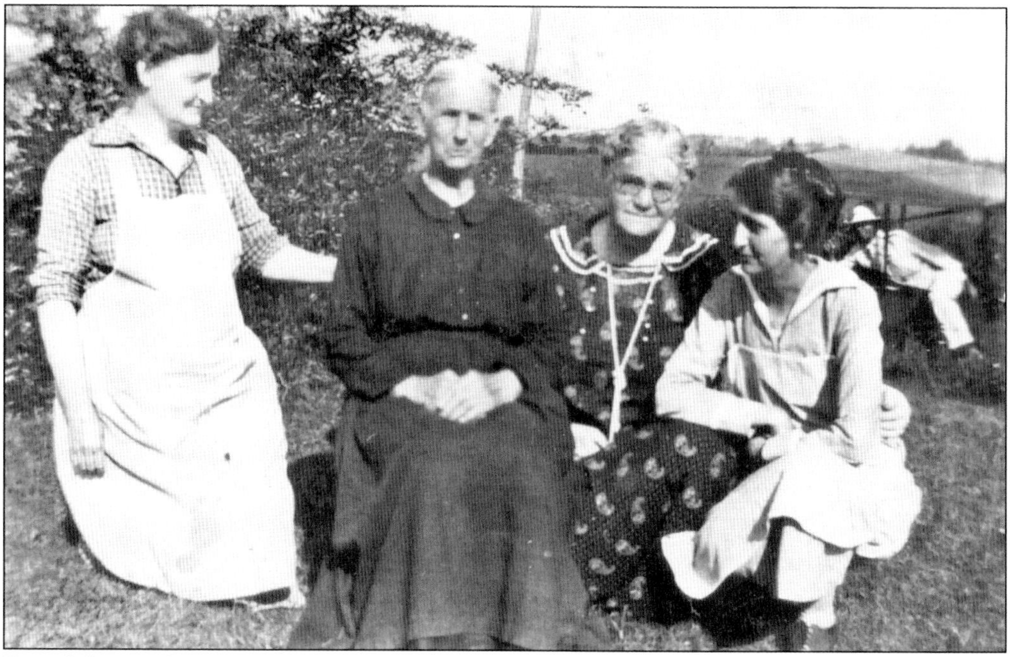

From left to right are unidentified, Mary Tharp, unidentified, and Sallie M. Hornback Tharp. Mary Tharp was the wife of Jasper Tharp. Note the gentleman stretched out in the back. He doesn't seem to be aware that he is being photographed. (Courtesy Joan Lorenz Waldbusser.)

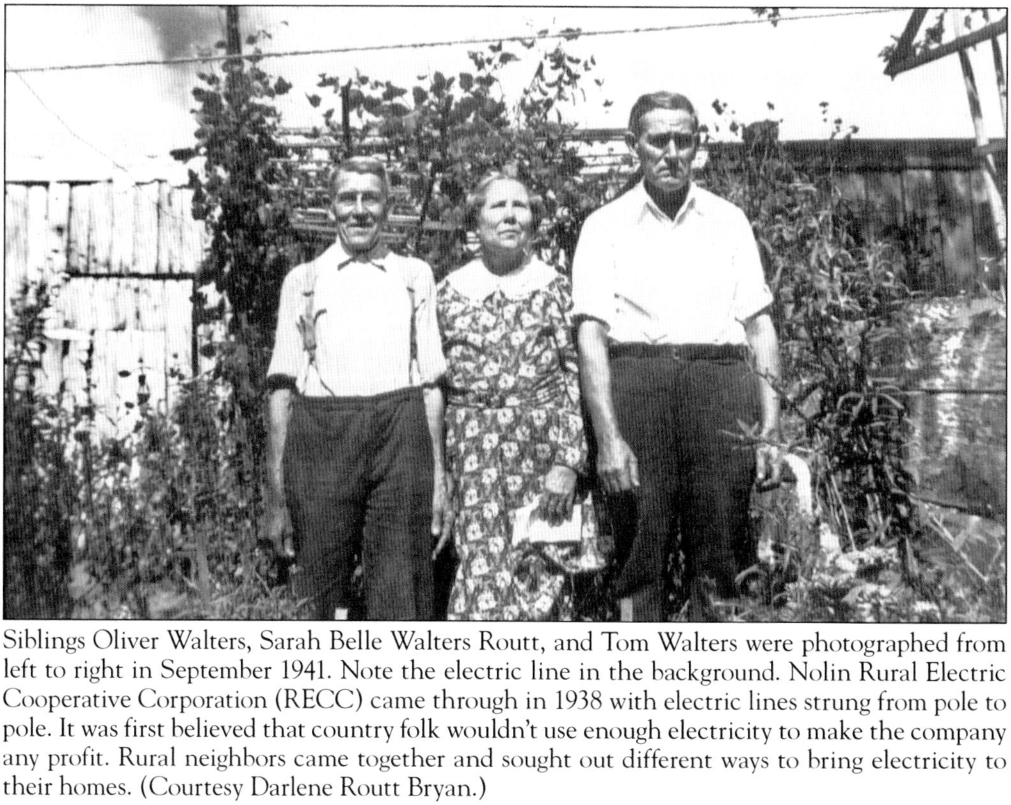

Siblings Oliver Walters, Sarah Belle Walters Routt, and Tom Walters were photographed from left to right in September 1941. Note the electric line in the background. Nolin Rural Electric Cooperative Corporation (RECC) came through in 1938 with electric lines strung from pole to pole. It was first believed that country folk wouldn't use enough electricity to make the company any profit. Rural neighbors came together and sought out different ways to bring electricity to their homes. (Courtesy Darlene Routt Bryan.)

Virgil Druien was born February 24, 1881, and died March 1, 1981, in LaRue County. Virgil married Sally Sprawles and is buried at Mount Tabor Cemetery in Buffalo, Kentucky. (Courtesy Pat Wheeler Lassonde.)

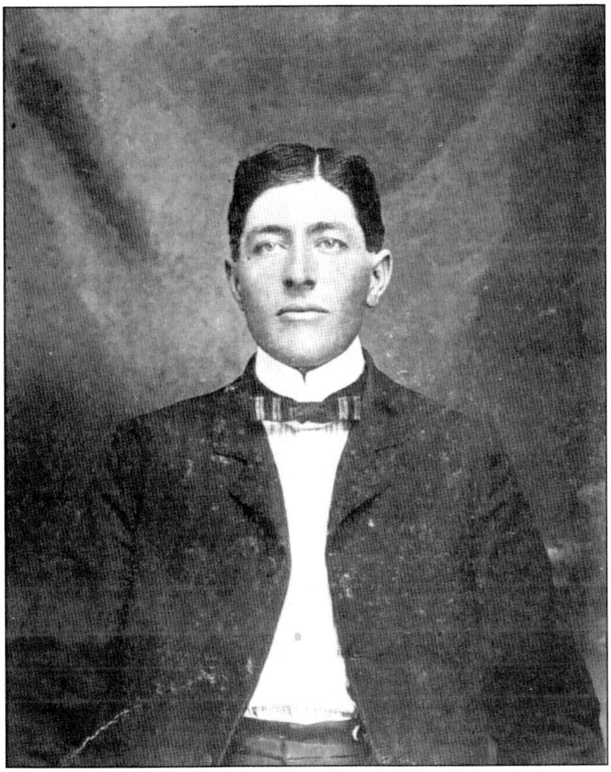

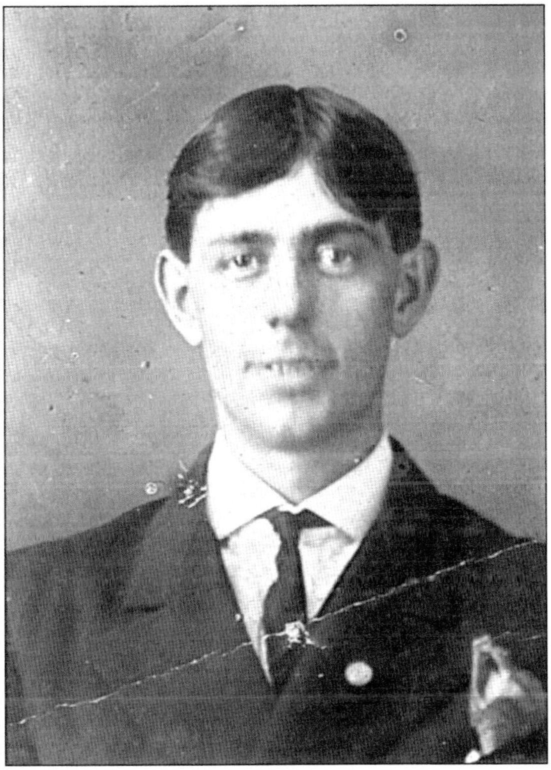

Joseph Druien was born June 18, 1884, in LaRue County, Kentucky. He died June 12, 1956, and is buried in Bloomington, Illinois, in McLean County. Joseph married Louri Ferril, who was born March 10, 1886, in LaRue County. His brother, Virgil, is pictured above. (Courtesy Pat Wheeler Lassonde.)

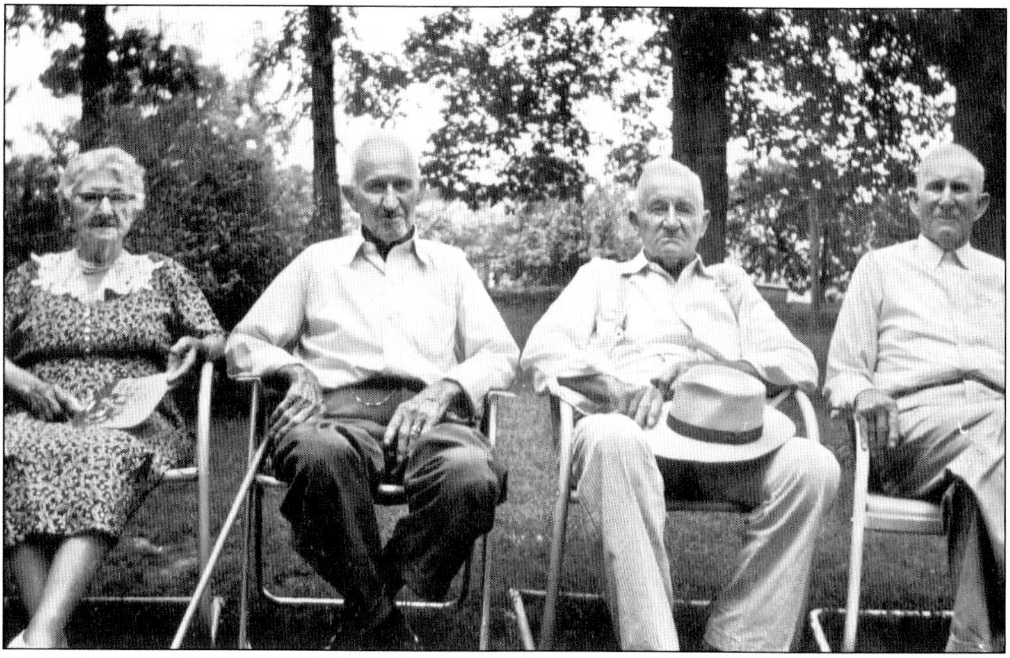

From left to right, Virgie, Jim, A. B., and Dave Ward were photographed at this family get-together. Virgie and Jim Ward raised Virgil Pennington after his parents, James and Martha, had passed away. A local road is named for A. B. Ward. (Courtesy Mary Kathryn Pennington Puckett.)

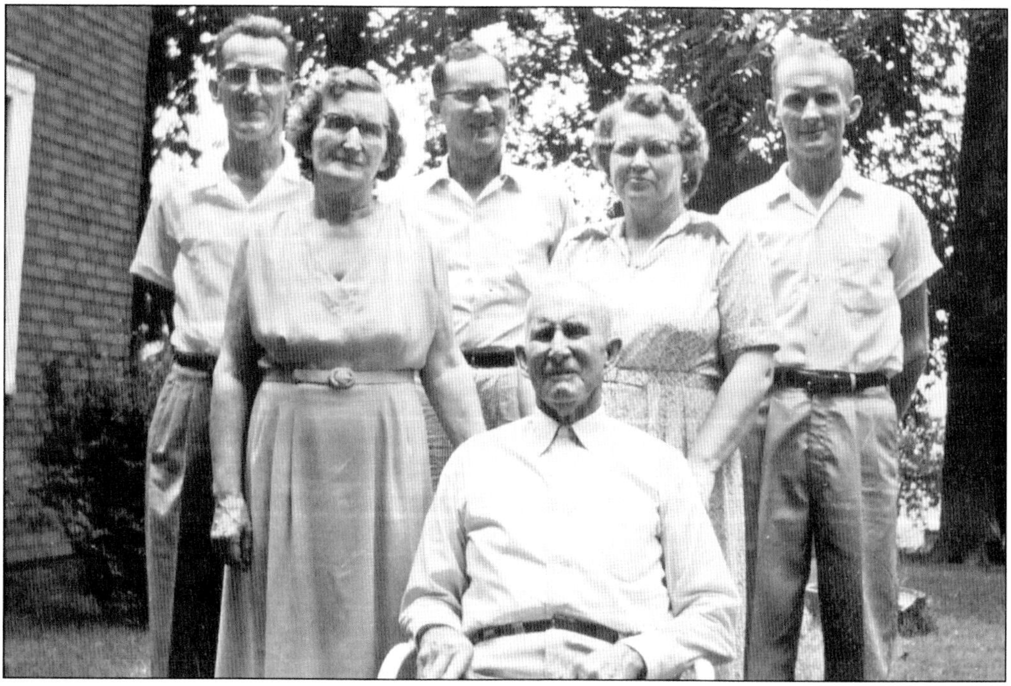

Dave Ward sits in the chair while behind him from left to right are Perry Ward, Edna Ward Cruse, Homer Ward, Mabel Ward Moore, and Stanley Ward. Stanley led the singing at Oak Hill Church during much of the 1970s and 1980s. This photograph was taken in August 1956. (Courtesy Mary Kathryn Pennington Puckett.)

Albert Hornback was the son of Benjamin Thomas and Ida Hornback. Albert married Eva, the daughter of Martin and L. W. Leasor, on January 30, 1925. At one time, Albert and Eva ran a country supply store out of their home called Creekside Store. (Courtesy Rhonda Hornback Nichols.)

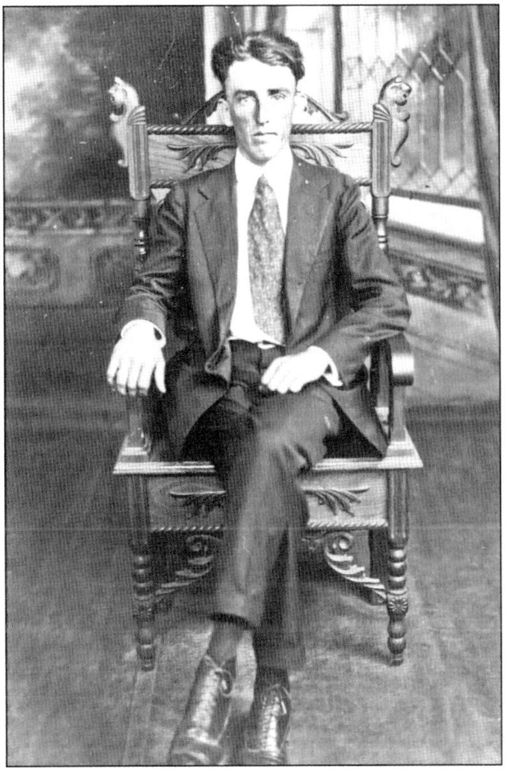

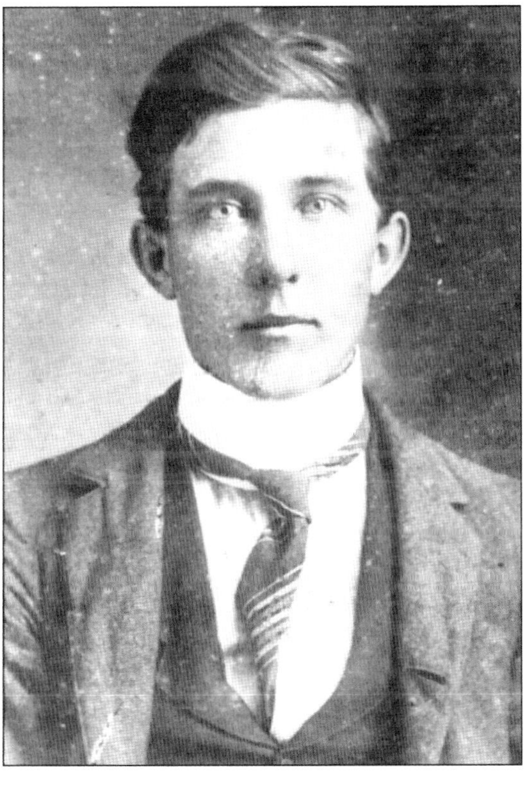

Weaver Robinson, the son of Marion Monroe Robinson, married Mary F. Hornback on March 23, 1905, having one daughter, Jo Robinson. The couple divorced when Jo was just a small child. Weaver Robinson was known for his sparkling gold tooth. He could be seen traveling in a horse and buggy with his second wife, Mary Belle Meers, en route to church in Sonora in the 1930s. In the 1930 census, the couple had four children: Elmo, Boyd, James, and Newton. (Courtesy Patricia Fields Hornback.)

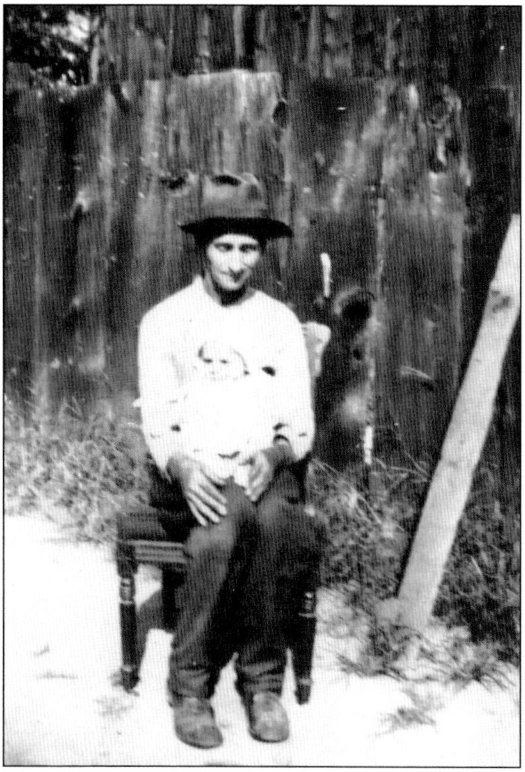

Amos Hornback holds an infant thought to be Leonard Tharp in front of an old barn. Timber frame barns were used to shelter livestock and kept hay and grains dry. (Courtesy Joan Lorenz Waldbusser.)

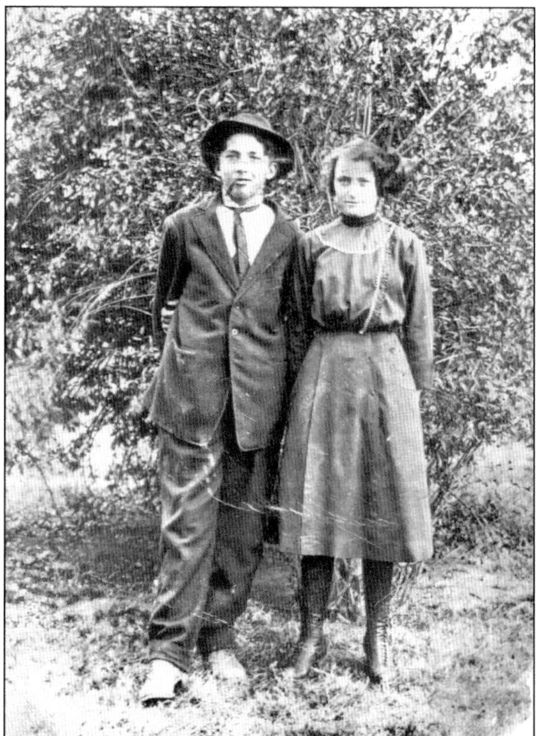

Herb Cruse and Ellen "Ellie" Gusler stand in front of this clump of trees. Ellen was the sister of Ollie and Jim Gusler. The Cruses and Guslers were mostly from the Barren Run area. (Courtesy Darlene Routt Bryan.)

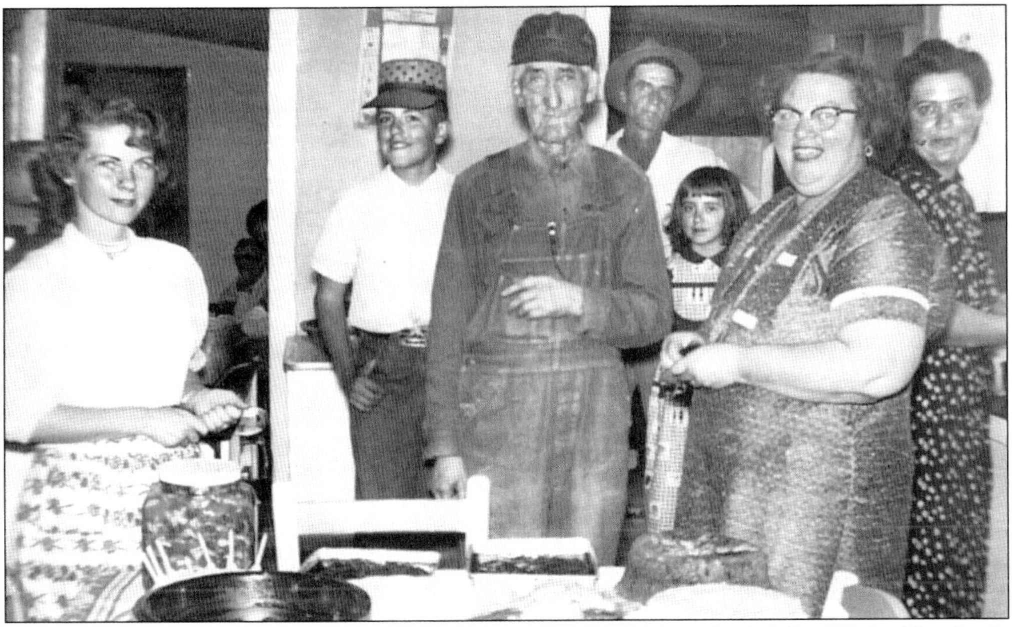

Pictured from left to right, Lucille Hornback Jaggers, Marion Lee Hornback, John Wesley Hornback, Herman Hornback, Doris Ann Hornback, Georgia Jaggers Hornback, and Juanita Hornback smile at John's birthday celebration in the mid-1950s. Note the cake with the candles on the table. (Courtesy Patricia Fields Hornback.)

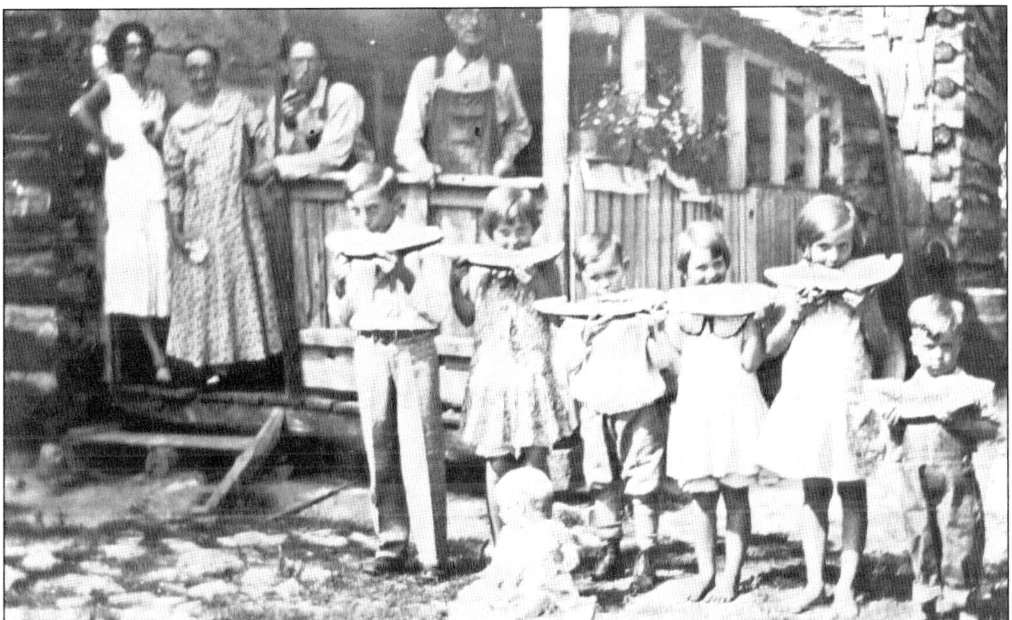

This family photograph was taken around 1932. Pictured from left to right are Irene Hornback Angel, Melvinia Hornback, Elzie Curtis Hornback, Benjamin Thomas Hornback, Wilburn "Webb" Hornback, Juanita Hornback, Calvin Hornback, Dorothy Hornback, Beatrice Hornback, and Delmar Hornback; the baby on the ground is Wilma Jean Hornback. The children are enjoying a watermelon as they pose for this photograph. (Courtesy Patricia Fields Hornback.)

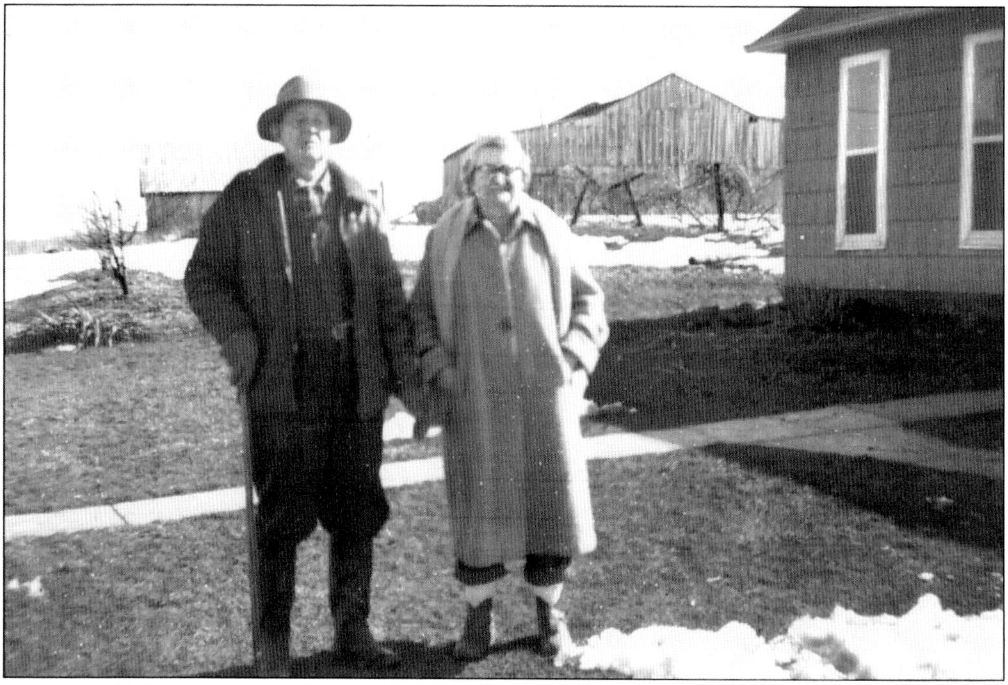

Brown and Ella Gusler Hornback stand together in the photograph taken in the 1960s, when the sunshine seems to have melted some of the snow away. Ella Gusler lived to be over 100 years old. (Courtesy Morna Humphrees Eastridge.)

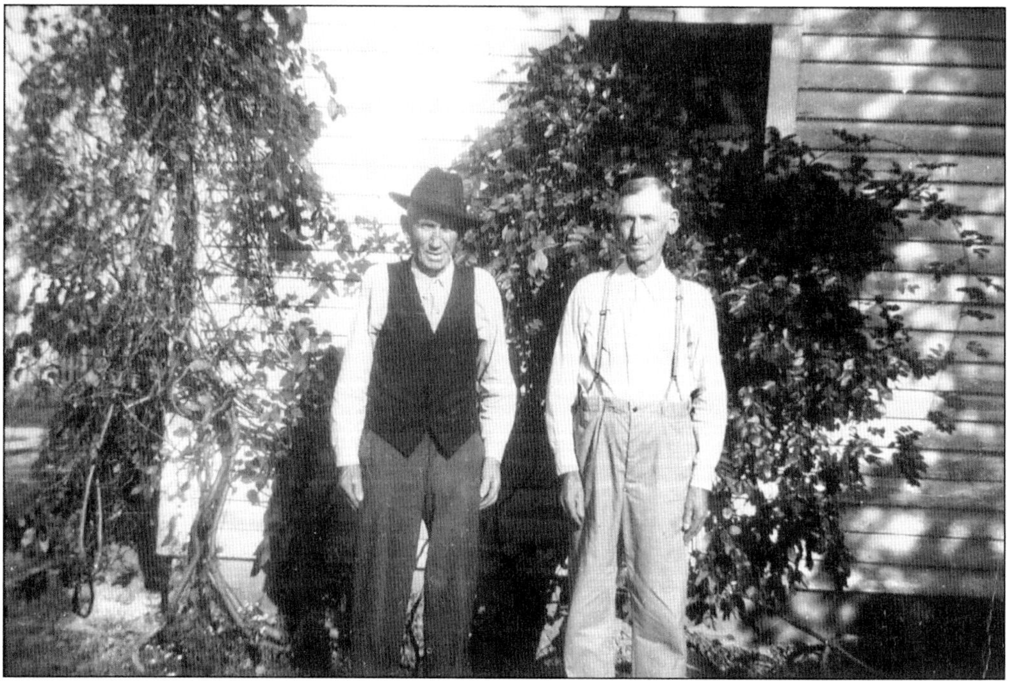

These brothers, David Clark Routt (left) and John Waller Routt Sr., stand beside each other to have their photograph taken. A third person in the window can barely be seen. (Courtesy Darlene Routt Bryan and Linda Routt Daniels.)

Mary Sullivan poses to have her photograph taken. In the 1920s, hairstyles became shorter and the Mary Jane ankle-strap button shoe became popular. Shoes were no longer just functional but fashionable as well. (Courtesy Darlene Routt Bryan.)

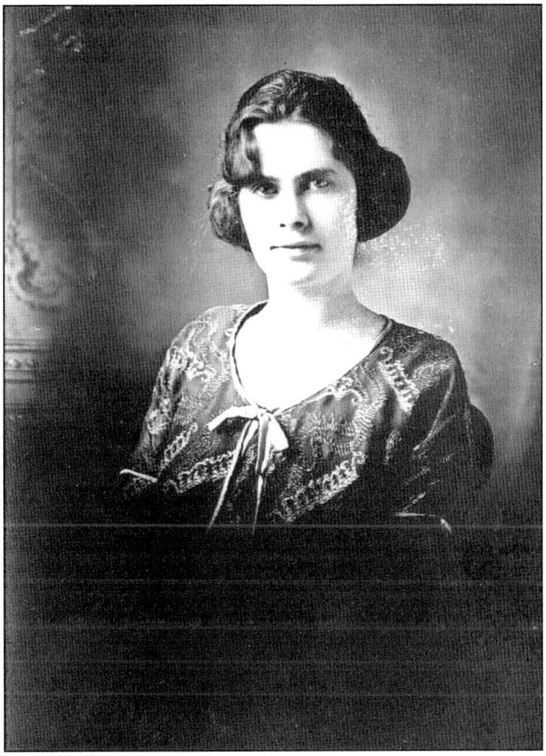

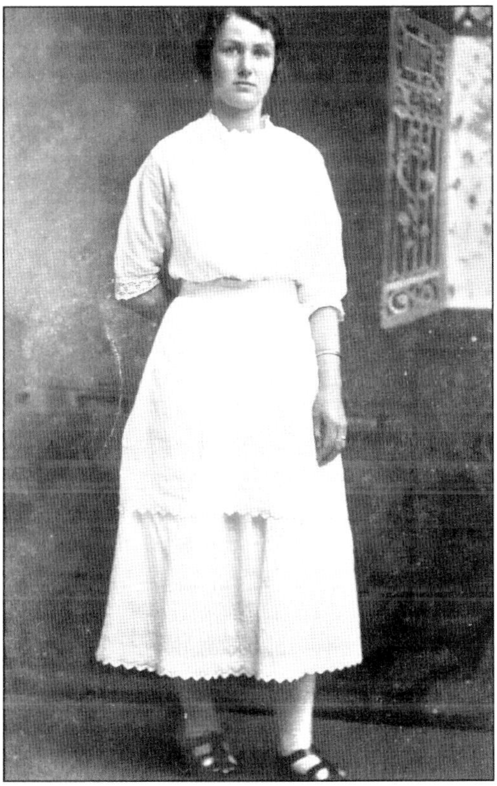

In 1915, Artie Routt, age 16, stands in a white tea dress. The *Titanic* and the teen years inspired these beautiful linen dresses that were considered evening wear. (Courtesy Darlene Routt Bryan.)

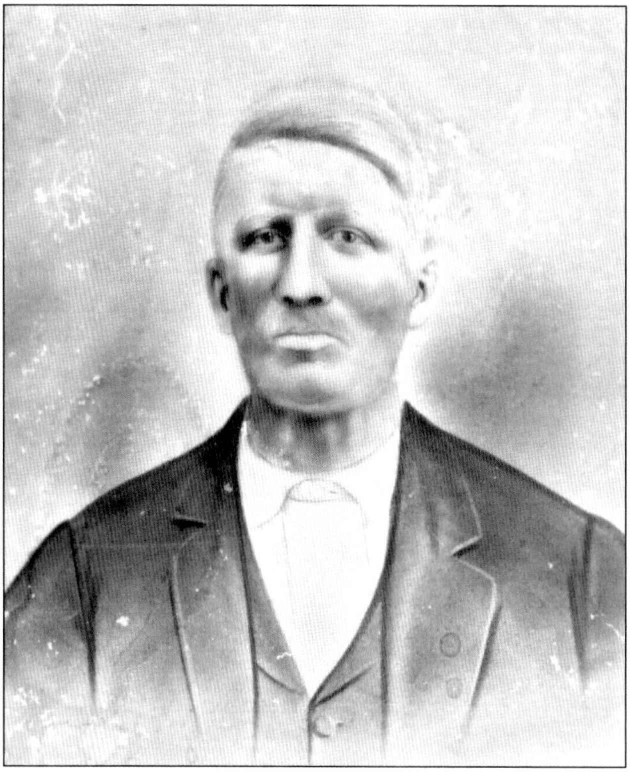

This is a charcoal drawing of James K. Pennington. James, who was born in 1833 and died in 1914 in LaRue County, was the father of Annie and Virgil. (Courtesy Mary Kathryn Pennington Puckett.)

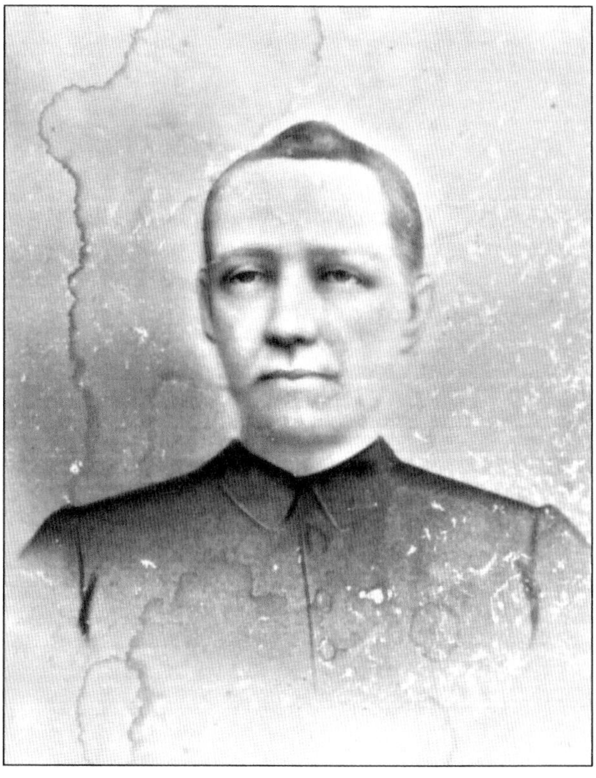

Martha "Mattie" Hornback Pennington was married to James, in the photograph above. Martha, the daughter of Henry Buckner and Martha Jane Hornback, was born in 1863 and died in 1918. (Courtesy Mary Kathryn Pennington Puckett.)

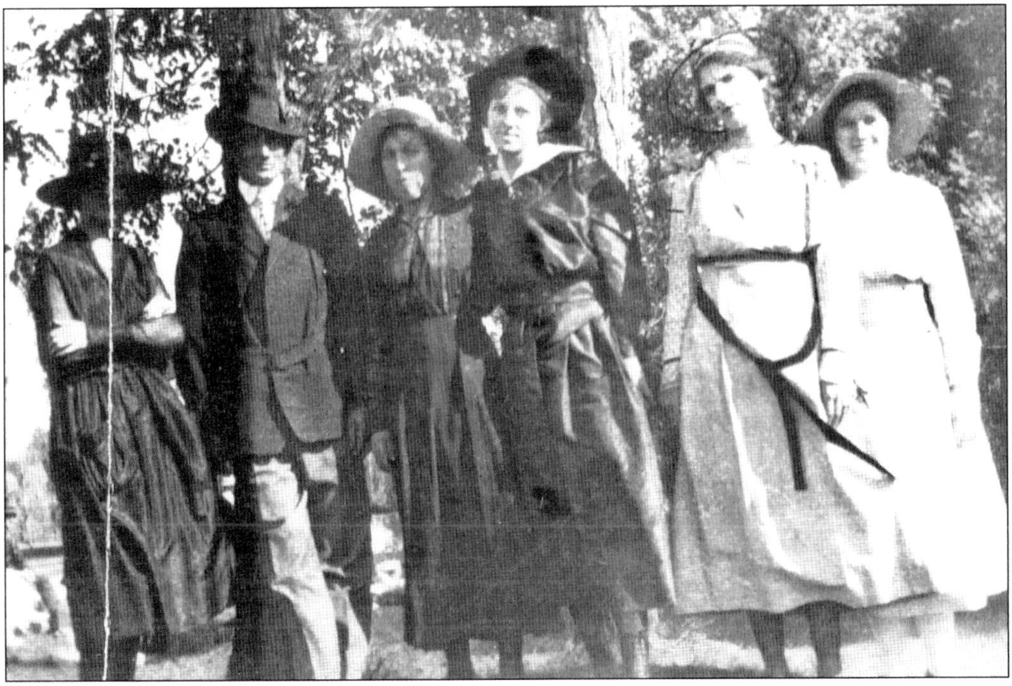

Sue Abell, Virgil Morrison, Nannie Vilther, Fanny McCandless, Margaret Redman, and Mary Orrender are photographed from left to right in this early-1900s photograph. Note that each one has a different kind of hat. In the early 1900s, hats were large with flowers, feathers, and ribbons. In the 1920s, women's hair became much shorter and the helmet-hugging hats with small brims became fashionable. (Courtesy Alva Martin Tharp.)

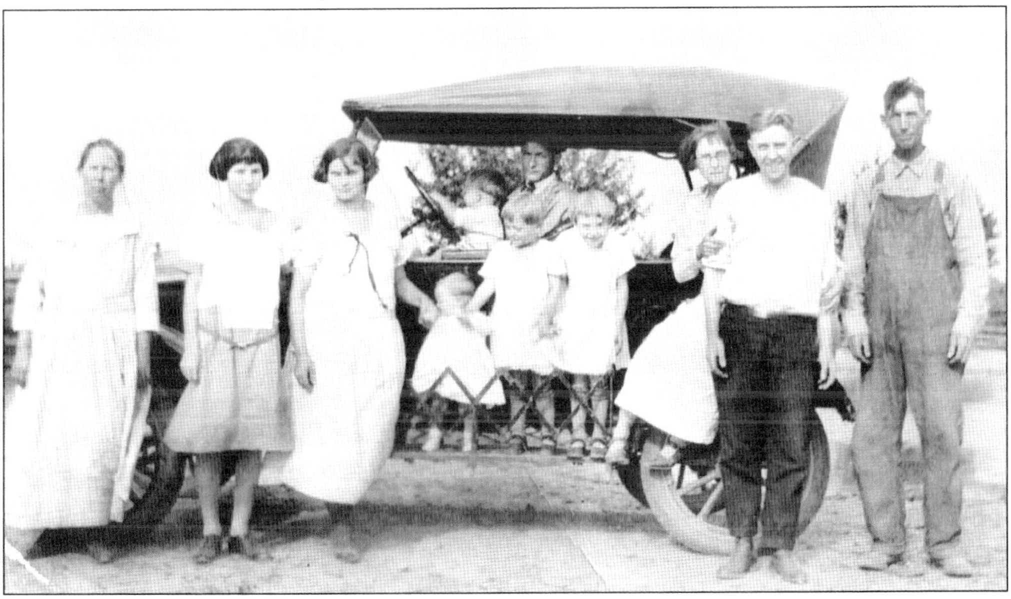

On July 5, 1924, three generations of the Routt family posed together around this automobile. By the 1920s, automobiles changed the American culture, starting a whole new industry. Automobiles provided more jobs to the American worker and the opportunity to visit other parts of the country. (Courtesy Darlene Routt Bryan.)

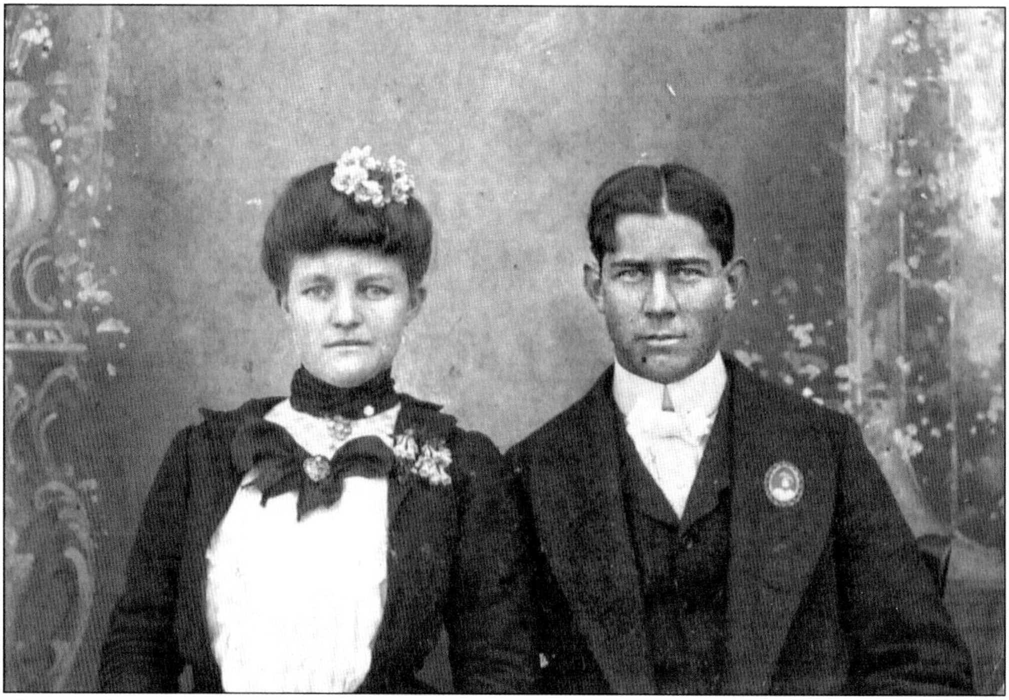

This is a photograph of Blanche and Anderson Walters taken around the early 1900s. The couple were lifelong residents of LaRue County. (Courtesy Darlene Routt Bryan.)

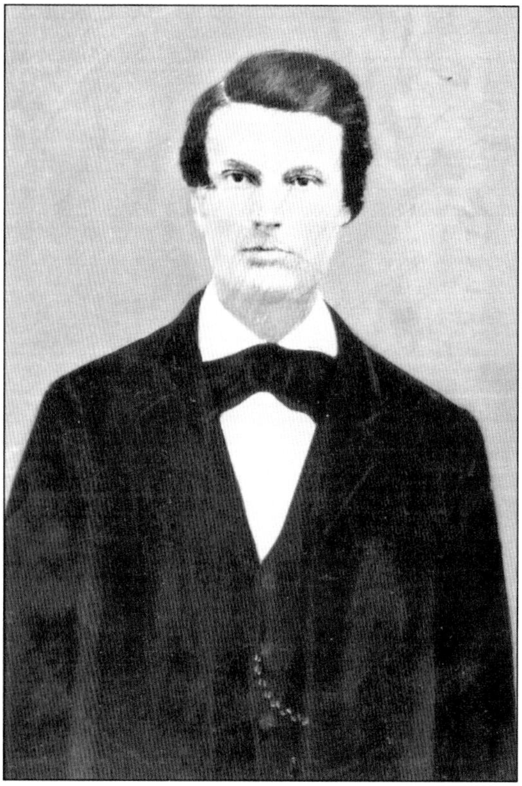

Charles W. Lee was born October 2, 1849, in LaRue County. Charles was the father of Minnie Belle Lee, who married Henry B. Jackson. (Courtesy William Leslie Hornback Jr.)

Odessa Priddy Hornback, Steve Hornback, and his youngest daughter, Joyce Lynn Hornback, are shown here. Odessa was Steve's second wife, and they were married in September 1967, residing in the Oak Hill community. Odessa Hornback was a babysitter for country music singer Loretta Lynn in Nashville, Kentucky, in the 1940s. (Courtesy Patricia Fields Hornback.)

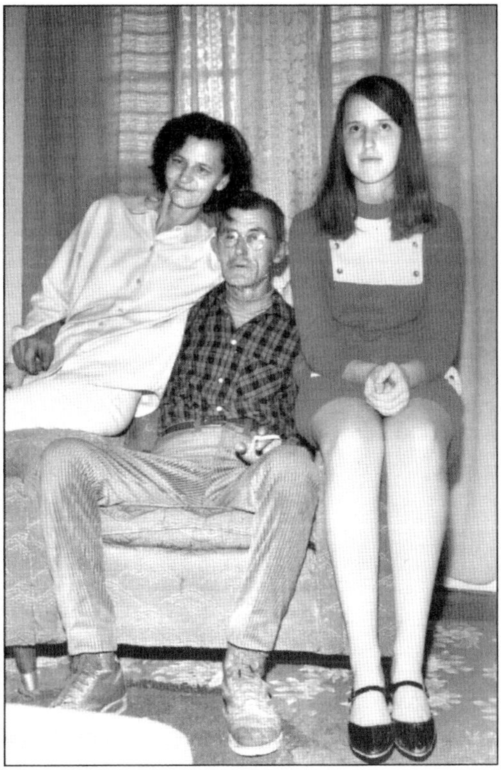

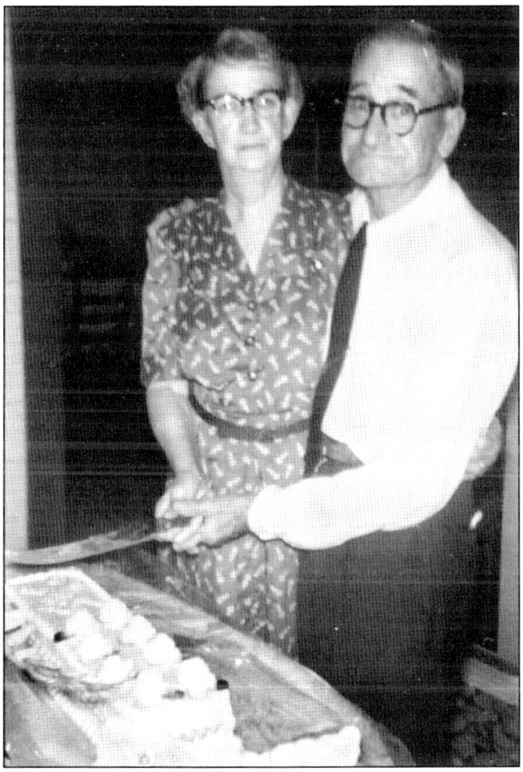

Ira Belle Hornback Angel and Charles Franklin Angel celebrate their 50th wedding anniversary. The couple was married November 15, 1908, in Bardstown, Kentucky. Ira was born June 29, 1890, in LaRue County and died July 28, 1968, in Pensacola, Florida. Charles was born September 6, 1887, in Roanoke, Virginia, and died December 11, 1969, in Pensacola, Florida. She was the daughter of Benjamin Thomas and Ida Hornback. (Courtesy William Leslie Hornback Jr.)

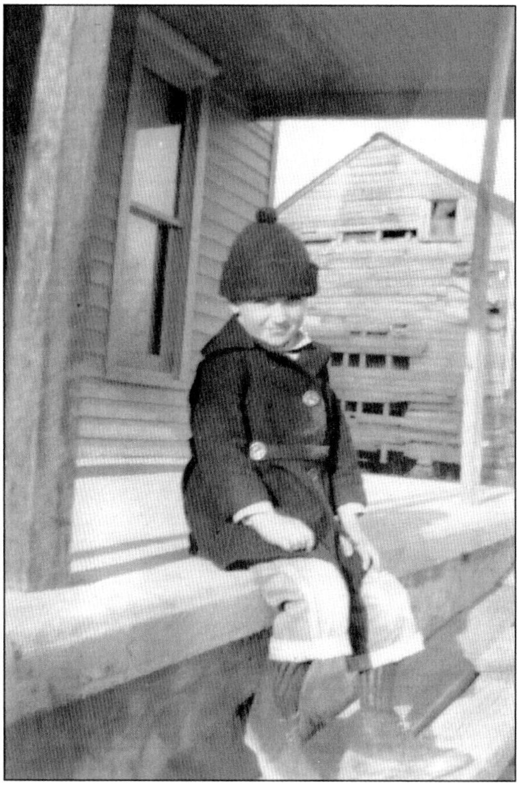

Vorice Turner is photographed sitting on the steps of Sarah and John Routt's house in March 1924. Vorice attended Barren Run School. (Courtesy Darlene Routt Bryan.)

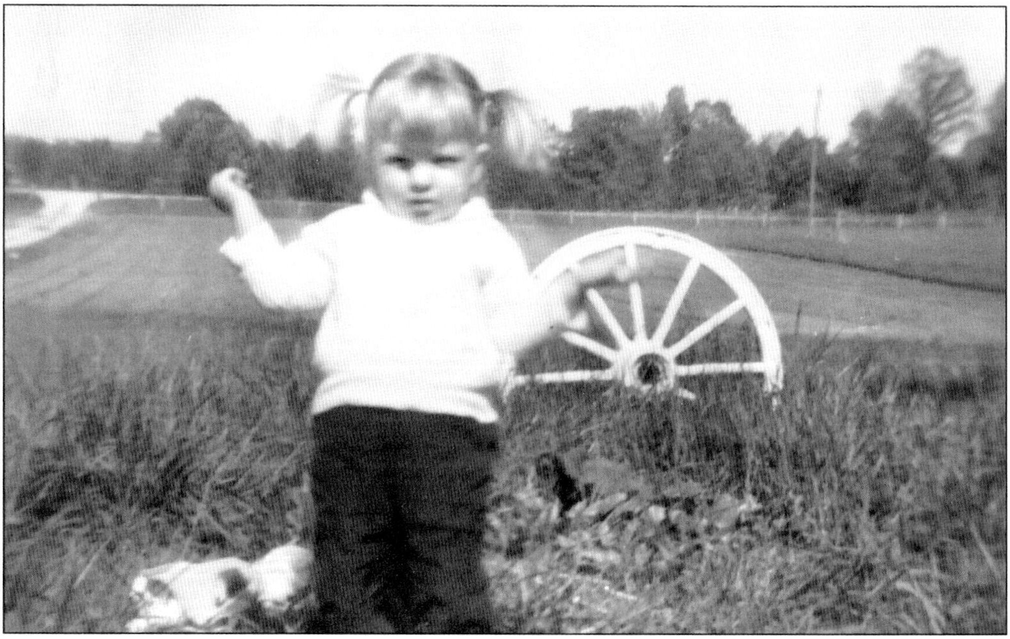

Cathy Jean Fields stands with her blonde ponytails at the old James and Cynthia "Cent" Hornback homestead. Cathy is the daughter of Raymond and Elizabeth Priddy Fields. Cathy Fields now lives in Hart County, where she is raising her son Charles "Charlie" Fields. (Courtesy Patricia Fields Hornback.)

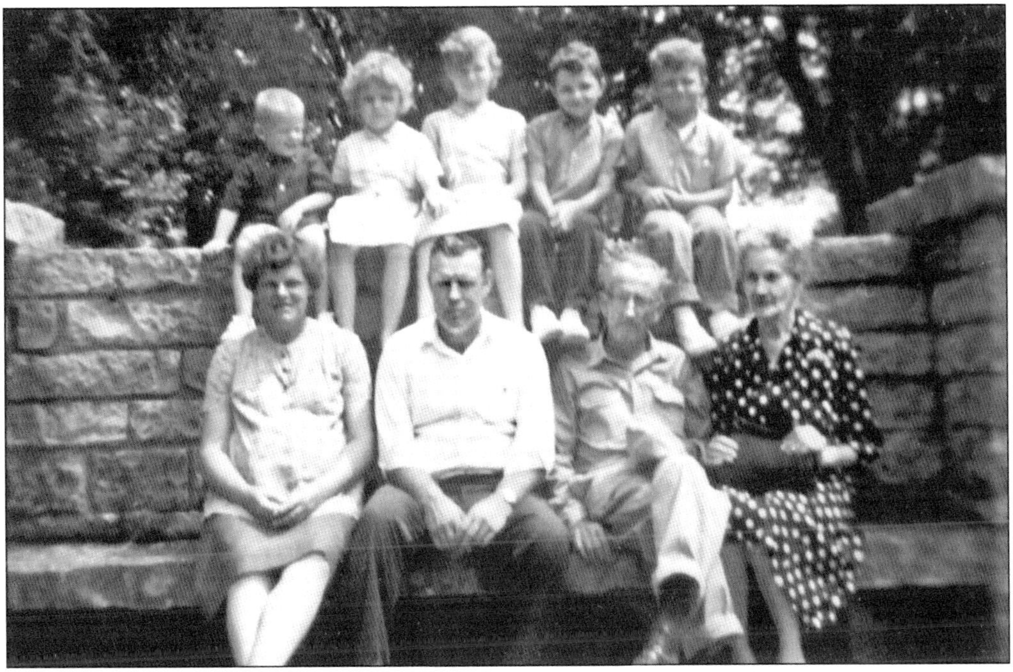

Abraham Lincoln's Birthplace in Hodgenville, Kentucky, is the site of this family photograph taken in May 1965. Shown from left to right are (first row) Elizabeth Priddy Fields, Raymond Dallas Fields, Albert Hornback, and Eva Leasor Hornback; (second row) Jesse Douglas Fields, Peggy Lynn Fields, Shirley Dean Fields, Frankie Nall, and Frankie's brother Donnie Nall. The group toured the birthplace and enjoyed a picnic lunch together. (Courtesy Patricia Fields Hornback.)

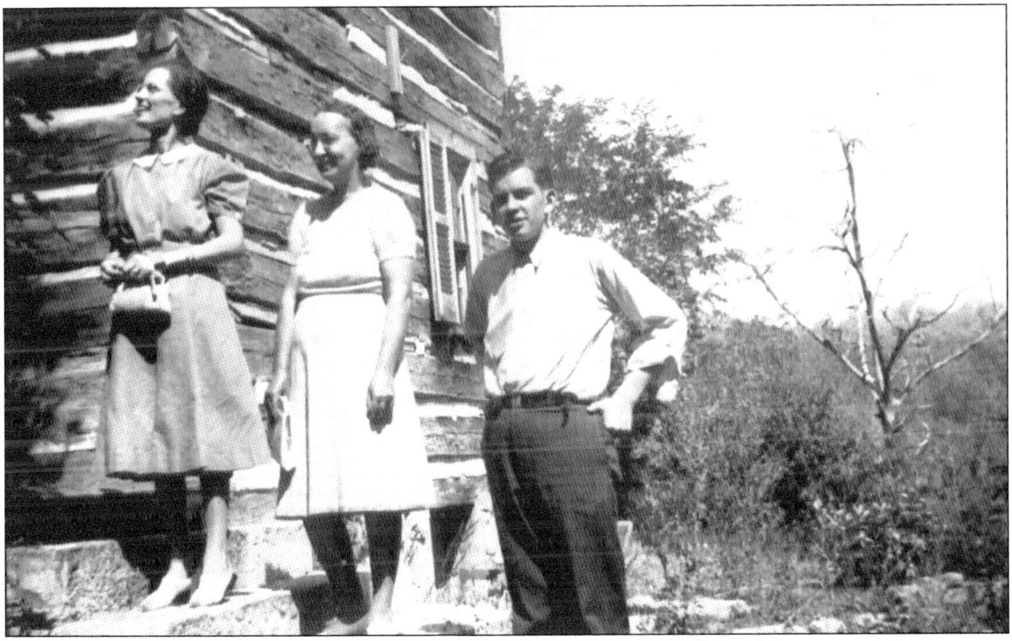

In 1943, Florence Routt Cook (left), Susan Abell Tharp, and Russell Cook Jr. enjoyed their visit to Rock City, Tennessee. Southern lore claims you can see seven states from Lover's Leap at nearby Lookout Mountain, although it is not true. (Courtesy Alva Martin Tharp.)

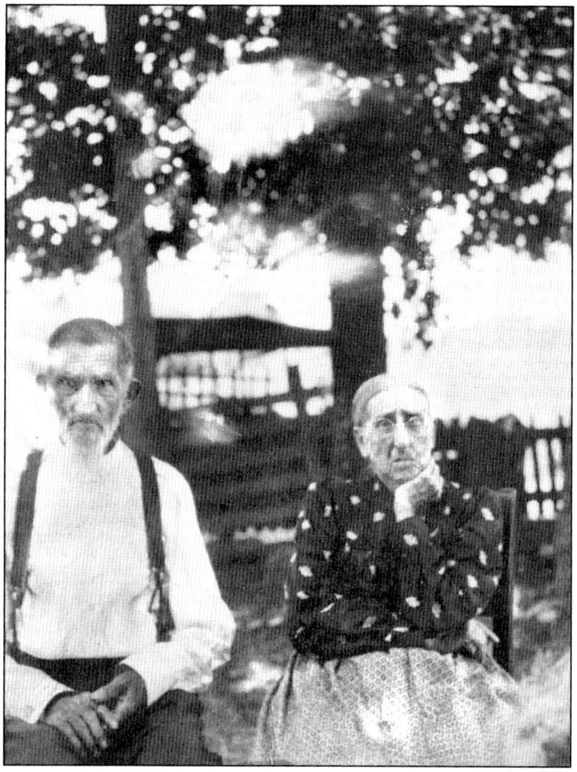

Henry Buckner and Martha "Mattie" Jane Hornback were photographed on July 30, 1919. Henry Buckner Hornback was the son of Isaac and Catherine Joseph Hornback. Isaac served in the War of 1812 and fought in the Battle of New Orleans. It was said he came to Kentucky from Virginia with a musket on his back. Catherine Joseph was born in 1801 in Athertonville, Kentucky, and was a schoolmate of Abraham Lincoln. (Courtesy Patricia Fields Hornback.)

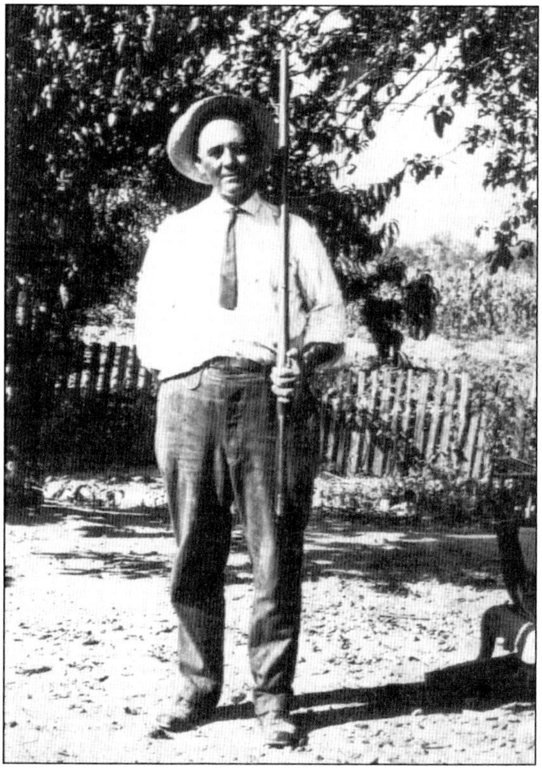

Robert Mathew Abell holds this cap and ball rifle bought at an estate sale of a neighbor, a Mr. Catlett, for 50¢. This photograph was taken August 19, 1917. Alva Martin Tharp now owns his great-grandfather's rifle, which is still in working condition today. (Courtesy Alva Martin Tharp.)

Alva Martin Tharp (left) and Marion Lee Catlett show off their instruments they used for entertaining friends and neighbors. The boys often played at square dances and local parties. This photograph was taken March 11, 1945. (Courtesy Alva Martin Tharp.)

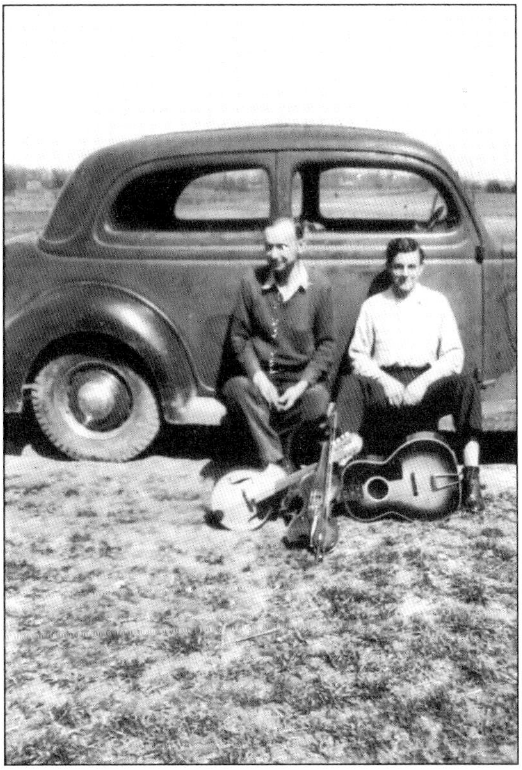

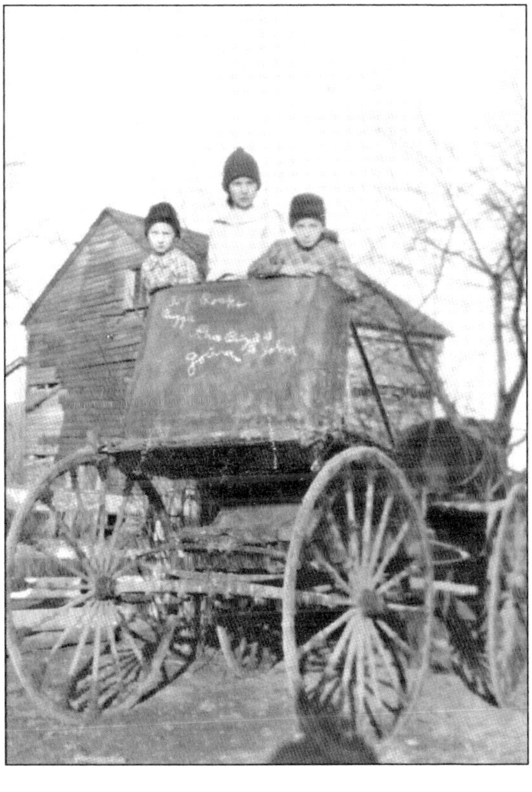

In 1921, Josie Routt stands in the middle of Roy Rock's buggy with Williams sisters on each side of her. Roy Routt used this buggy when he would court his future wife, Ruby. (Courtesy Darlene Routt Bryan.)

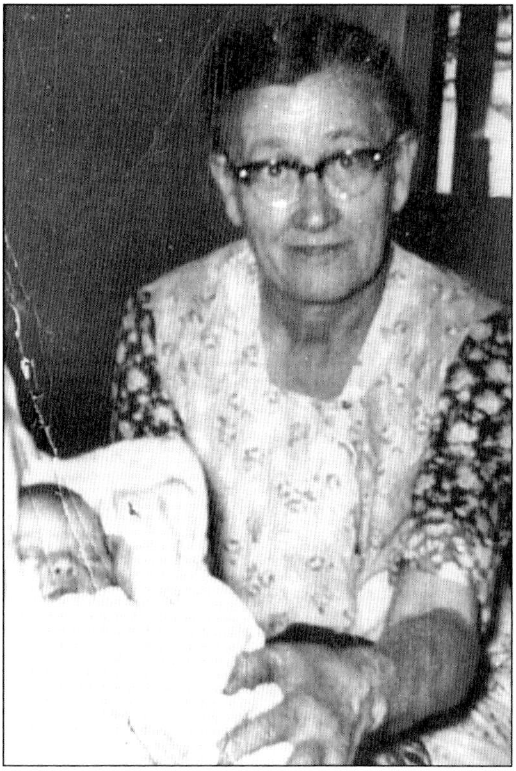

Effie D. Curry Hornback holds her granddaughter Marsha Hornback in this photograph dated April 1954. Marsha is the daughter of Robert and Geraldine Gusler Hornback. Effie was the wife of Jeff Hornback. (Courtesy Eula May Brooks Hornback.)

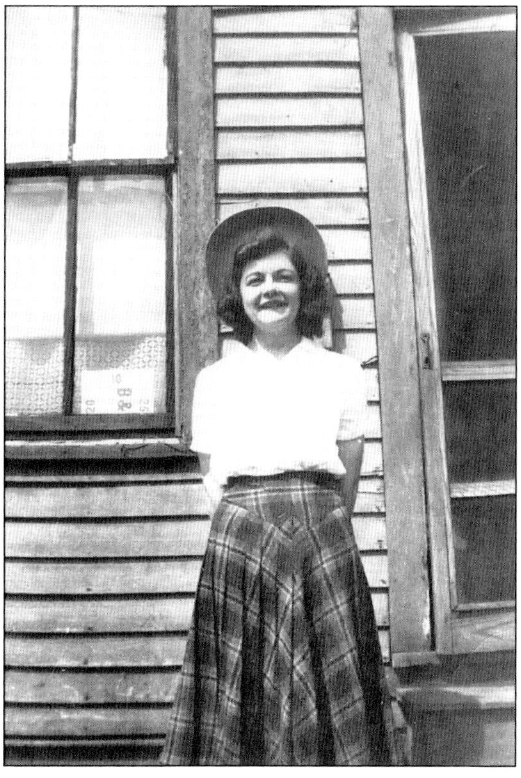

This photograph was taken of Gladys Walters on September 1941. In 1941, Franklin Roosevelt was elected for a third term as president. The U.S. Naval Base in Pearl Harbor was bombed by the Japanese on December 7, 1941. (Courtesy Darlene Routt Bryan.)

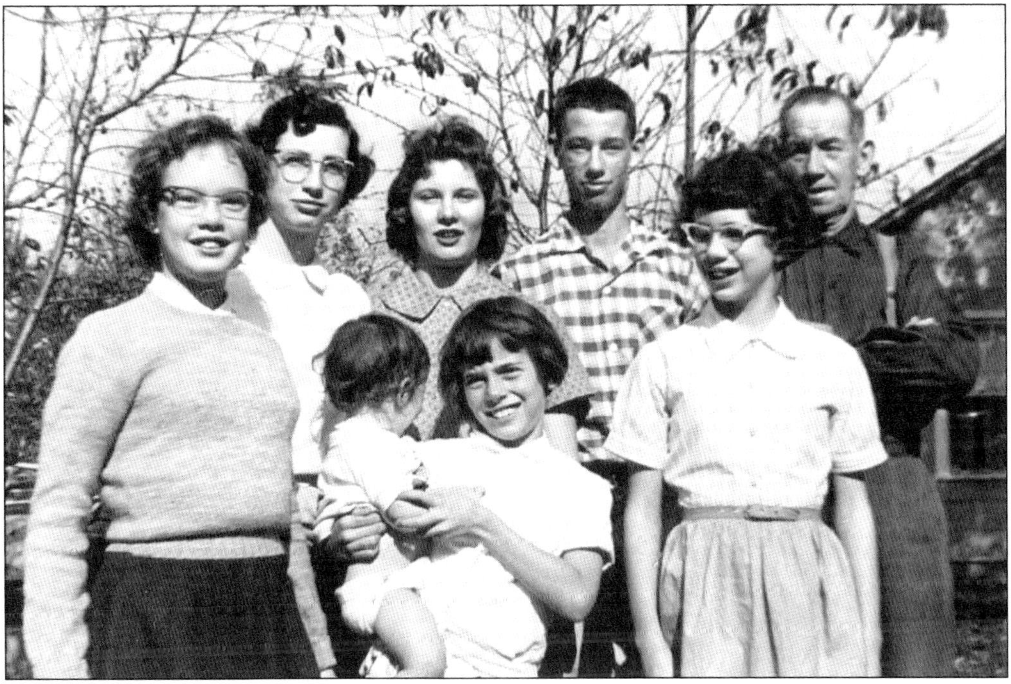

On November 1, 1959, pictured from left to right are (first row) Patricia Rock, baby Ramona Lynn Routt, Bitty Routt, and Linda Routt; (second row) Darlene Routt, Sarah Lou Routt, Clayton Rock, and Pa Bowly. (Courtesy Darlene Routt Bryan.)

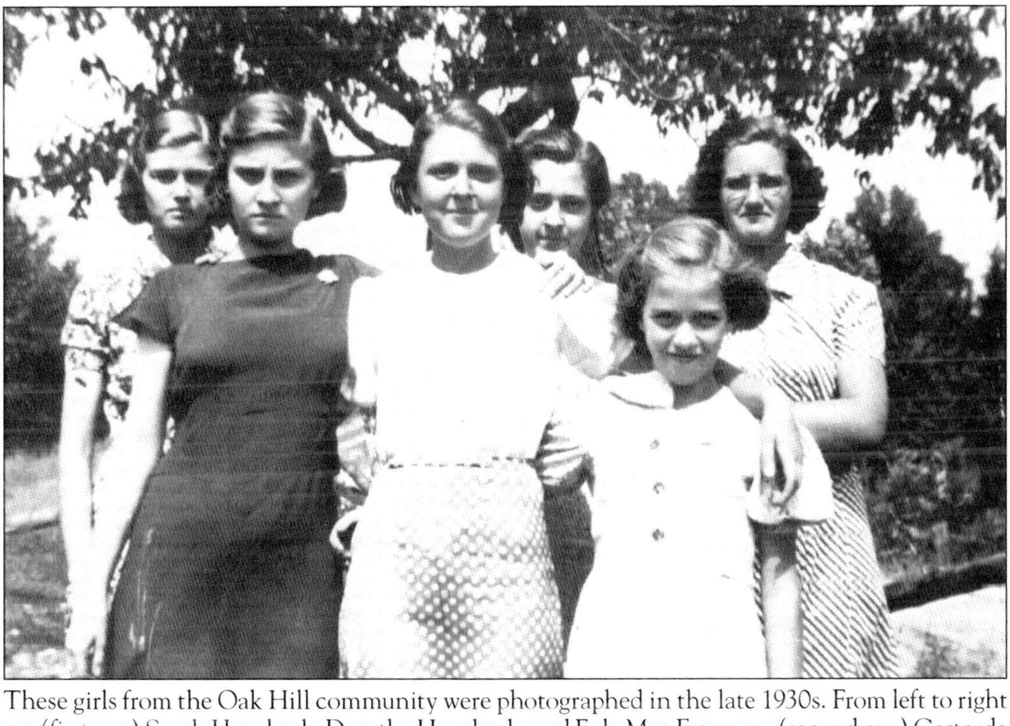

These girls from the Oak Hill community were photographed in the late 1930s. From left to right are (first row) Sarah Hornback, Dorothy Hornback, and Eula Mae Freeman; (second row) Gertrude Hornback, Juanita Hornback, and Lenora Watkins. (Courtesy Beatrice Hornback Gibson.)

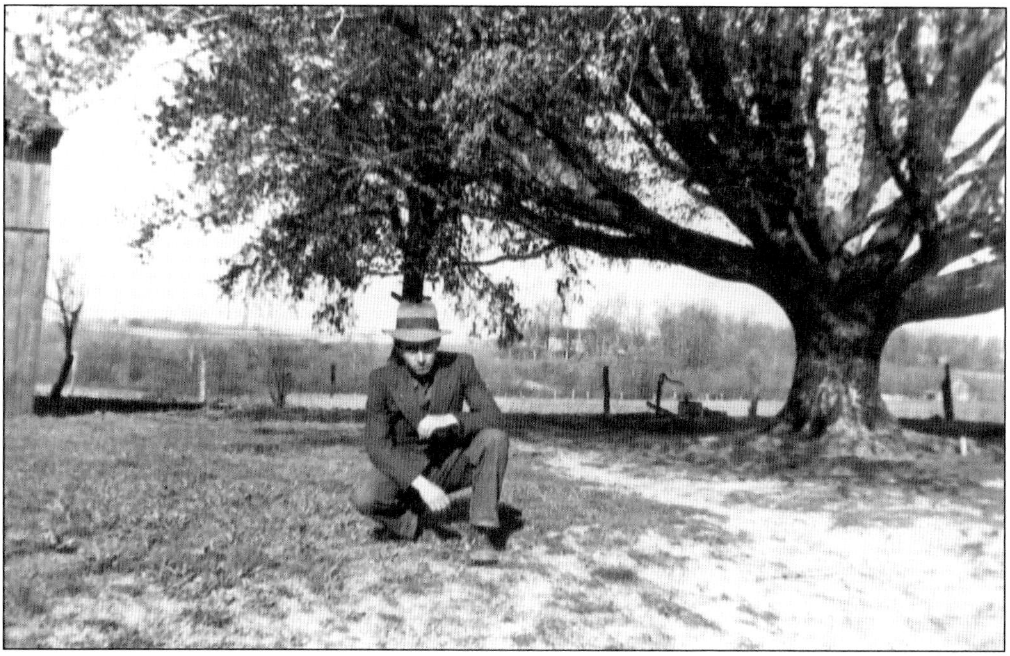

Wilburn "Webb" Hornback is pictured in front of this large beech tree, which all of the children in the neighborhood would climb. It was said by different members of the community that there were over 100 names carved in the tree. The farm was owned by Ollie and Nannie Hornback on Oak Hill Road. (Courtesy Beatrice Hornback Gibson.)

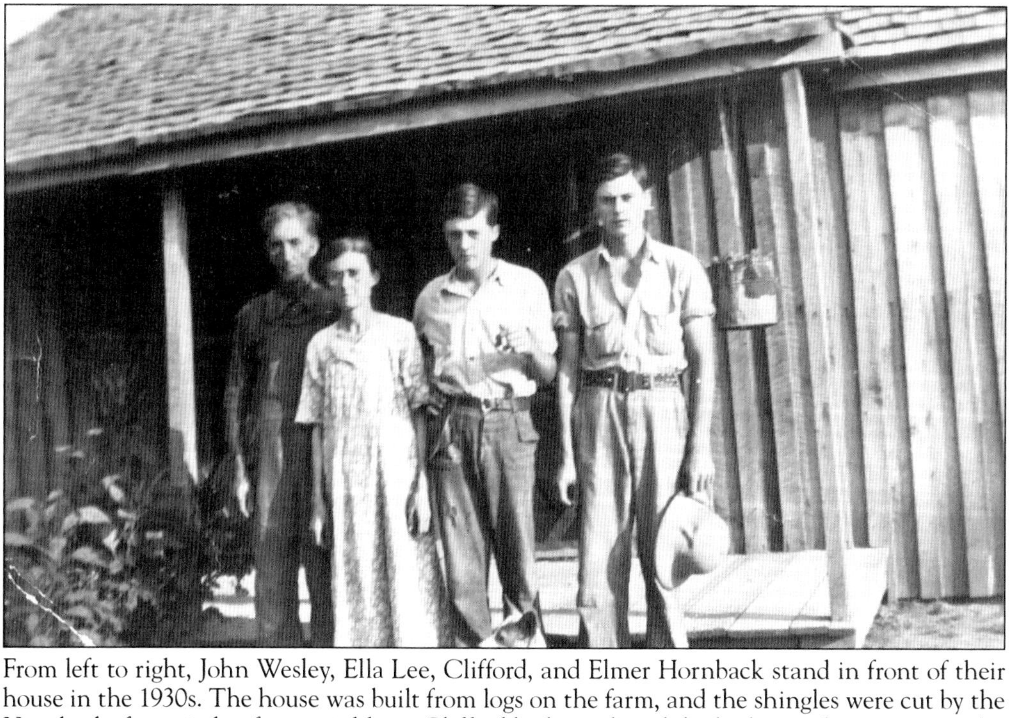

From left to right, John Wesley, Ella Lee, Clifford, and Elmer Hornback stand in front of their house in the 1930s. The house was built from logs on the farm, and the shingles were cut by the Hornbacks from timber from neighbors. Clifford looks as though he had something to say to the photographer. (Courtesy Clifford Hornback.)

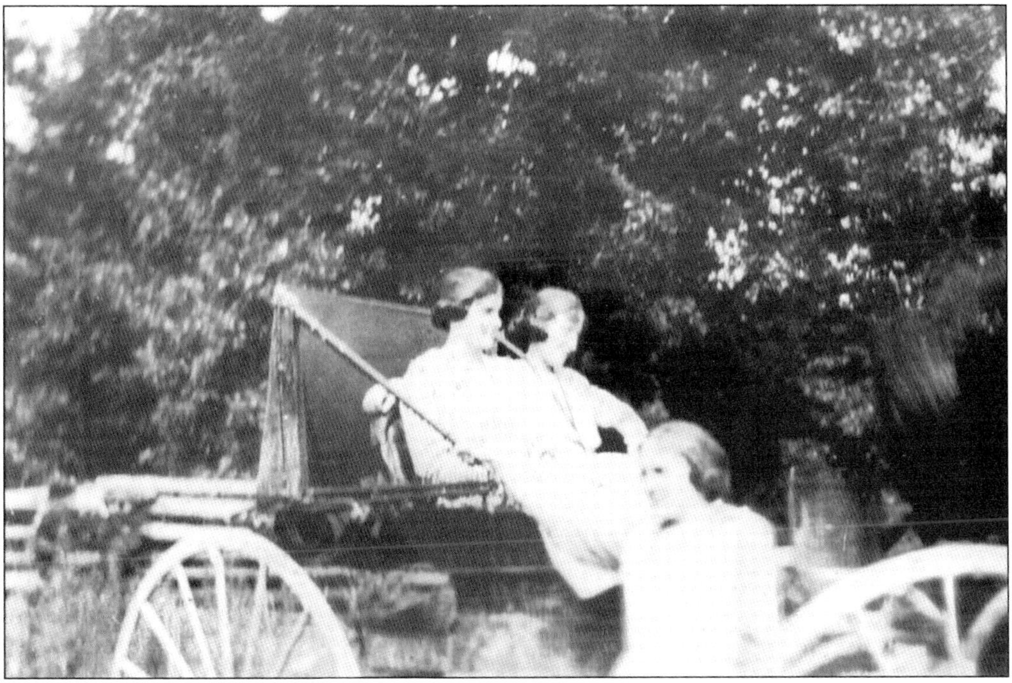

Edna Ward (left), Sophia Meers Sullivan (center), and ? Meers are photographed in this buggy. Horse and buggies provided women the means to travel, visit sick neighbors, and attend social events instead of walking for miles. (Courtesy Evelyn Cruse.)

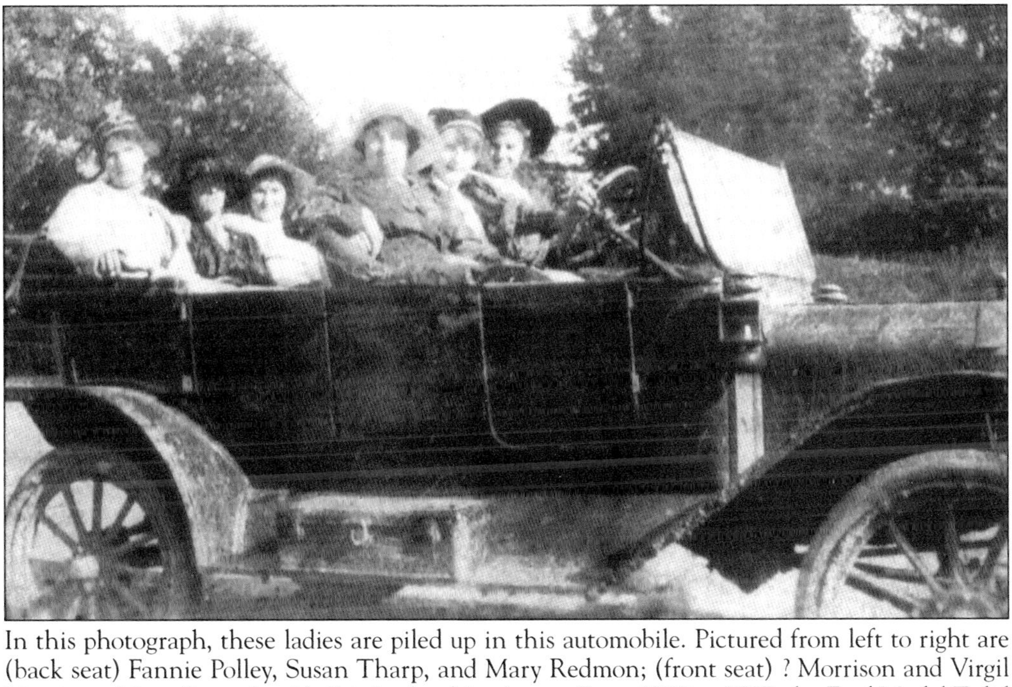

In this photograph, these ladies are piled up in this automobile. Pictured from left to right are (back seat) Fannie Polley, Susan Tharp, and Mary Redmon; (front seat) ? Morrison and Virgil Morrison; Mary Orrender Abell is in the driver's seat. From 1908 to 1927, the Ford Model T did not change much in appearance. This photograph was taken in the early 1900s. (Courtesy Alva Martin Tharp.)

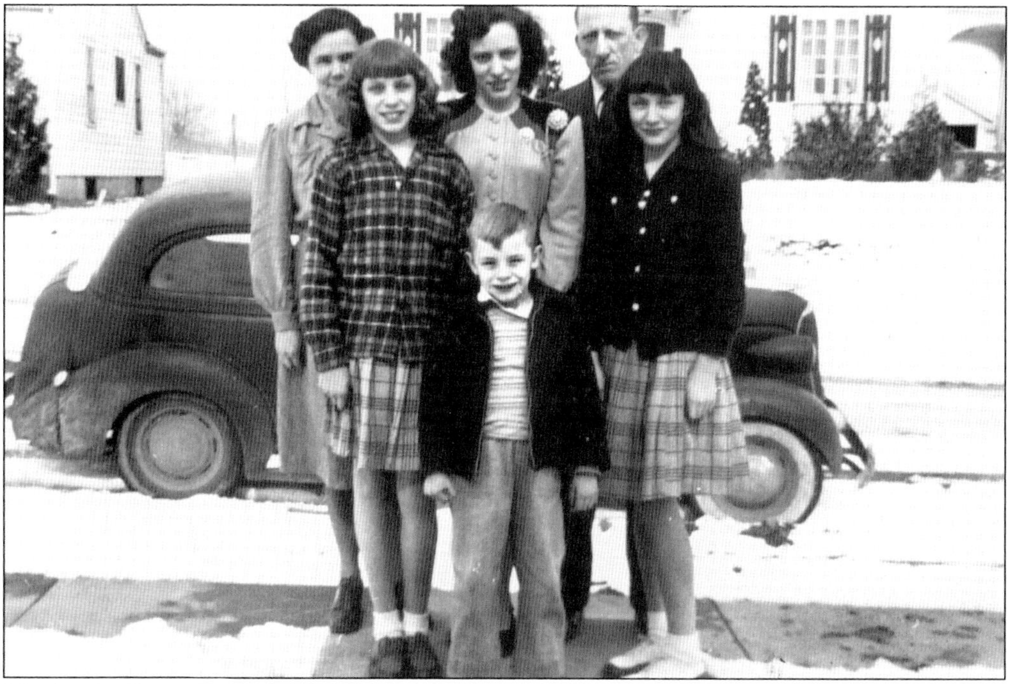

The family all stands together for this family photograph in the snow. Pictured from left to right are Thelma, Mary Kathryn, Nancy, Virgil, Yvonne, and the little boy is Robert "Bobby" Pennington. (Courtesy Mary Kathryn Pennington Puckett.)

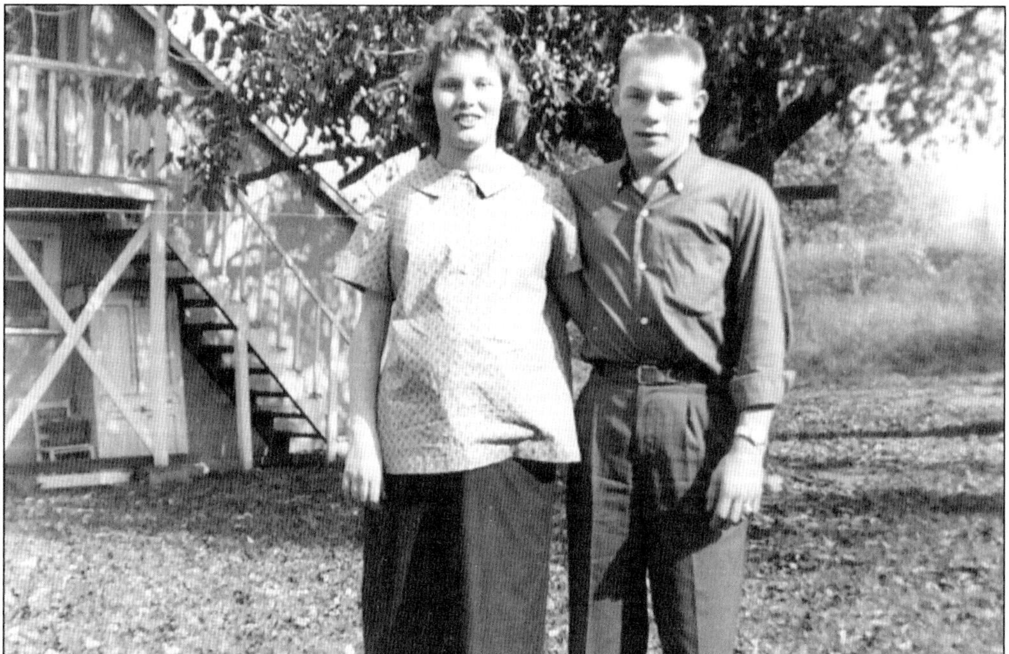

Sarah Lou Routt Pennington and Robert "Bobby" Pennington stand side by side for this photograph dated November 1, 1959. (Courtesy Darlene Routt Bryan.)

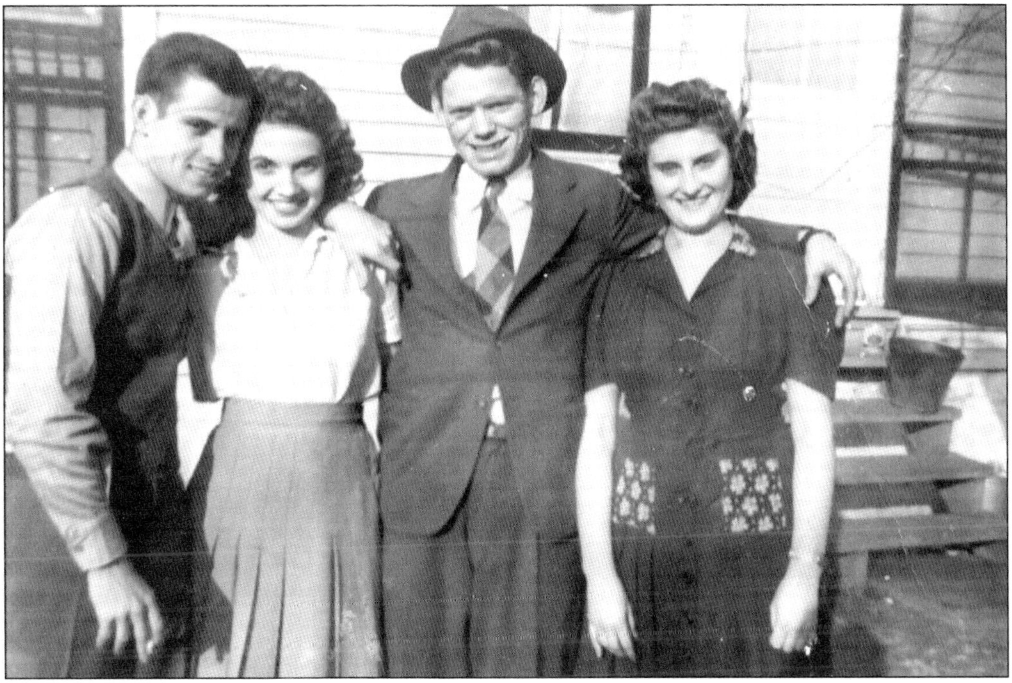

Listed from left to right, Jesse "J. C." Hornback, Beatrice Hornback, Calvin Hornback, and Sarah Hornback huddle in close together to be photographed. J. C. and Calvin are brothers and cousins of the girls. During World War II, Beatrice and Sarah moved from their homes in LaRue County to work at a factory for a while in Louisville, Kentucky. (Courtesy Beatrice Hornback Gibson.)

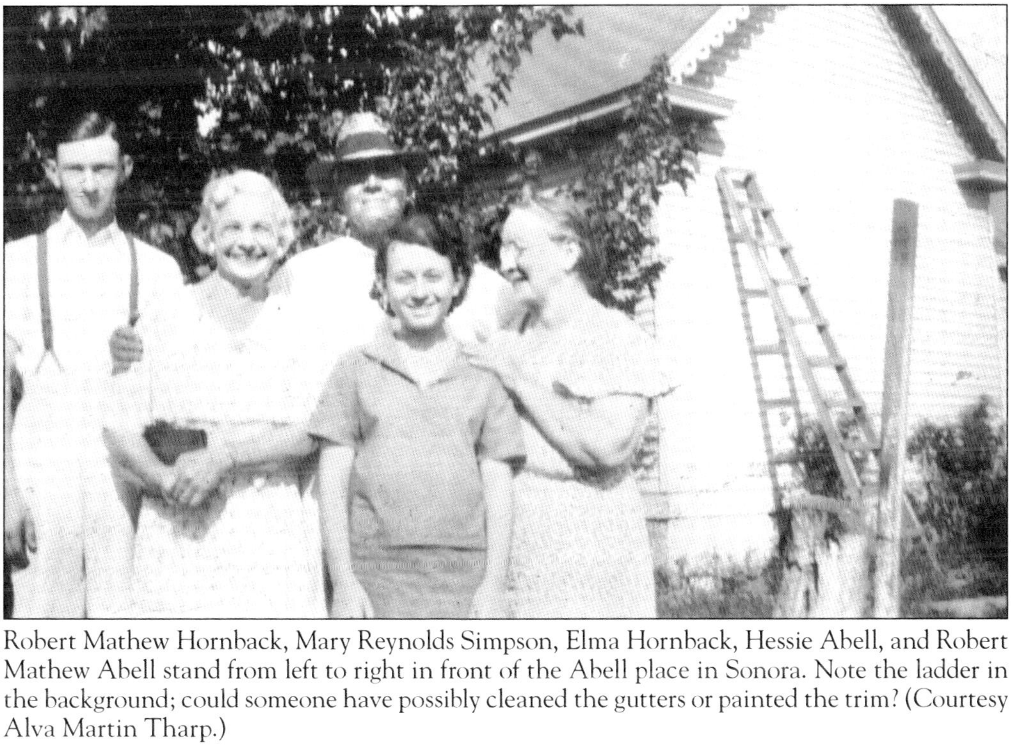

Robert Mathew Hornback, Mary Reynolds Simpson, Elma Hornback, Hessie Abell, and Robert Mathew Abell stand from left to right in front of the Abell place in Sonora. Note the ladder in the background; could someone have possibly cleaned the gutters or painted the trim? (Courtesy Alva Martin Tharp.)

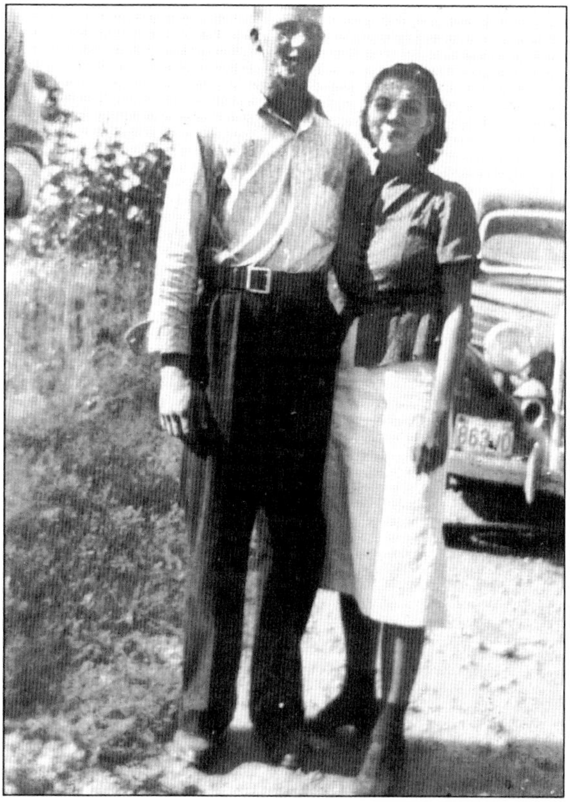

Arthur and Morna Humphrees Eastridge pose in front of their car in 1939. Note the license plate number: 863J0. The first license plates used on automobiles were seen in New York in 1901. The first plates were made of leather pads or flat metal plates with the owner's initials. (Courtesy Morna Humphrees Eastridge.)

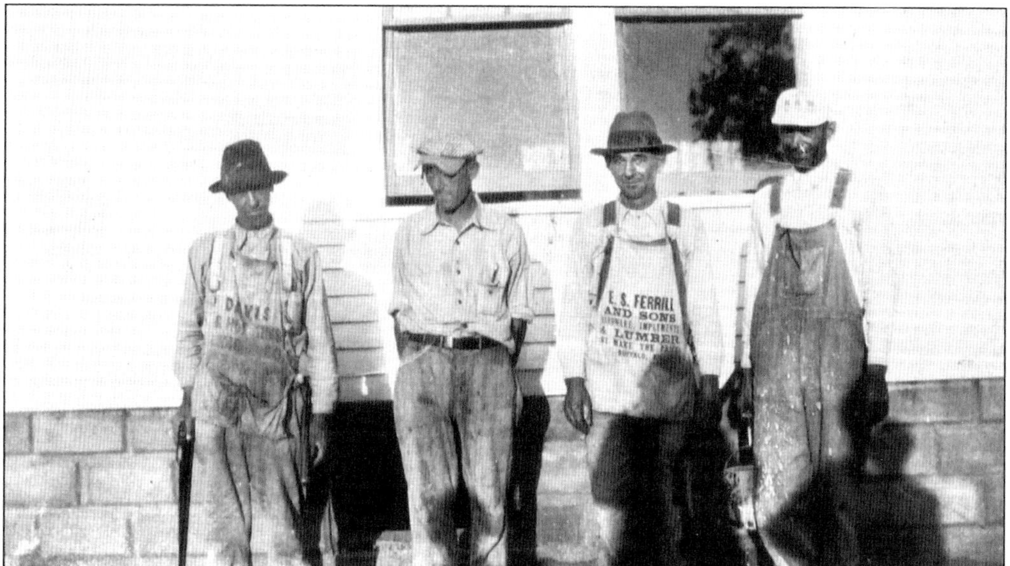

Although it is not clear who these gentleman are in this photograph dated October 13, 1931, it is clear they had been working very hard. The first gentleman has a saw in his hand, and the fourth gentleman has a paint bucket. The photograph came from the private collection of Virgil and Thelma Pennington. (Courtesy Mary Kathryn Pennington Puckett.)

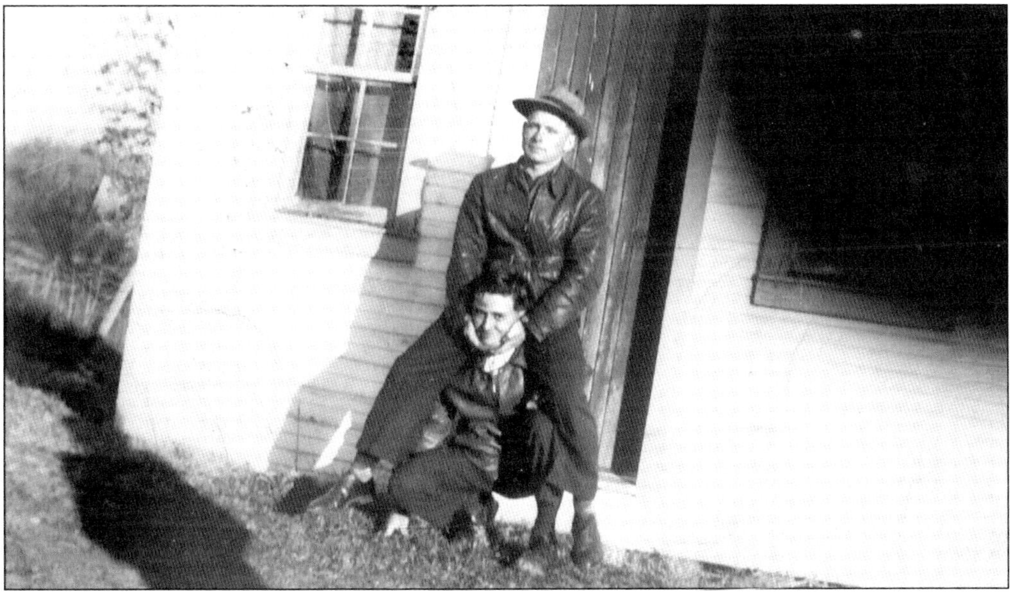

Pete Wheeler (top) and Clifford Hornback clown around in this photograph. These two young men, often makers of mischief, remained friends throughout their lives. Pete was the son of Ollie Wheeler and farmed in the Sonora area. Clifford served in the U.S. Army from June 15, 1945, until June 15, 1948, as an engineer in the General Service Battalion and a combat engineer. Clifford retired from Leggett Platt, Inc., in Simpsonville, Kentucky, where they made furniture. Clifford married Georgia Jaggers, and the couple had three children—Janit, Craig, and Ricky. (Courtesy Shirley Hornback Miller.)

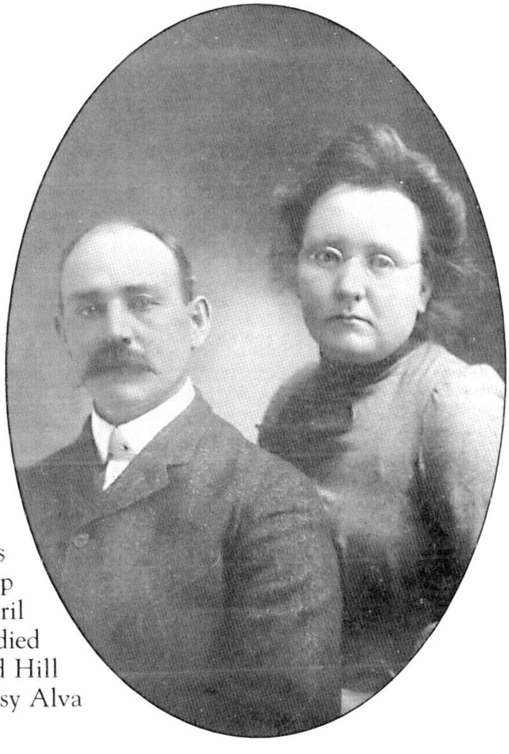

Robert Mathew Abell and Hester Jane Adams Abell were grandparents of Alva Martin Tharp in Sonora. Robert was born c. 1867 and died April 23, 1950. Hester "Hessie" was born c. 1875 and died March 13, 1941. The couple is buried at Red Hill Cemetery in Hodgenville, Kentucky. (Courtesy Alva Martin Tharp.)

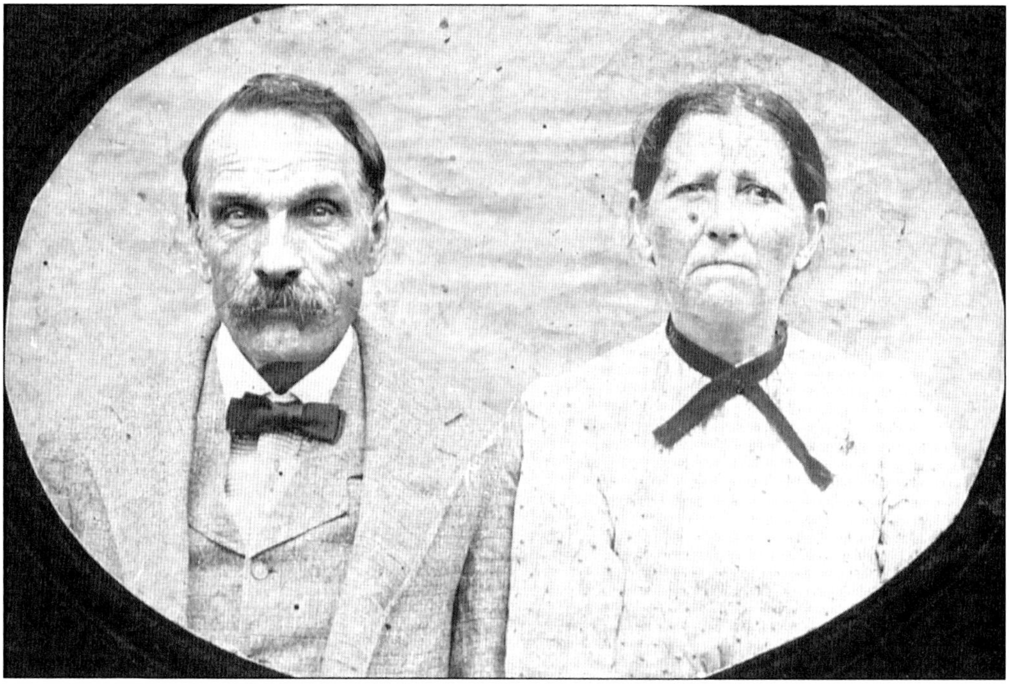

Greenberry Benjamin Druien and Mary Frances Pearce Druien are shown in this oval frame. Greenberry, son of George William and Celia "Cola" Perkins Druien, was born January 8, 1846, and died January 13, 1921. Mary Pearce was born October 25, 1849, and died January 13, 1921. James Wesley Wheeler was their son-in-law. (Courtesy Pat Wheeler Lassonde.)

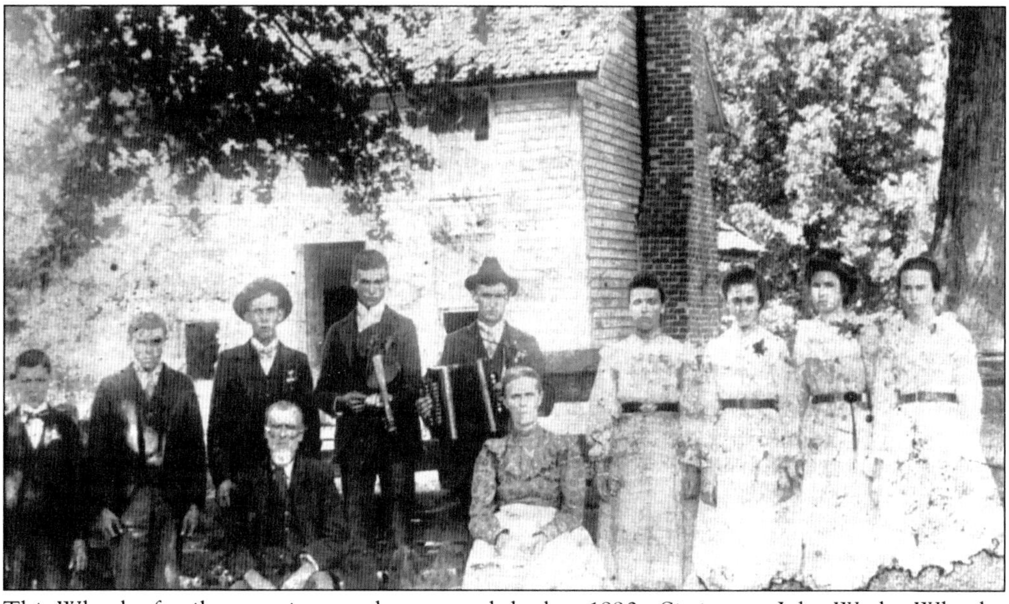

This Wheeler family portrait was taken around the late 1890s. Sitting are John Wesley Wheeler and his wife, Thurzia or Therissa Wheeler. Their children from left to right are ? Wheeler, James Wesley Wheeler, thought to be Edward Wheeler and two other Wheeler boys, ? Wheeler, Ella Lee Wheeler, ? Wheeler and Martha Jane Wheeler. Note the musical instruments in the boys' hands. (Courtesy Clifford Hornback.)

Three

God's Creatures Working Together

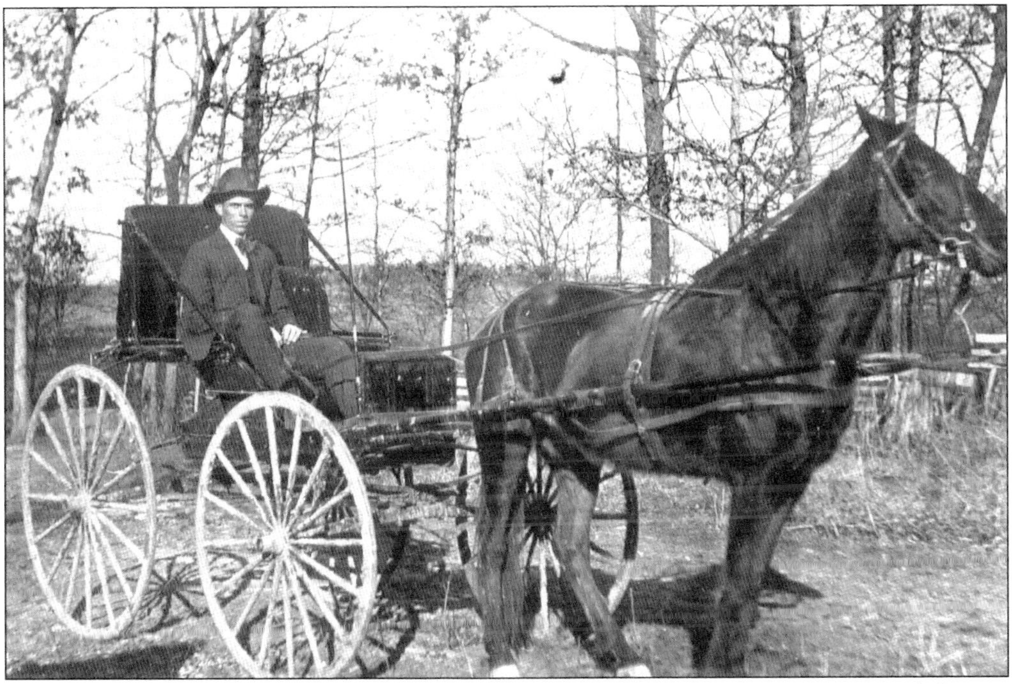

Aylette Lively Cruse is seen with his horse and buggy in the 1920s. The horse was a central element in urban life. It plowed fields, hauled supplies, and sprinted with people in elegant buggies and carriages. The increasing urban population created a new industry for horses. Aylette was born c. 1887 and died October 20, 1960. (Courtesy Evelyn Cruse.)

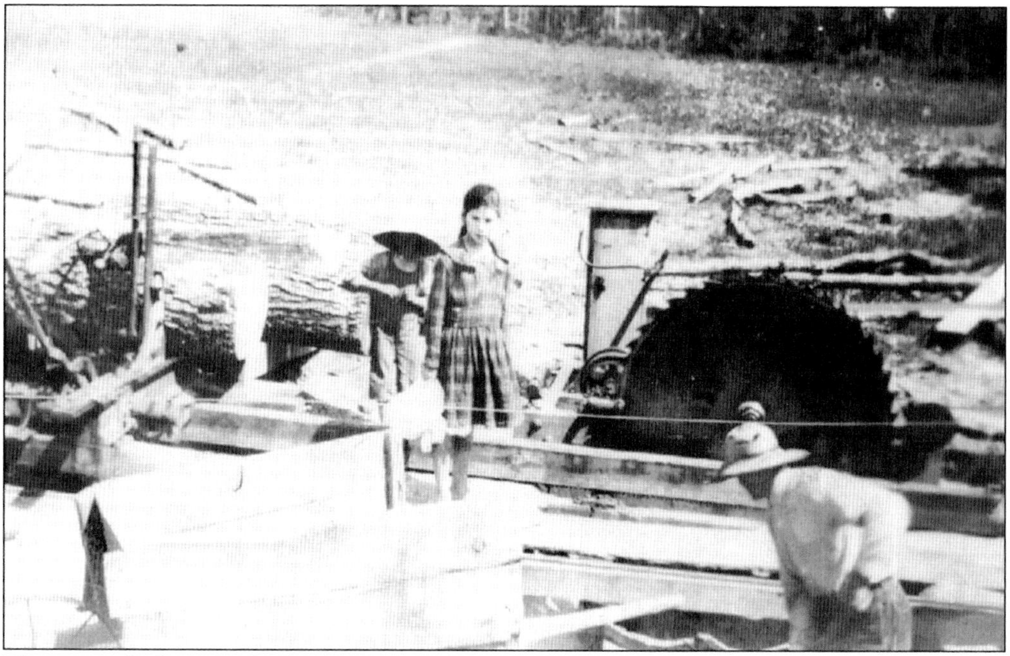

This sawmill photograph of Lee Routt and his children Eston "Eck" and Josie Routt was taken in the 1920s. Note the size of the blade on the sawmill. These large blades, flywheels, and long exposed belts were all left unguarded. The large saw blade sat vertically between two sliding wooden arms. (Courtesy Darlene Routt Bryan.)

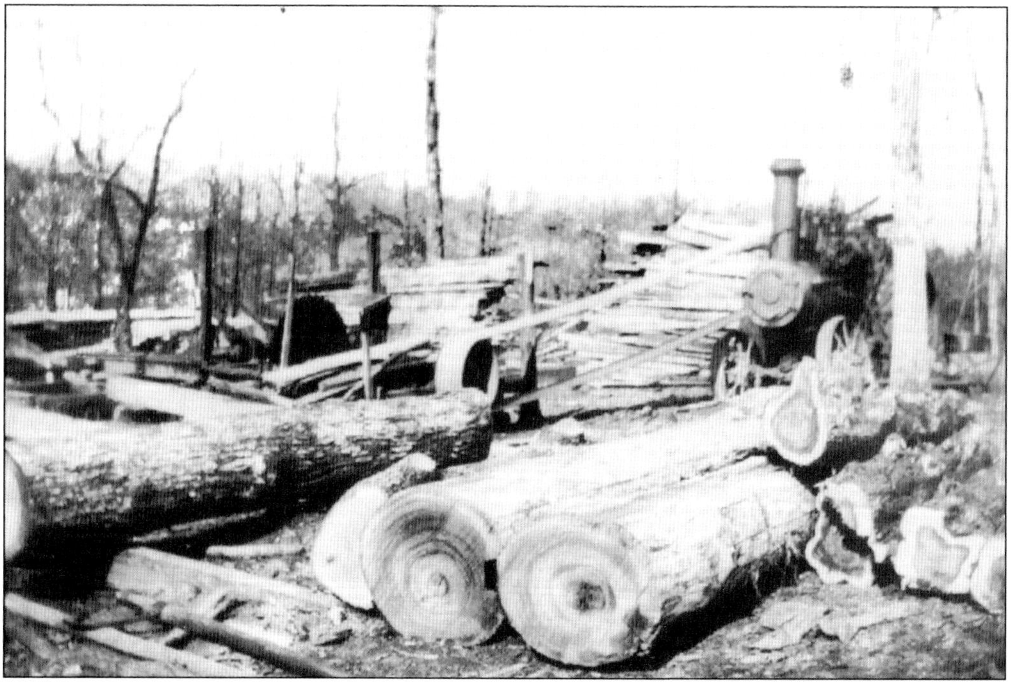

A load of lumber has been evenly cut and stacked in this photograph. The steam machine sits at the back of the sawmill. The system of pulleys and belts transferred power from the main drive wheels to the saw. (Courtesy Darlene Routt Bryan.)

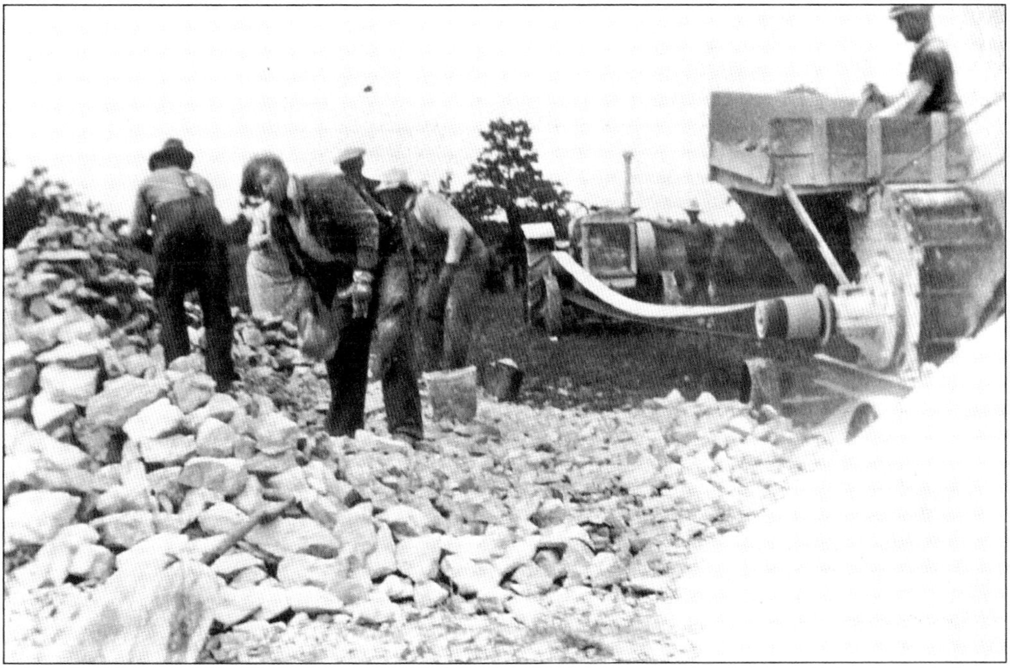

This rock-crushing machine was located on Oak Hill Road in Sonora on the farm of Granville and Clliffoord Cruse. These men hauled limestone rocks from the farm and threw them into the box of the rock crusher. County roads were provided with gravel produced from the rock crushers. (Courtesy Evelyn Cruse.)

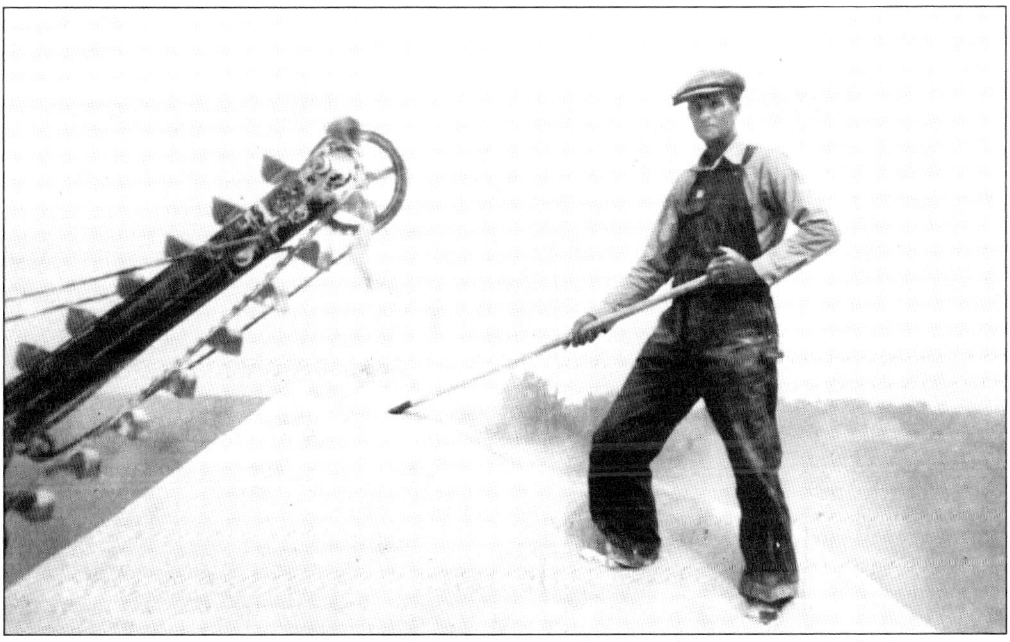

Granville Cruse stands on this pile of limestone rocks after they were crushed. The ground powder was used for fertilizer. Some of the limestone rocks had been used to construct the porch of Alva Martin Tharp's house, less than a mile down the road on Chestnut Fork Road. (Courtesy Evelyn Cruse.)

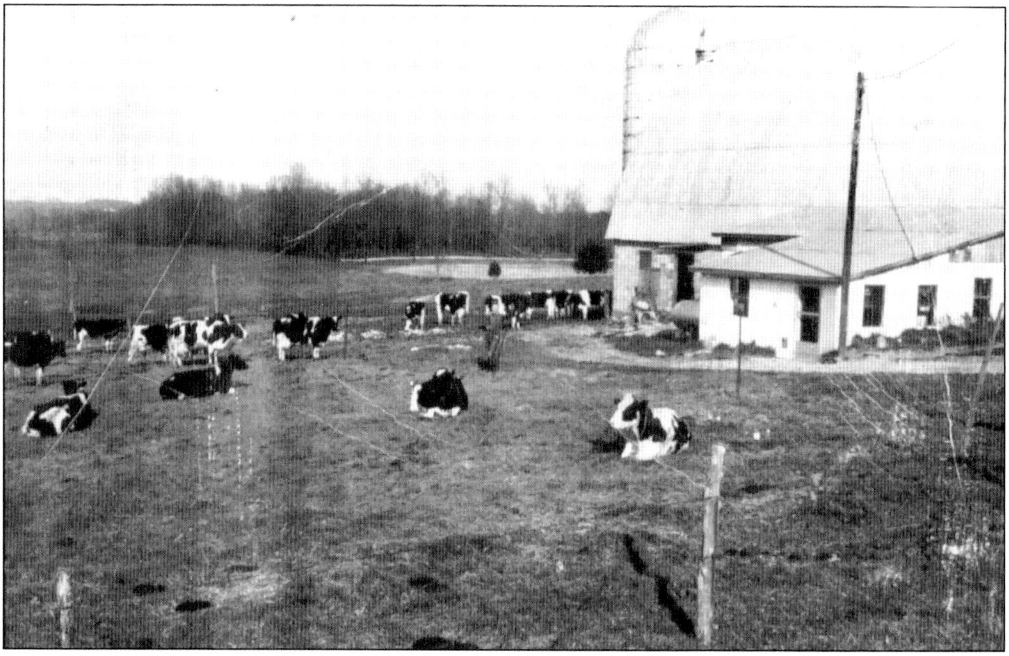

This dairy barn of Arthur and Morna Eastridge was built out of scrap metal from the Fort Knox, Kentucky, barracks. Fort Knox is a U.S. Army post in Kentucky. A new armored force was constructed in 1940, leaving scrap materials behind. (Courtesy Morna Humphrees Eastridge.)

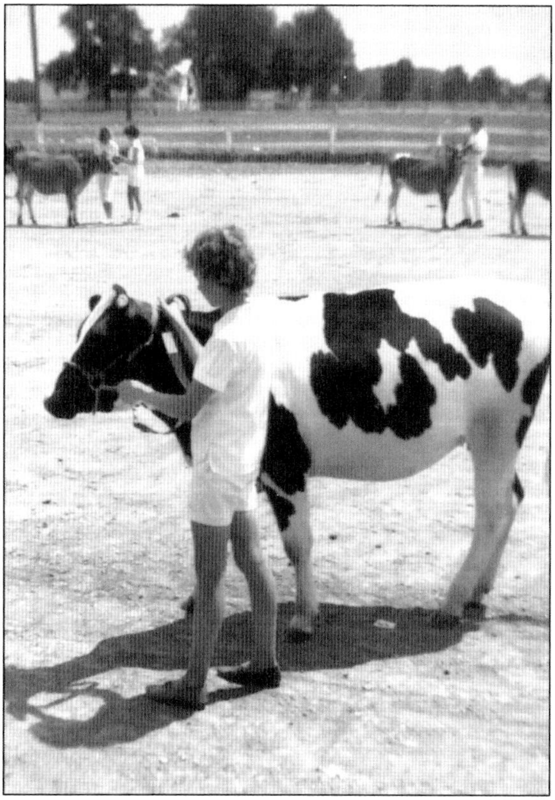

Violet Eastridge, a member of 4-H, shows off her prized Holstein heifer at the LaRue County Fair Grounds. Holsteins are black and white or red and white. They are a very stylish animal. Healthy newborn calves weigh approximately 90 pounds at birth. Holstein cattle are dairy cows. The LaRue County Fair is the oldest continuously running fair in Kentucky. (Courtesy Morna Humphrees Eastridge.)

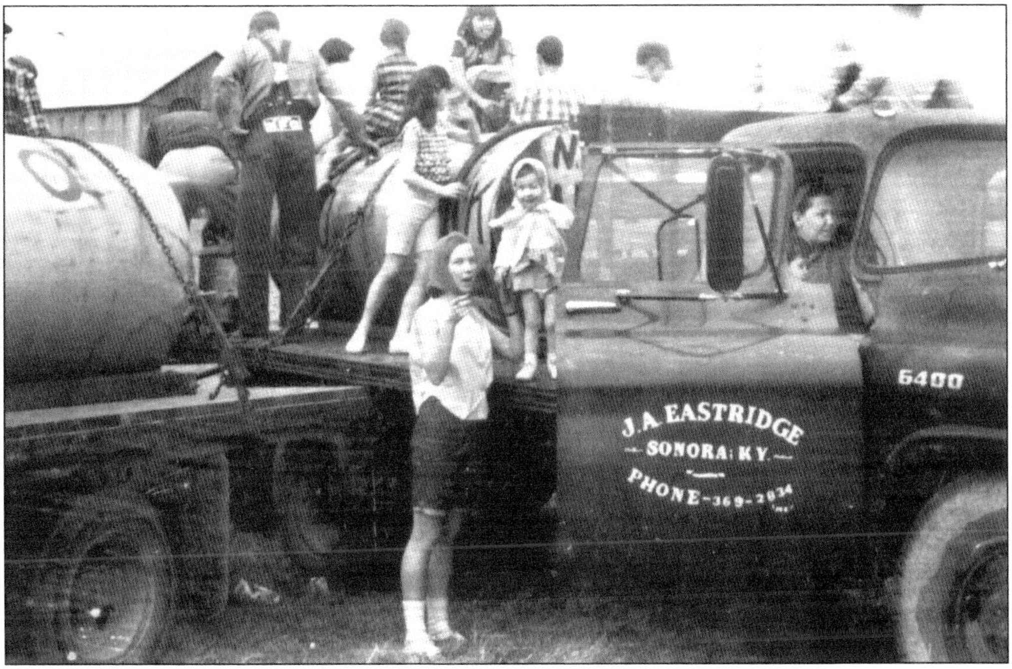

Violet Eastridge points her finger at the photographer while farmers are pouring out gallons of milk after the profit of milk dropped. By pouring out the gallons, it brought milk back in demand. The milk production of one cow twice a day has been known to produce 67,914 gallons of milk in one year. Of the 3.6 million dairy farms in business in the 1950s, just 116,000 are left. (Courtesy Morna Humphrees Eastridge.)

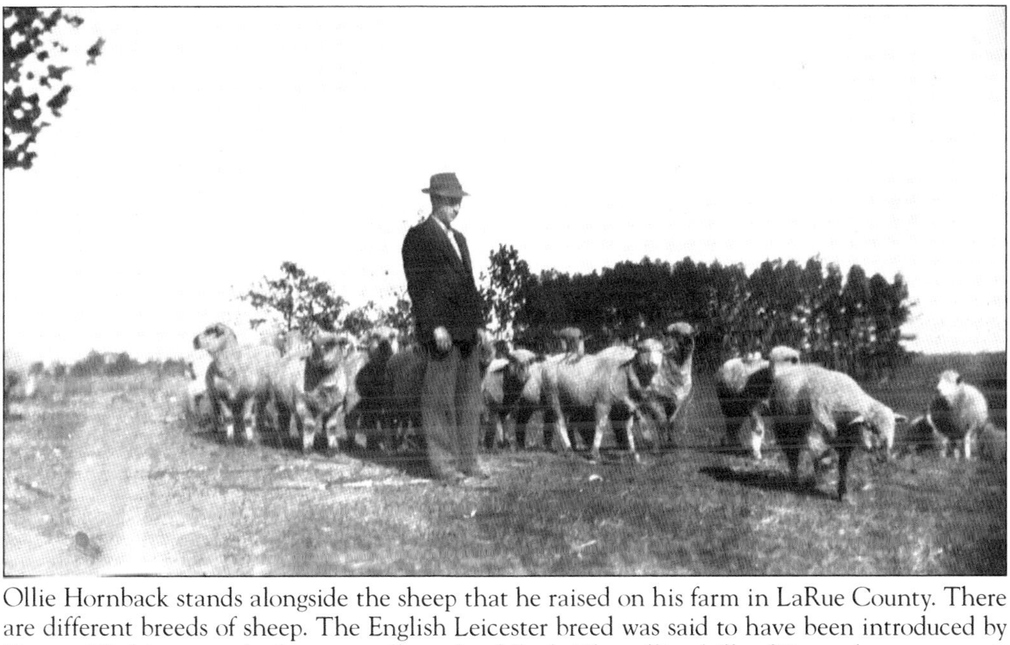

Ollie Hornback stands alongside the sheep that he raised on his farm in LaRue County. There are different breeds of sheep. The English Leicester breed was said to have been introduced by George Washington, who kept a small purebred flock. The rolling hills of Kentucky seem to suit the Leicester with limestone-based pastures; not much supplemental feeding is needed. (Courtesy Beatrice Hornback Gibson.)

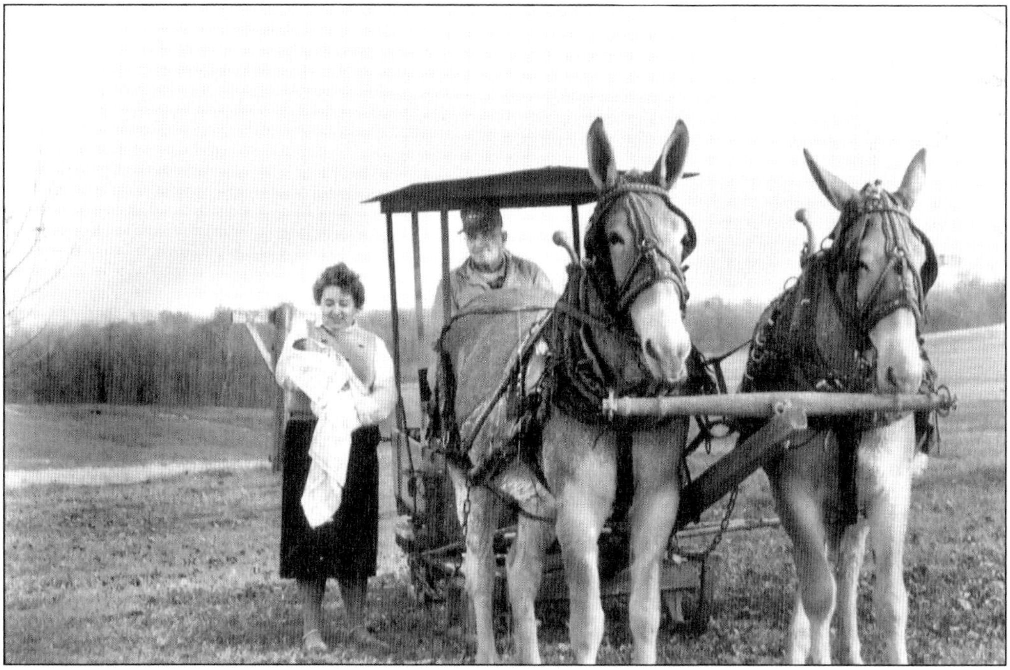

Charles "June" Routt has worked around mules his whole life. June holds the record of selling the most expensive mules in all Hardin and LaRue Counties. He has a table full of trophies and ribbons he received showing his prized mules. He remembers his father working with mules before tractors came along. June is seen photographed with his daughter, Sharon, and his granddaughter, Dawn. (Courtesy June Routt.)

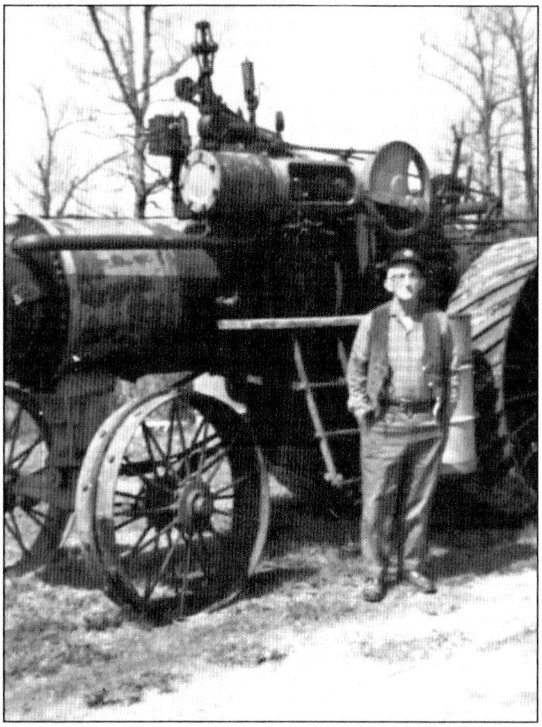

Elmo Doc Routt is seen here with an old steam machine. In the 1920s and 1930s, farmers used horses to plow the soil and plant the seeds, but machines were used to shell corn and thresh grain. Farmers would pitch in and buy a large piece of machinery and split the costs. Other times, one owner could rent the machine out, moving from farm to farm during harvest time. (Courtesy June Routt.)

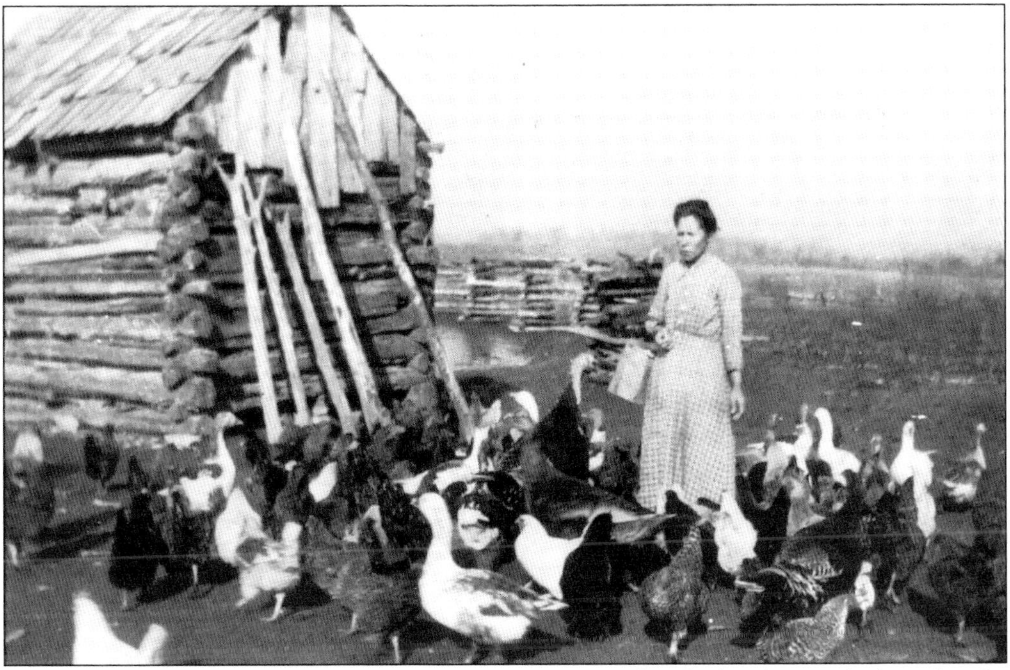

Sarah Belle Walters Routt feeds her chickens and geese. The chicken houses had perches for roosting and nest boxes for laying eggs. Chickens and geese like to scratch for bugs and eat fresh greens. This is what gives the yolk a nice orange color. This photograph was taken around 1915. (Courtesy Darlene Routt Bryan.)

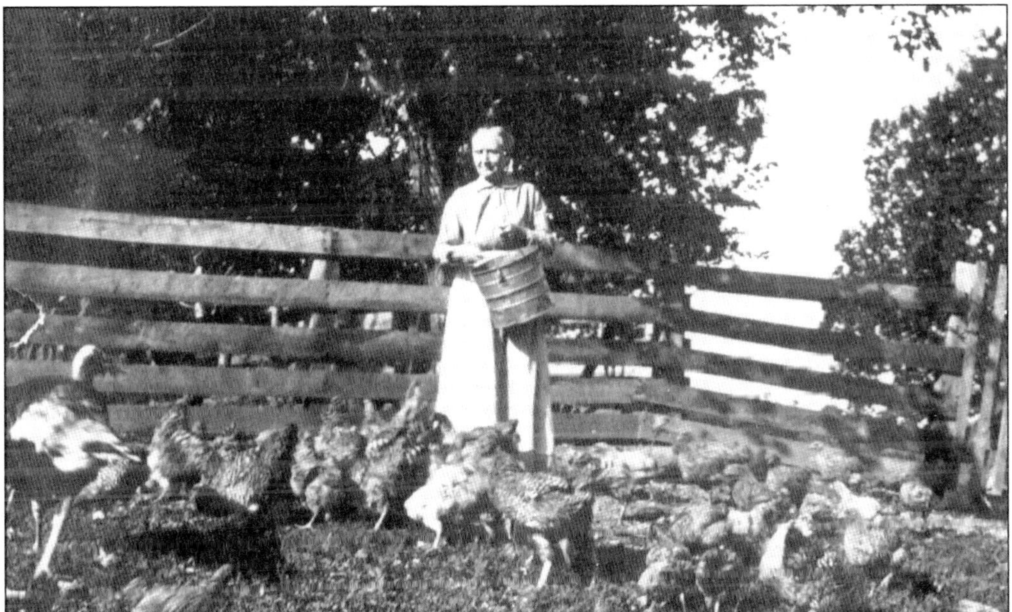

This photograph was taken on August 18, 1916, of Susannah Adams feeding her turkeys. Corn or different grains would be scattered on the ground for the turkeys to scratch for. Like chickens, turkeys like to scratch for bugs, berries, and seeds. Tom turkeys (males) average in size from about 20 to 24 pounds while hens weigh 14 to 16 pounds. (Courtesy Alva Martin Tharp.)

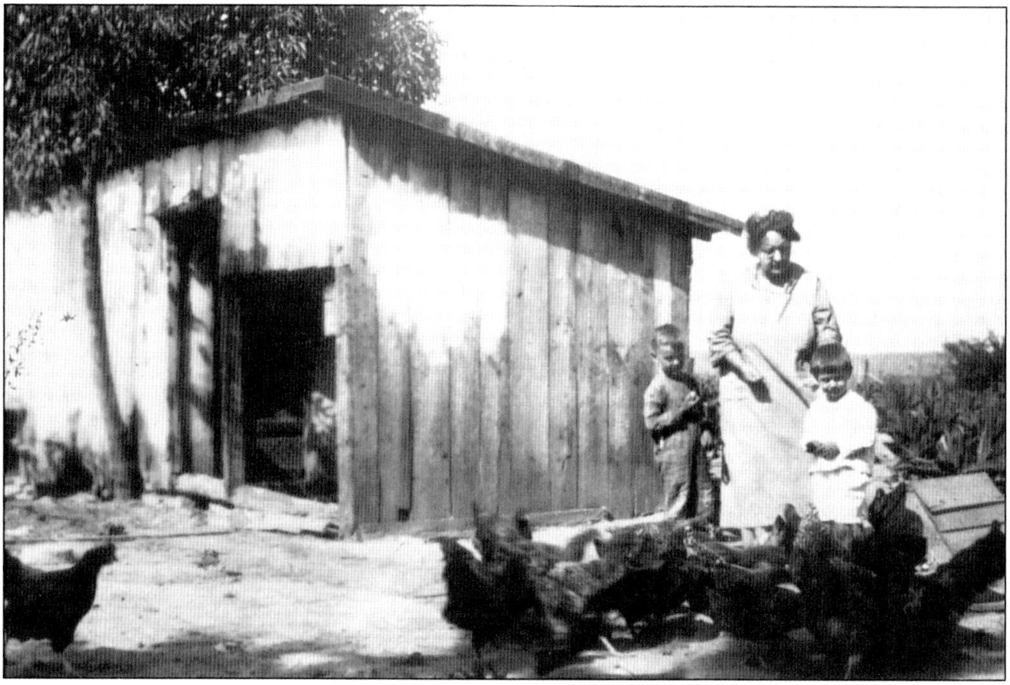

Alva Martin Tharp (left), Hester Abell, and Robert Henderson feed the chickens and gather fresh eggs. Farmers' wives would gather eggs for the family daily or sell fresh eggs to make extra money to neighbors or the country store down the road. (Courtesy Alva Martin Tharp.)

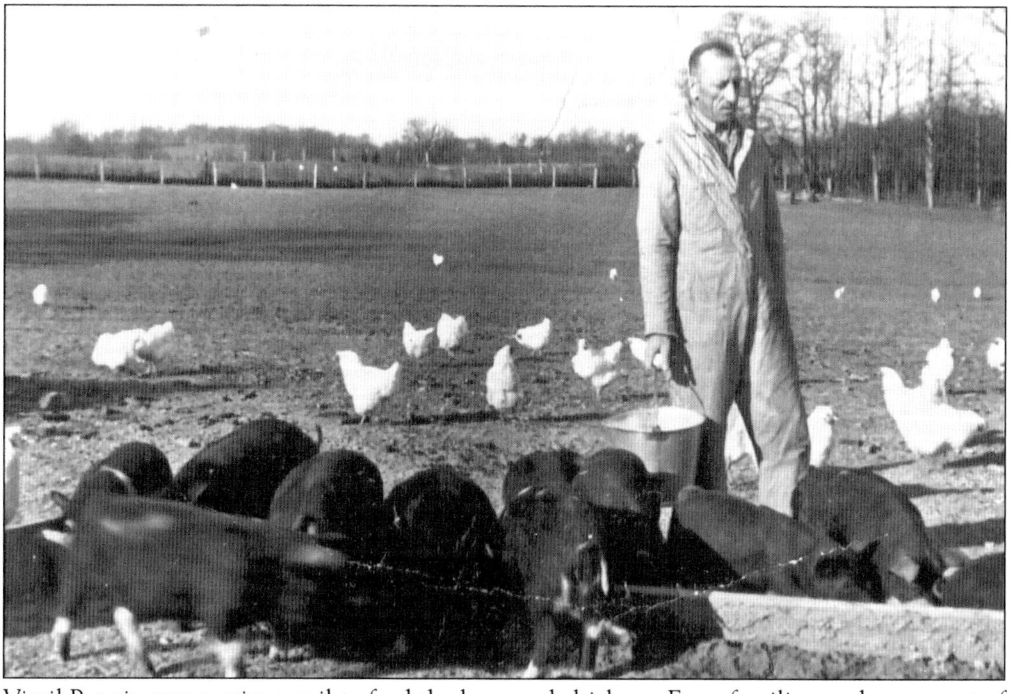

Virgil Pennington carries a pail to feed the hogs and chickens. Farm families used every part of the hog. Meat was smoked or cured for ham, bacon, and sausage because most farms did not have electricity, and the meat could spoil. (Courtesy Mary Kathryn Pennington Puckett.)

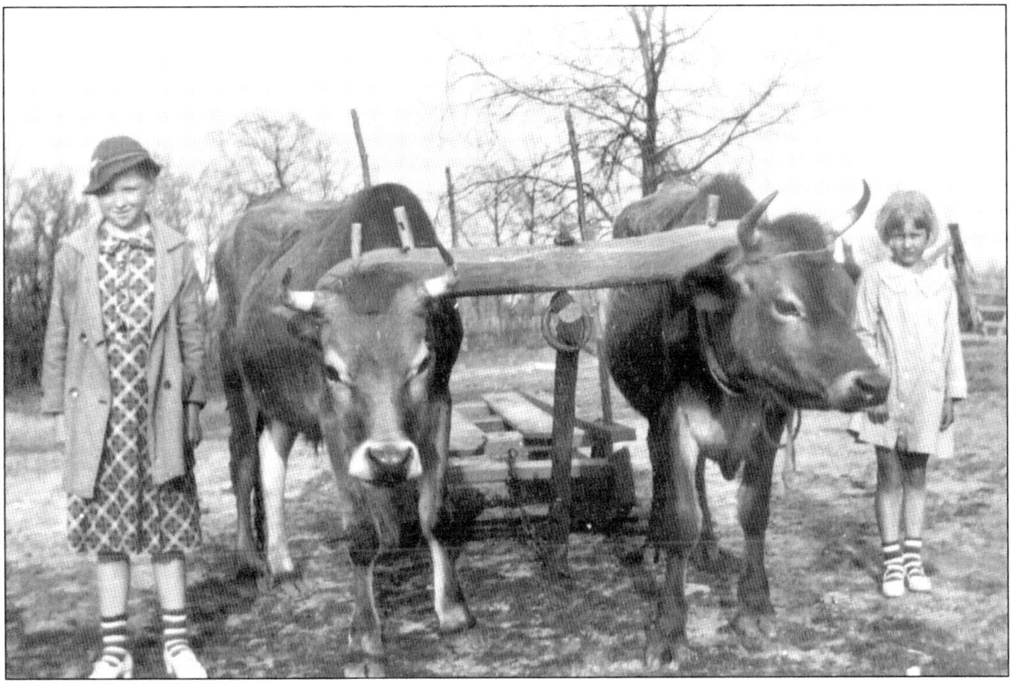

Mona (left) and Nats Wells are photographed with these large oxen. Brown Swiss oxen tend to be calm and easygoing. These oxen are hitched together by a wooden frame called a yoke. Brown Swiss cows are a mixture of Holstein and Brown Swiss. (Courtesy Evelyn Cruse.)

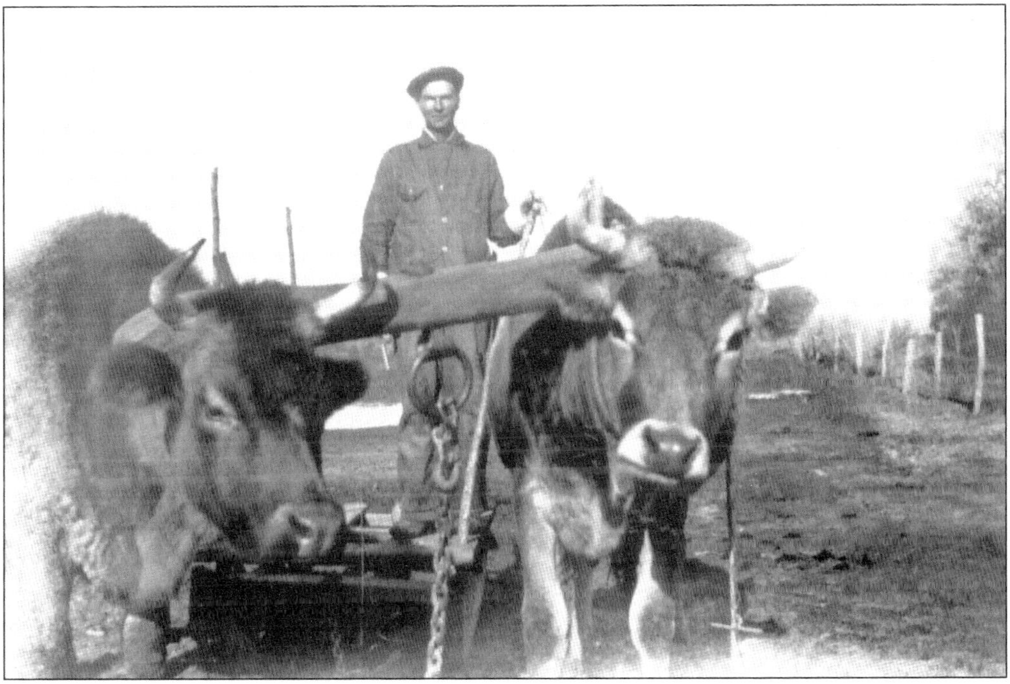

Granville Cruse is photographed with his oxen. Oxen are much stronger than horses and can be used to pull wagons, plow fields, and remove stumps. These oxen were used to carry large limestone rocks. (Courtesy Evelyn Cruse.)

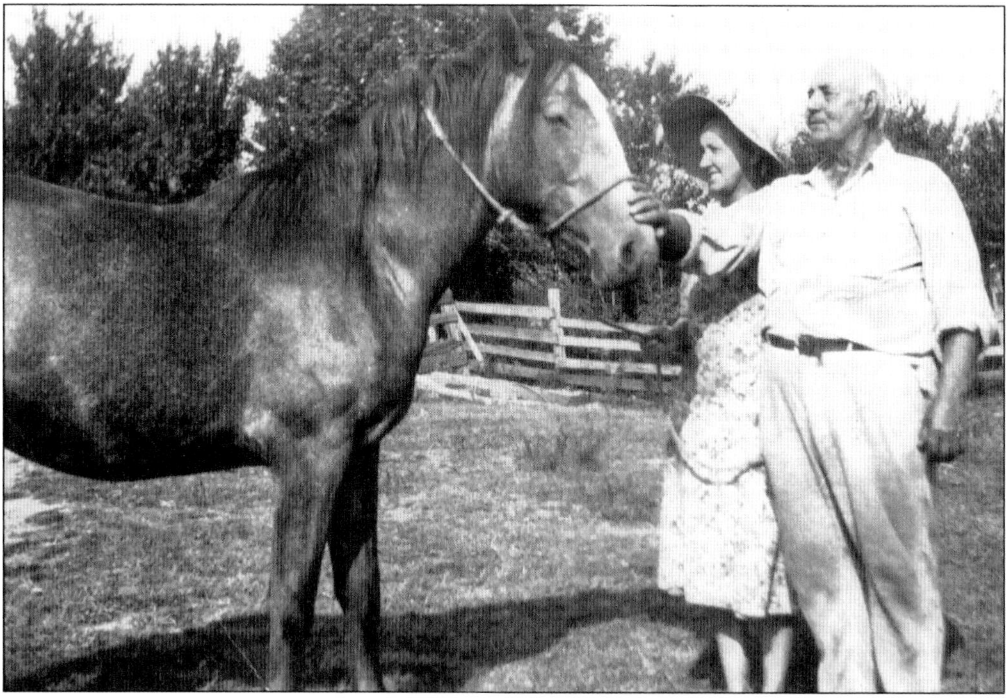

Susan and Robert Mathew Abell give ole Frank a good nose rubbing. Work horses took a lot of the heavy burden off of farmers and became a part of the family. (Courtesy Alva Martin Tharp.)

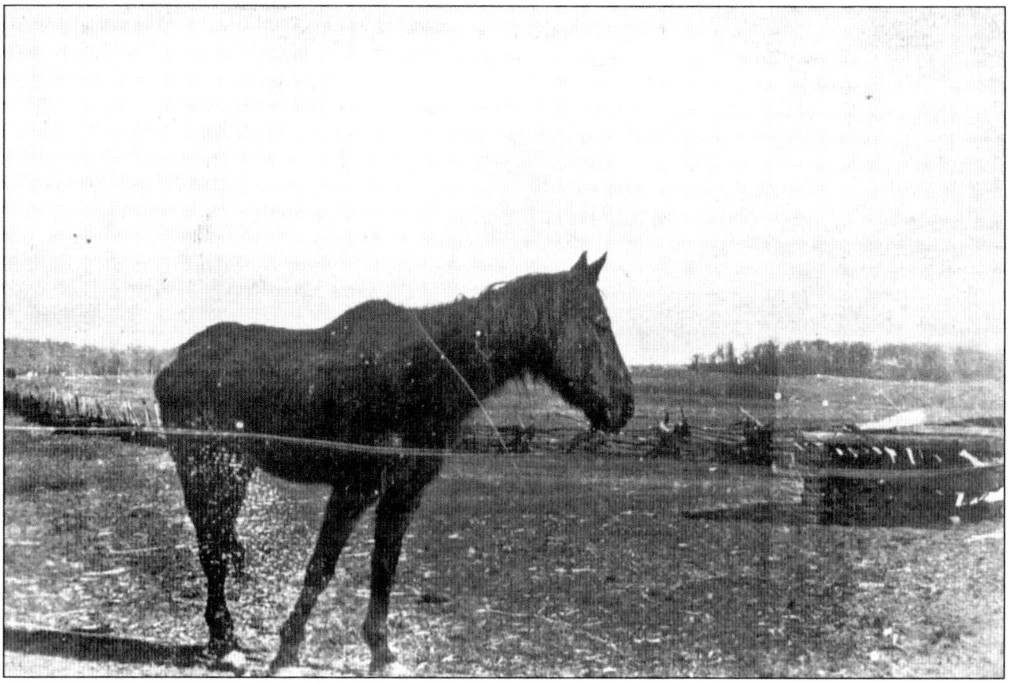

Jake was 23 years old when this photograph was taken on March 19, 1919. The mule belonged to John Routt Sr. A horse mule is the proper name for a mule. Mules are the product of a male donkey and a female horse. (Courtesy Darlene Routt Bryan.)

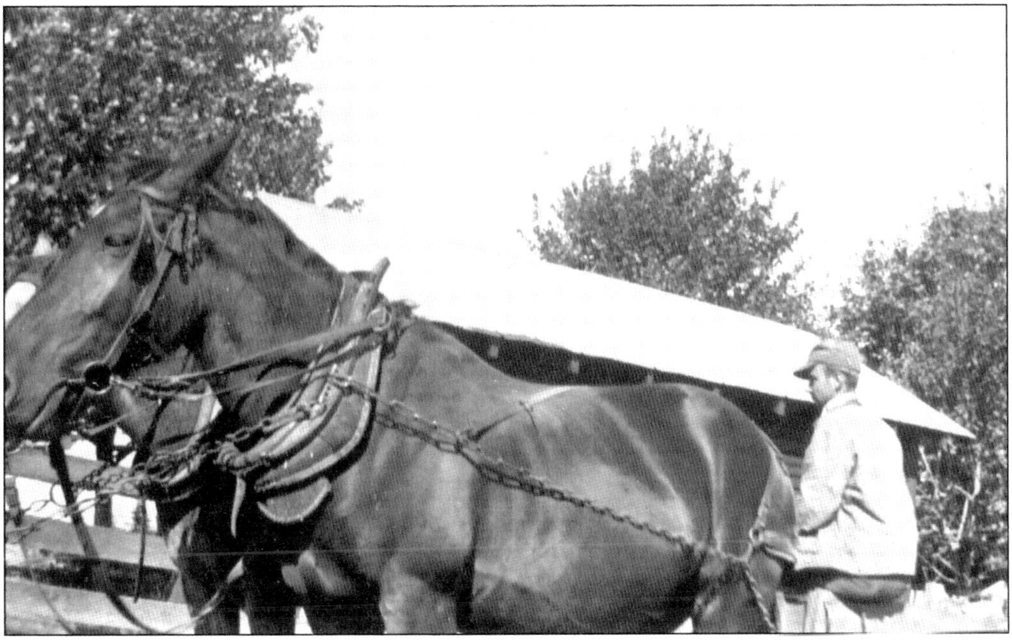

Baldy and Frank, work horses, bring Alva Martin Tharp back with a load of firewood. Working animals sacrificed themselves for the working needs of humans. Note the equipment draped over the horses. A harness is a set of devices and straps that attach to the horse and wagon. (Courtesy Alva Martin Tharp.)

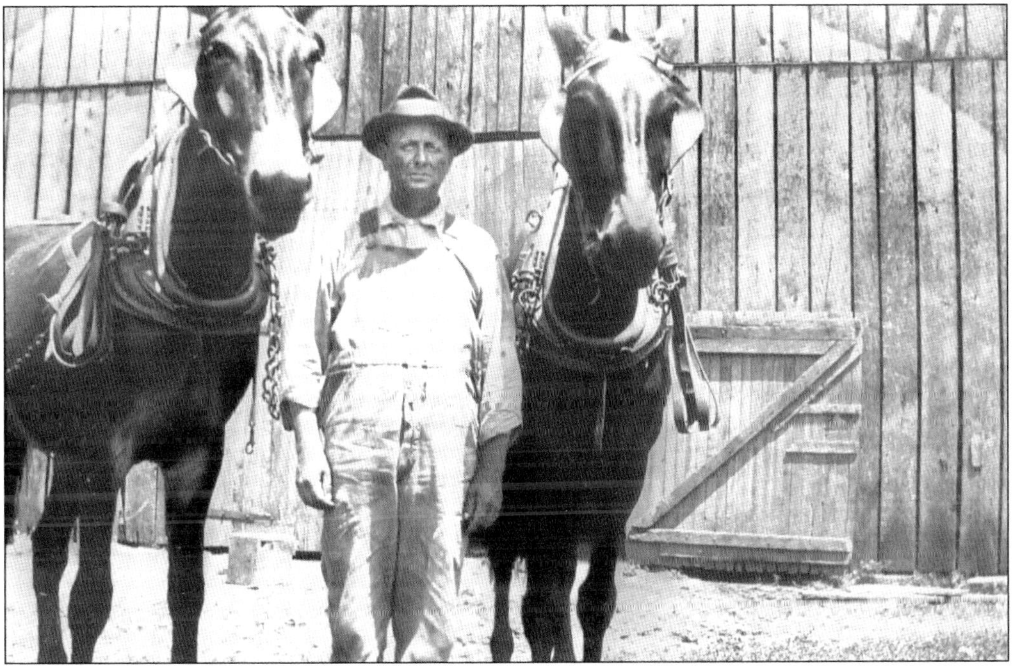

This pair of distinguished horses stands proud and tall with Grover Hodge between them. One could almost imagine their regal nature. Tack is the term used for any equipment and accessories used by domesticated horses, such as blinders, bridle, yoke, saddle, bit, reins, halters, and harnesses. (Courtesy Evelyn Cruse.)

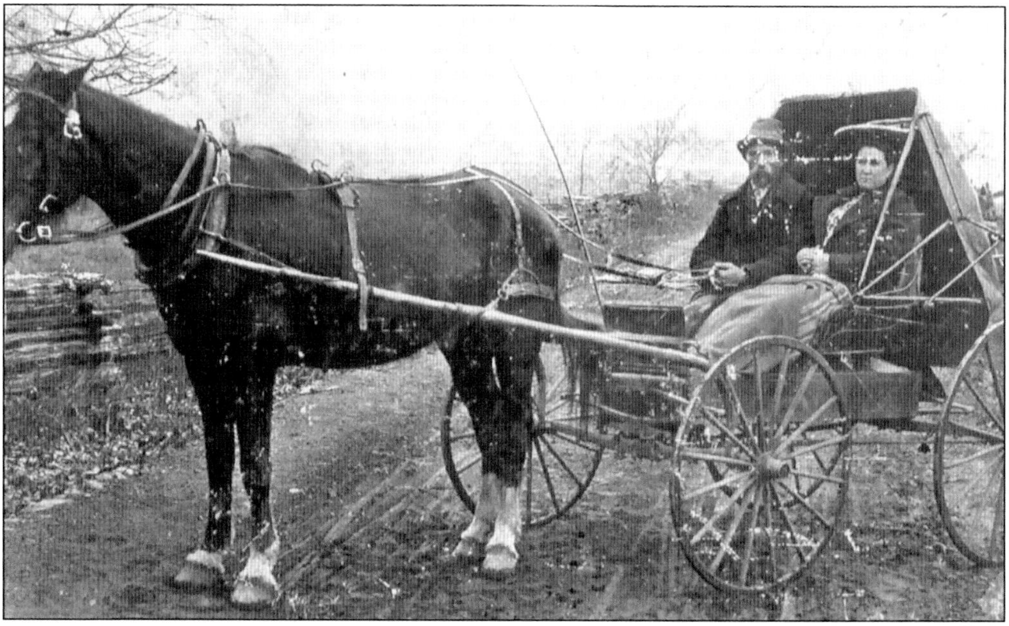

William and Myrtle Hines, photographed in a horse-drawn buggy, traveled this dirt road beside the split-rail fence. Split-rail fences were easily constructed and often used in areas where timber was plentiful. The couple was from the Leafdale area on the other side of Hodgenville, Kentucky. (Courtesy Jay Wheeler.)

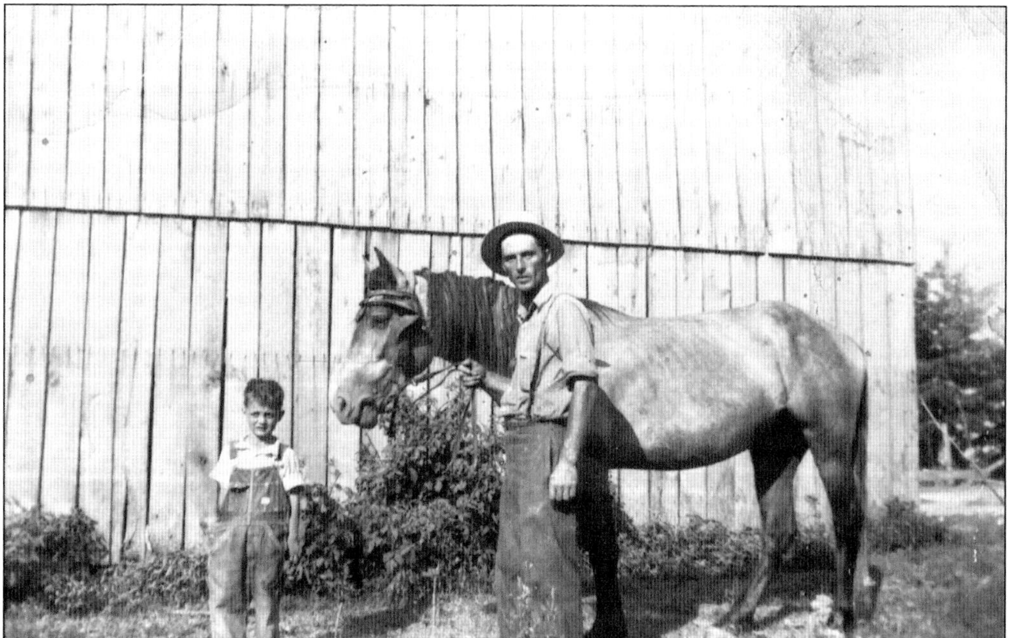

Albert Ray Hornback stands beside his father, Herman, and their horse. Each member of the family played a vital role in farm life. Rural children were responsible for feeding chickens, taking care of the horses, milking cows, and chopping wood. (Courtesy Shirley Hornback Miller.)

Mick jumps up as a trick and brings a smile to Alva Martin Tharp. Canines have always been the most popular pet in America. Leisure time could be spent playing fetch or just wandering over the farm together. This photograph was taken around 1930. (Courtesy Alva Martin Tharp.)

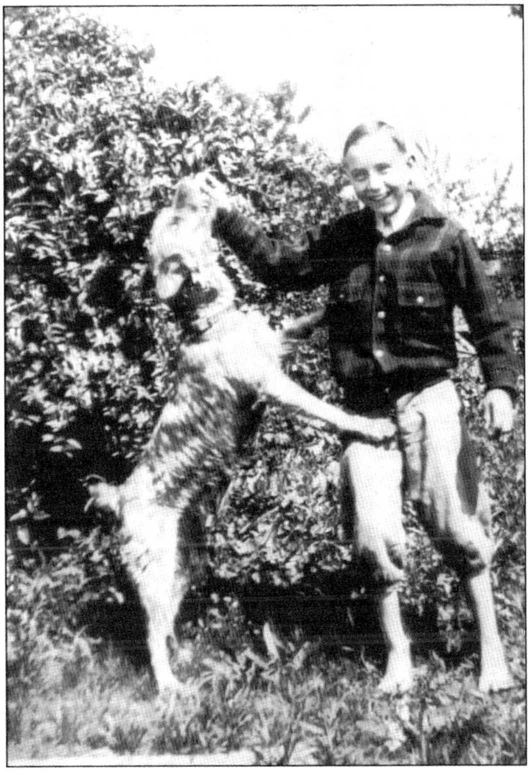

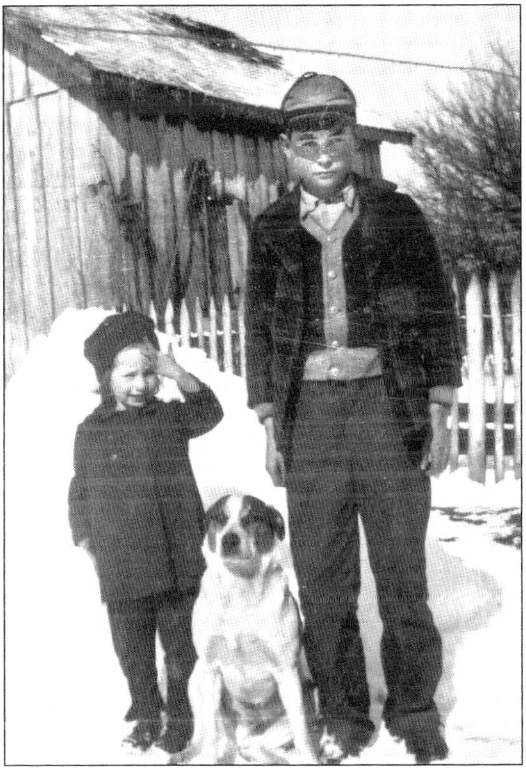

Snowball sits among his best friends, Darlene Routt and Walter Lee Tucker, as they play outside on this wintry day. Pets become intertwined with their owners' lives and often people find the best times spent with these little creatures. (Courtesy Darlene Routt Bryan.)

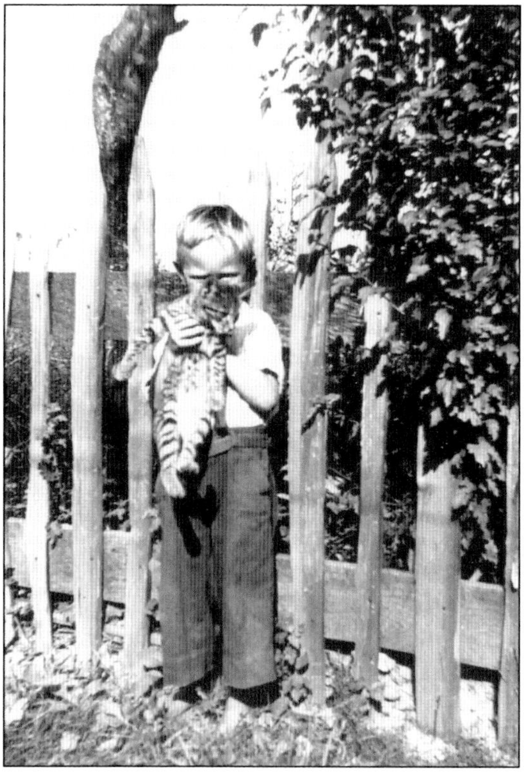

James R. "Blue Eyes" Routt stands in front of this wooden fence holding up his kitten to have their picture made together. James is the son of William and Dorothy Routt. (Courtesy Darlene Routt Bryan.)

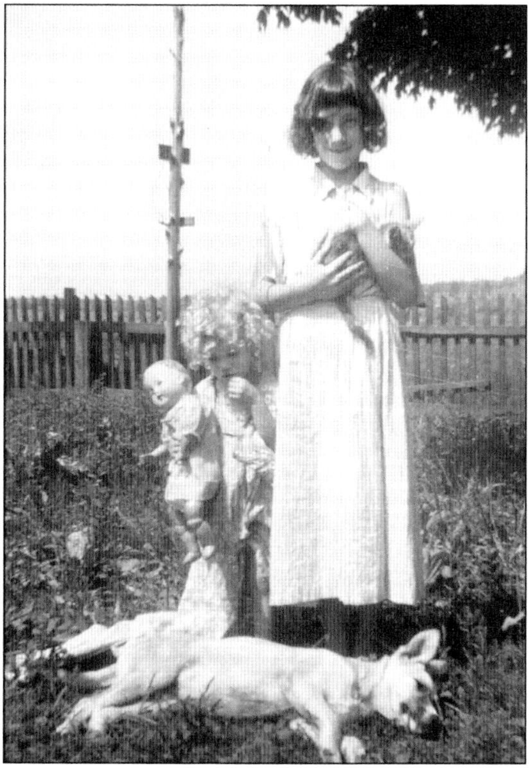

Sisters Linda and Darlene Routt pose for a photograph. Linda holds her baby doll while her sister Darlene cradles her kitten. Queenie, their dog, seems to be pretty relaxed at their feet. This photograph was taken in the 1940s. (Courtesy Darlene Routt Bryan.)

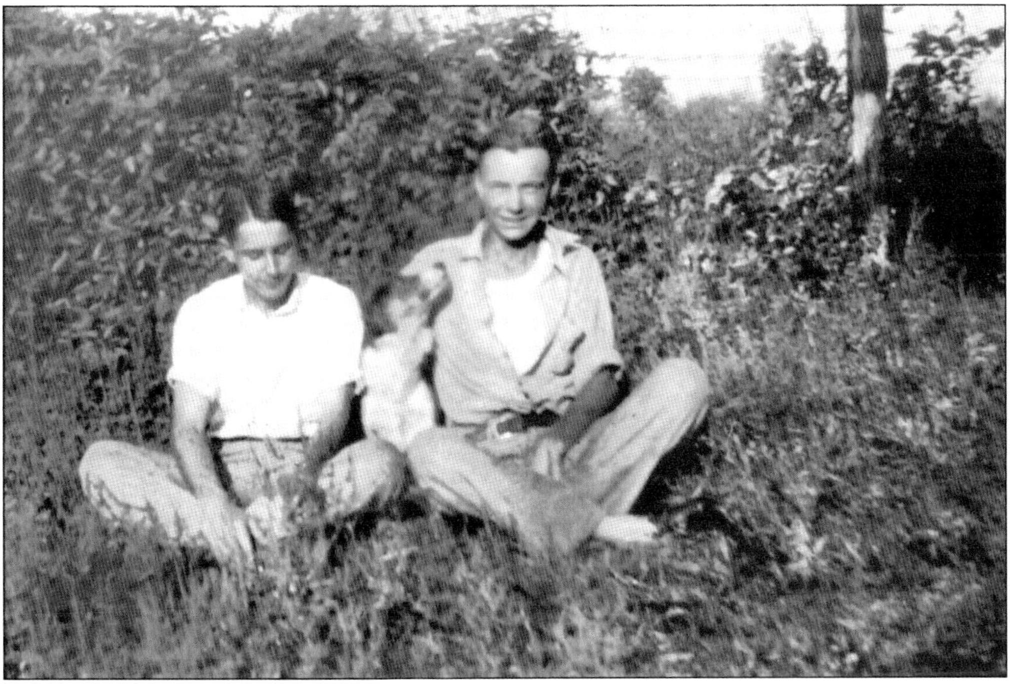

Marion Lee Catlett and Alva Martin Tharp buddy around with this old mix. The dog seems to be looking up for approval. (Courtesy Alva Martin Tharp.)

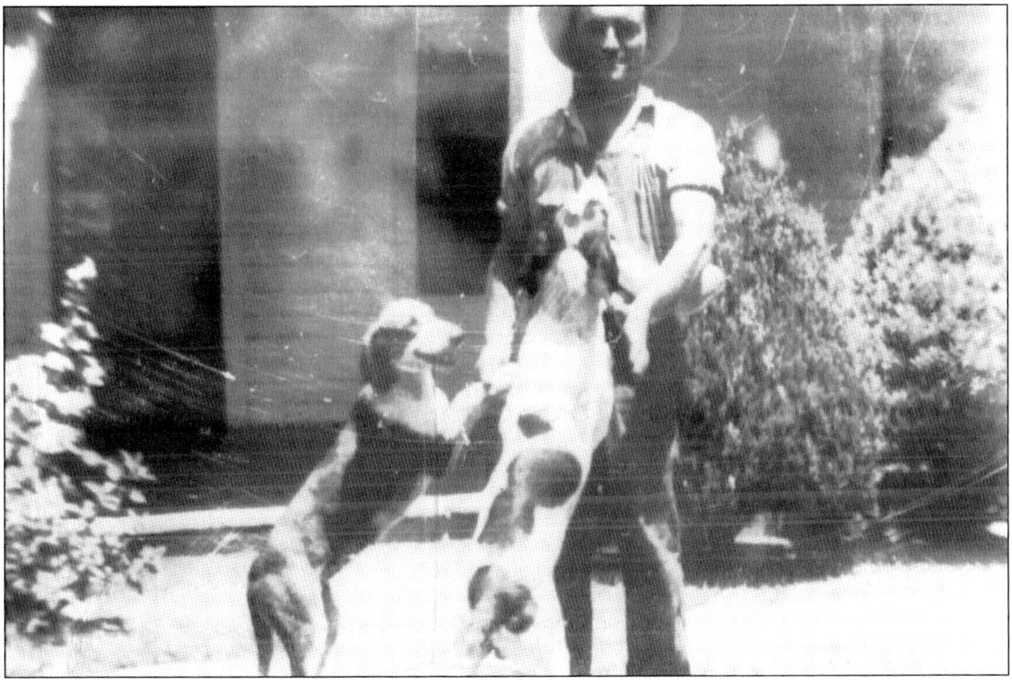

Queen and Cain, these foxhounds, share a happy moment with their friend June Routt. There are generally two types of foxhounds, the English and the American, which is the oldest breed of sporting dog. Men and boys in the rural communities would get their hounds together and hunt. (Courtesy June Routt.)

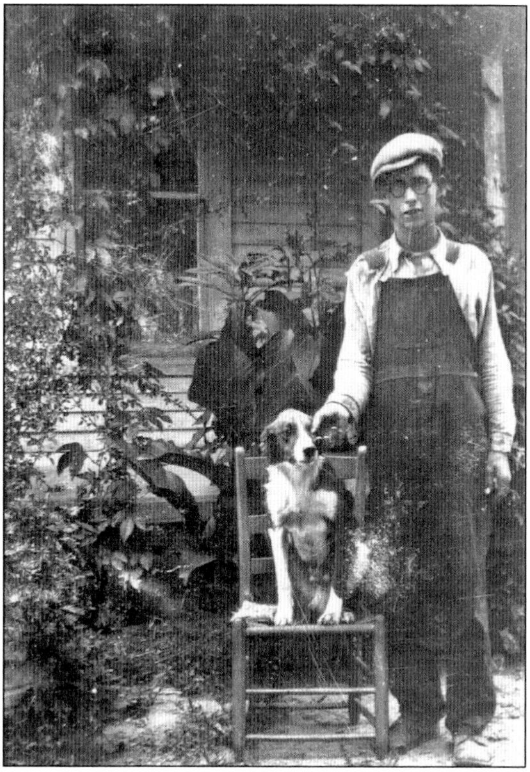

John W. Routt Jr. gently strokes the face of his dog as the photographer captures the moment between them. A chair was placed for his beloved pet to sit beside him. In the 1930s and 1940s, dogs and cats were popular pets, but squirrels and hamsters would make a claim as a favorite family pet. (Courtesy Darlene Routt Bryan and Linda Routt Daniels.)

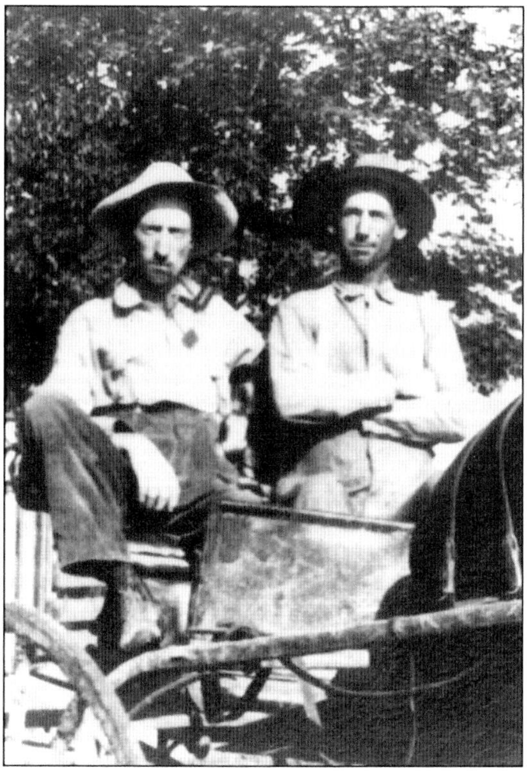

John Waller Routt Sr. (left) and Billy Bob Adams hold still long enough to get their photograph taken in the early 1920s. The two were possibly on their way back to the field or to run into town for supplies. Note the tobacco pipe sticking out from John's mouth. (Courtesy Darlene Routt Bryan.)

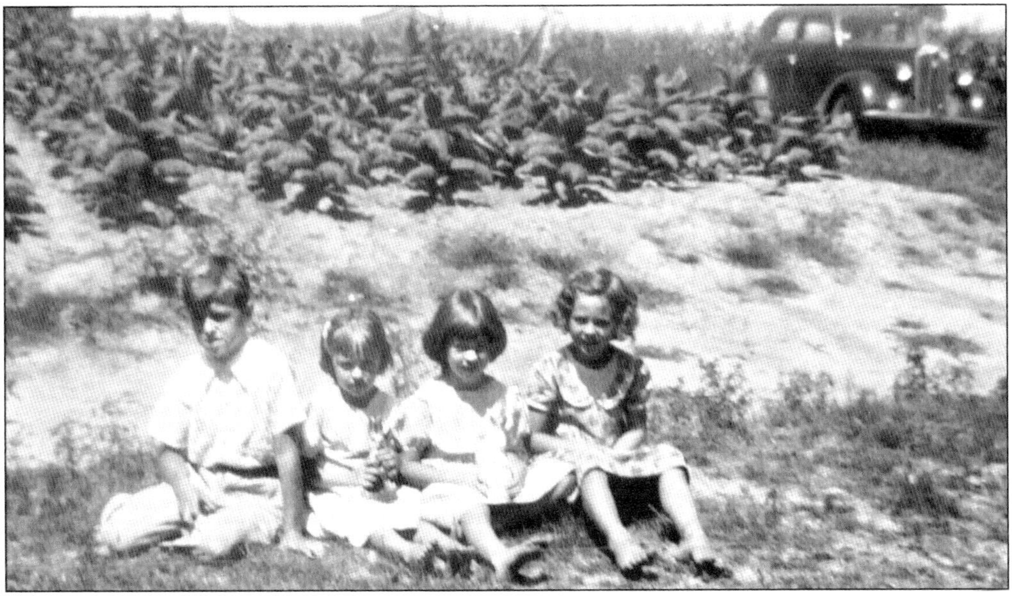

Marion Lee Hornback, Shirley Jean Hornback, Doris Ann Hornback, and their cousin, Anna Mae Philpott, (identified from left to right) sit at the edge of the tobacco patch. Tobacco seeds are planted in the spring in a tobacco bed. In the summer, the plants are pulled and transplanted to a nearby field. A couple months later, the tobacco is topped by plucking off the bloom at the top of the plant, then it's cut and housed in a barn. By fall, the tobacco is stripped of its leaves into different grades and later sold to a tobacco barn. This tobacco is still in the early stages. (Courtesy Patricia Fields Hornback.)

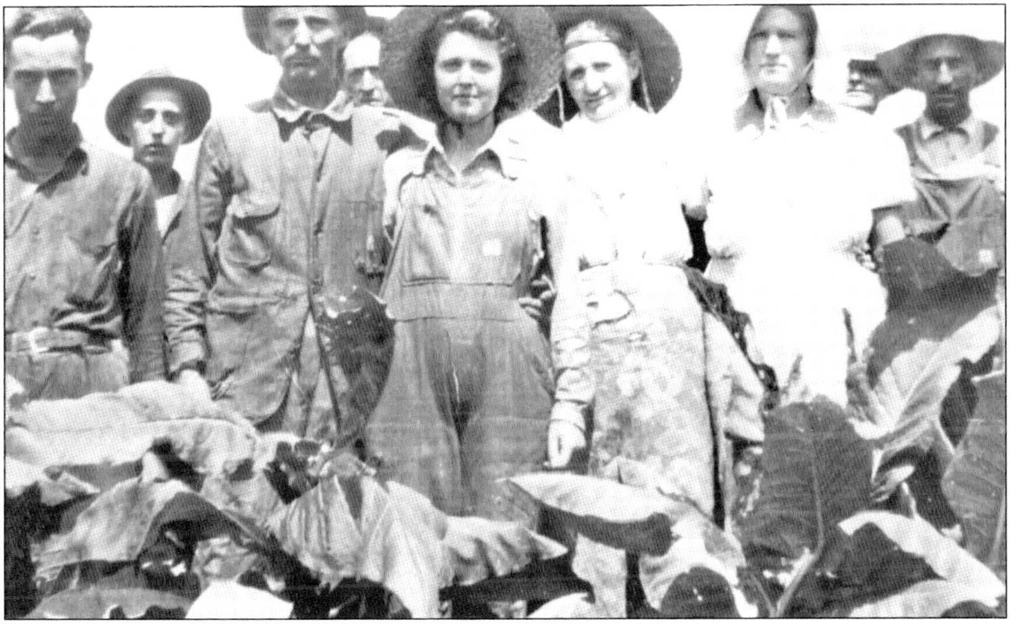

From left to right, Webb Hornback, Herman Hornback (the son of Elma and Mildred Hornback), Curt Philpott, Elzie Hornback, Dorothy Hornback Philpott, Mrs. ? Philpott, Jennie Hornback, Wilbur Hornback, and Ollie Hornback have just either topped the tobacco or are getting ready to cut the tobacco. (Courtesy Dorothy Hornback Philpott.)

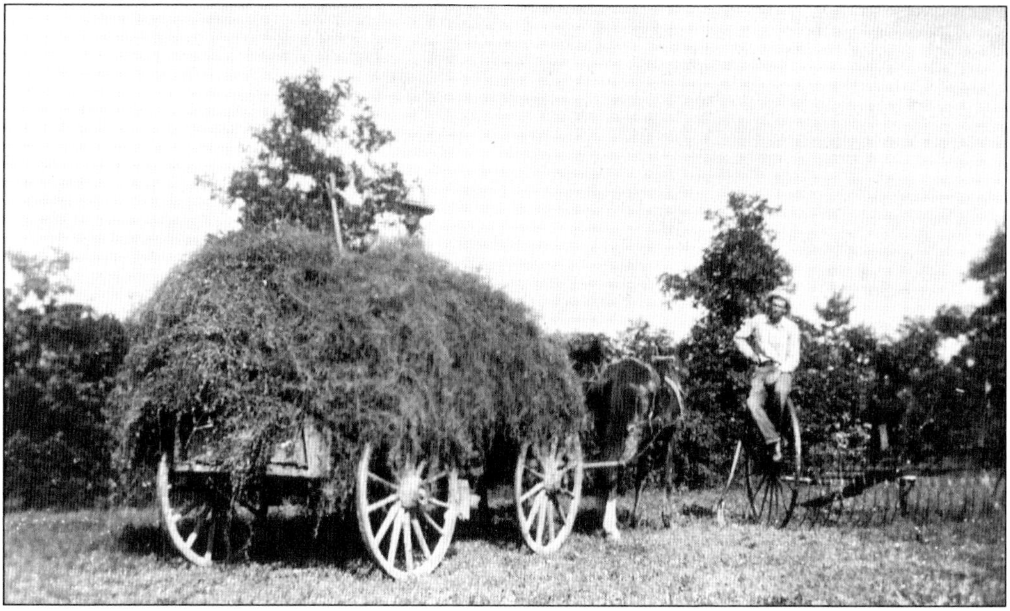

Granville Cruse stands on this wagonload of hay brought in by the team of horses. The introduction of different farm machinery made it easier on the farmer. Crops no longer had to be gathered by hand. Note the gentleman sitting on the hay rake. (Courtesy Evelyn Cruse.)

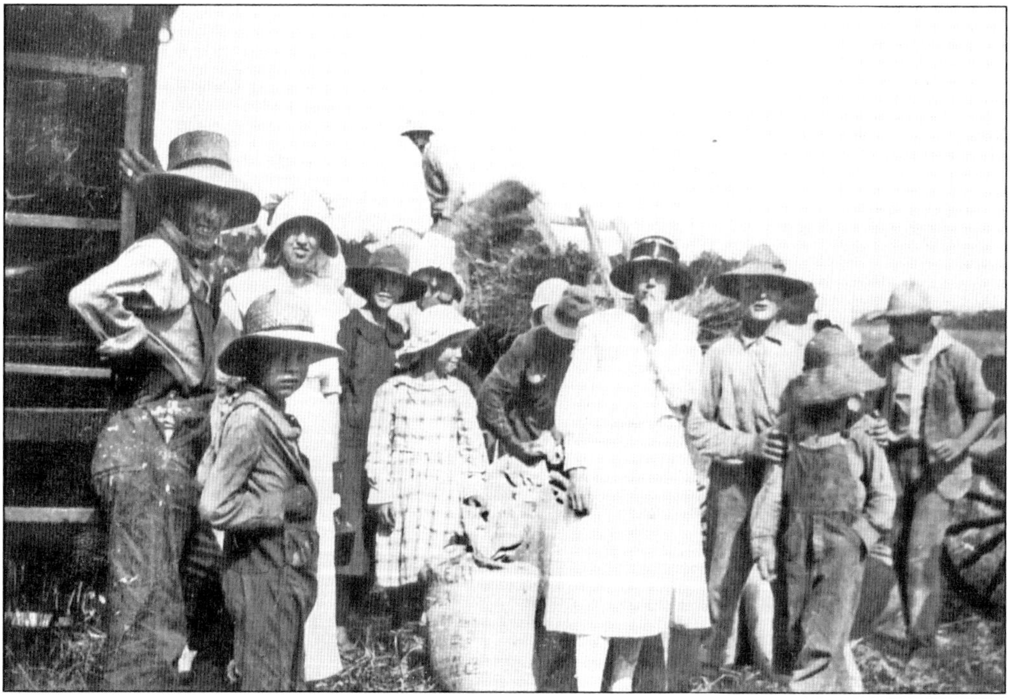

The only people identified in the photograph are Jim and Lilly Gusler to the left, Josie Routt (the little girl with the white hat), John Routt Sr. (the man tying the wheat bag), and Ola Routt (standing with the black hat and white dress). Eston Routt stands along beside her with a smaller boy. The wagon behind them is filled with wheat that will soon be fed into the wheat thrasher. After the wheat is thrashed, it will spit out grain to be put into bags. (Courtesy Darlene Routt Bryan.)

Four

GOING TO SCHOOL

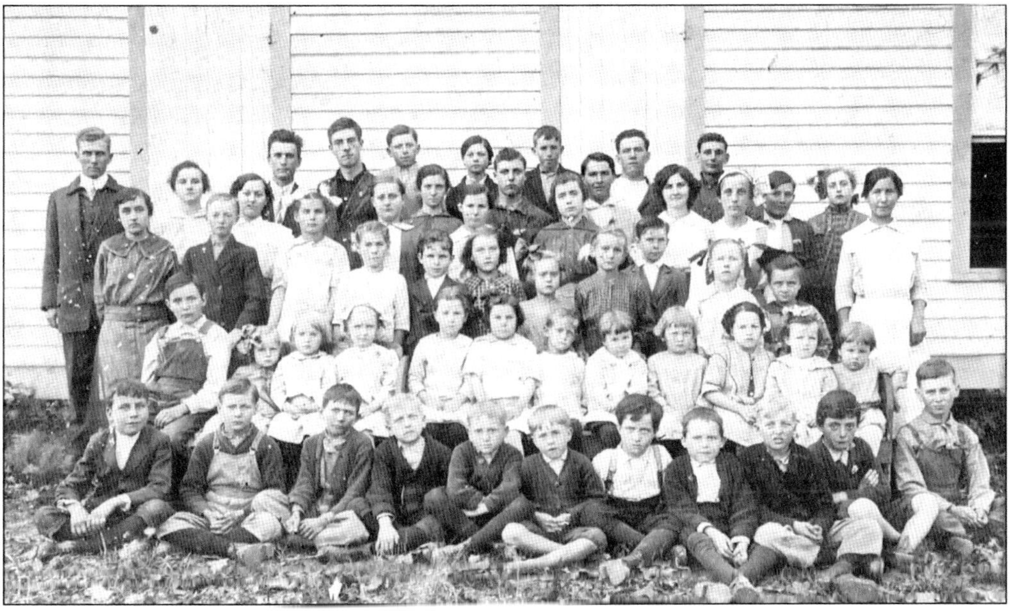

This photograph is of Talley School in LaRue County. Photographed from left to right are (first row) Alfred Miller, Archie Humes, Charlie Cruse, Allen Gardner, Monta Tucker, Raymond Ward, Grover Hornback, H. T. Johnson, Walter Bush, Guy Sullivan, and Herbert Massie; (second row) Walter Cruse, Ruby Bush, unidentified, Stella Gardner, Zelma Tucker-Walsh, Stella Akers, Roy Grimsley, Mildred Tucker, Ruth Massie, Lillie Hornback, Laura Hornback, and Layton Tucker; (third row) Lula Talley Dixon, Clifford Bush, Alice Akers, Agnes Akers, John Albert Tennison, Clara Massie Bergenson, Carrie Grimsley Hodge, Ruby Grimsley, Rom Tennison, Annie Mae Whitman, Zelma Miller, and Ruby Akers McCubbin; (fourth row) Jesse Gardner (teacher), Gladys Ward Bale, Janie Taylor, Maeola Humes Goldsmith, Lillie Taylor Morris, Ida Akers, Arvil Sullivan, Erman Talley Tharpe, Claud Hornback, Lena Taylor, and Iva Miller; (fifth row) Biven Cruse and Edith Sullivan Riggs; (sixth row) Robert Willian, Lynn Sullivan, Coy Tucker, Elmer Taylor, Walter Ward, Lawrence Hornback, and Leonard Kessinger. (Courtesy Adeline Bush Chappell.)

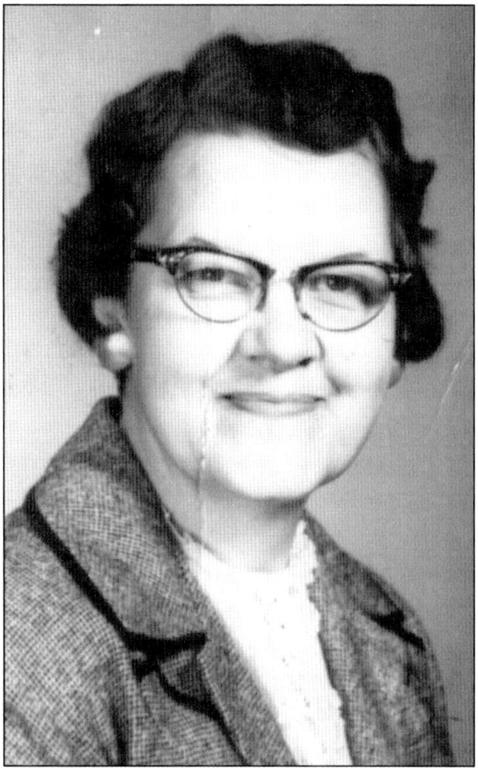

Marie Lawless taught school at Magnolia Elementary School in the 1950s. There are three remaining elementary schools in LaRue County. Magnolia Elementary was established in 1847, Buffalo Elementary in 1936, and Hodgenville in 1939. By the fall of 2007, Magnolia and Buffalo will completely merge to create Abraham Lincoln Elementary School. Magnolia has kept their mascot—Magnolia Majors—for decades. (Courtesy Patricia Fields Hornback.)

These students of Keith School were photographed in 1928. From left to right, they are (first row) Walter Lee Salsman, Ruel "Cat" Rock, Rueben Poore, James Thomas, Robert Abell, Harvey Curry, and John Robert Curry; (second row) Ruby Rock, Lawrence Brooks, Joe Rock, Jessie Poore, Charles Burton Poore, Mildred Bowling, George Thomas, Aletha Vancleaver, Margaret Middleton, Lucille Spratt, and Marjorie Abell; (third row) Arveil Durrett, Walter Polly, Owen T. Miller, Beulah Mae Thomas, Martha Poore (teacher), Bessie Bowling, Leonard Bowling, Arthur Salsman, and Edgar Curry. (Courtesy Darlene Routt Bryan.)

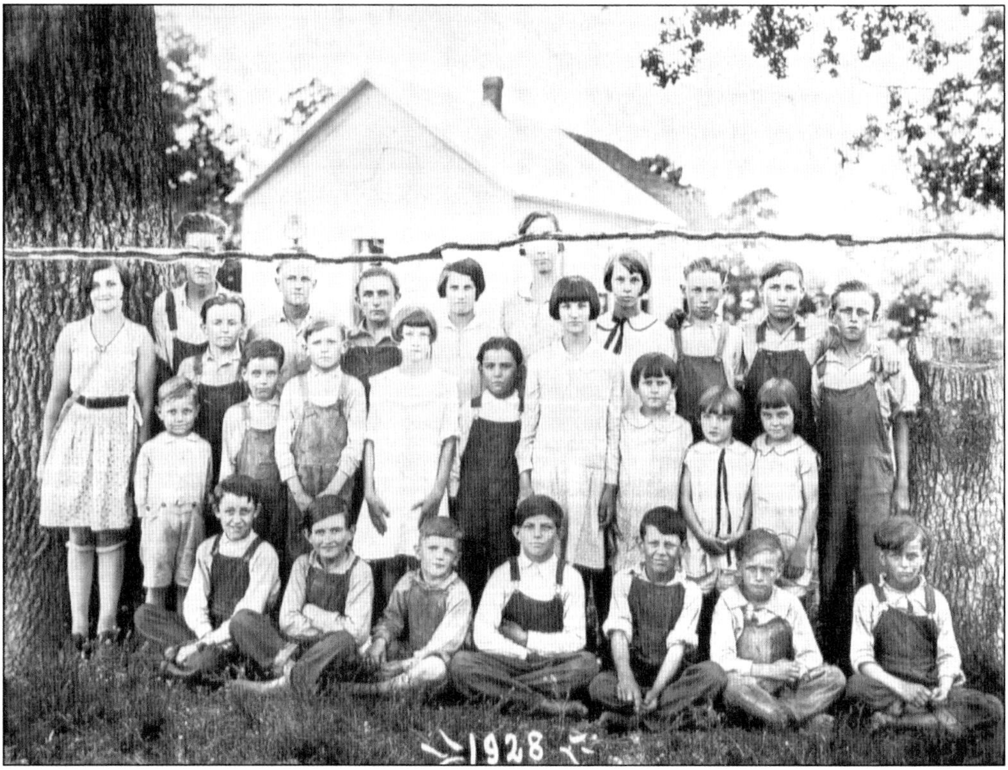

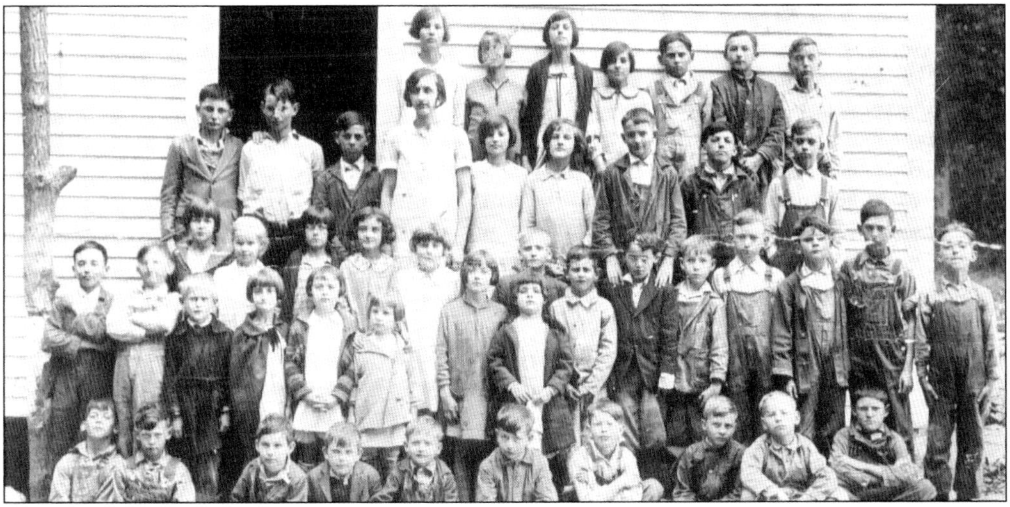

Photographed on October 22, 1928, at the Barren Run School in LaRue County in Sonora, Kentucky, are, from left to right, (first row) Biven Thurman, George Burba, John Durris, Dee Durris, Vernon Thurman, Robert Mather, Raymond Burba, Richard Arnett, Harding Catlett, and William Catlett; (second row) James Brown Routte, Vorice Turner, Chester Polley, Beulah Tharp, Mae Alma Hornback, Lucille Routte, Bernice Routte, Ralph Catlett, Marion Lee Catlett, Otis T. Blankenship, Robert Hornback, Leroy Routte, Herman Burba, and Norman Tharp; (third row) Stella Polley, Evelyn Routte, Edna Miller, Maude Routte, Marjorie Dixon, Evelyn Catlett, and Harold Routte; (fourth row) Wilburn Hazle, James H. Catlett, Madison Mather, Zelma Corum (teacher), Catherine Catlett, Lura Tharp, Carl Routt, Carl Underwood, and Leo Hornback; (fifth row) Gladys Catlett, Leona Mather, Mabel Miller, Mary Willia Dixon, Clyde Corum, Ollie Catlett Jr., and Alva Martin Tharp. This was the first school that Zelma Corum taught. (Courtesy Alva Martin Tharp.)

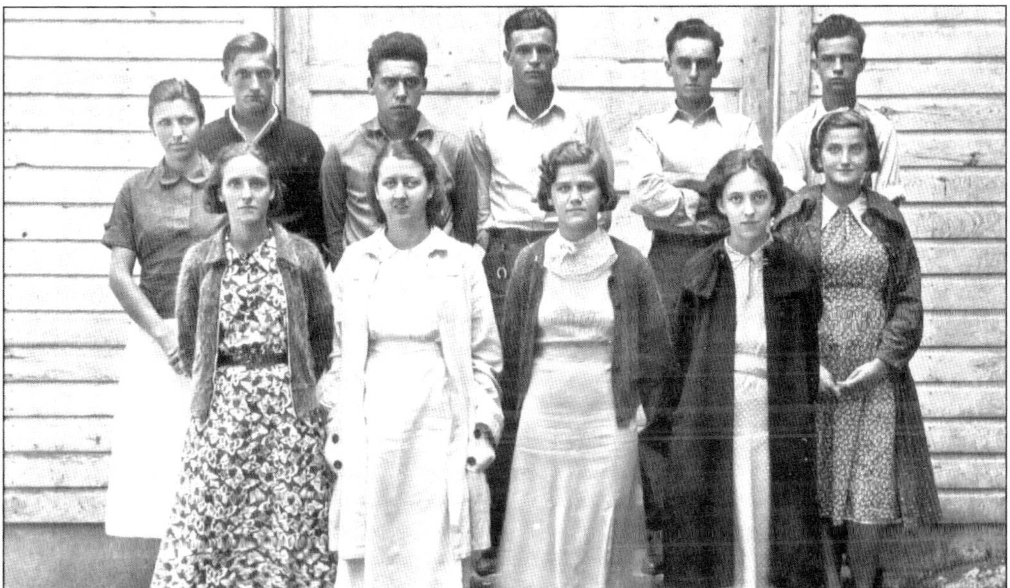

Students from Buffalo, Kentucky, stand next to Mount Tabor School to be photographed. The only student identified is the back row, fourth person from the left, Arleigh Monroe Gibson. (Courtesy Beatrice Hornback Gibson.)

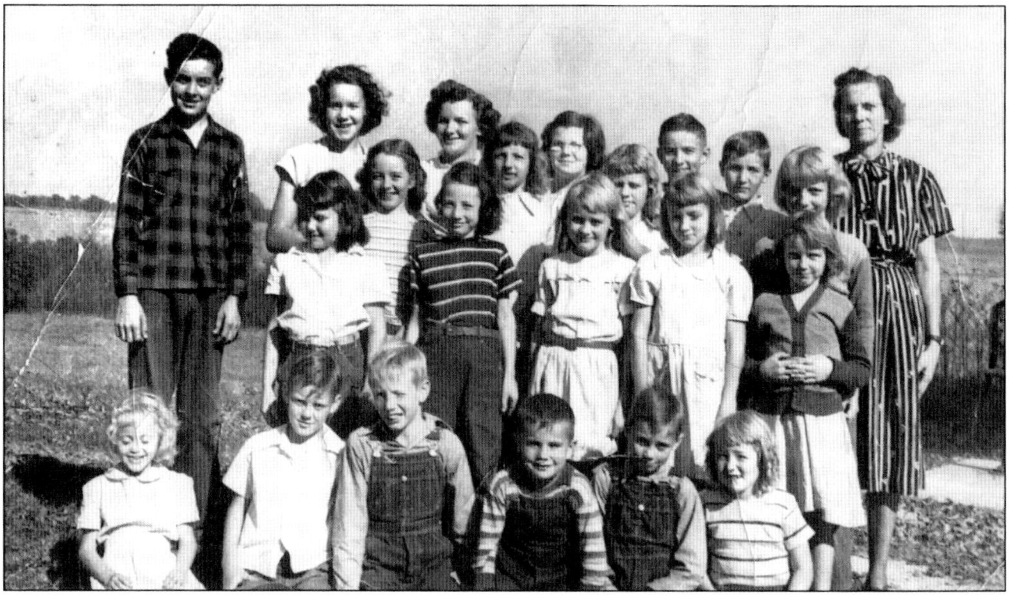

Siberia School students were photographed in 1949–1959 in Sonora, LaRue County. They are, from left to right, (first row) Joyce Smith, Windell Terry, Sonny Walters, Junnie Hudgins, Eston Carol Routt, and Marilyn Routt; (second row) Ann Hazelwood, Darlene Routt, Joyce Cruse, Mary Smith, and Karen Walters; (third row) Penny Routt, Elsie Smith, Wanda Daniels, and Shelly Jean Walters; (fourth row) Junior Wheeler, Shirley Hazelwood, Deloris Smith, Martha Hudgins, Randall Routt, Roy Smith, and Mrs. Martha Poore (teacher). (Courtesy Darlene Routt Bryan.)

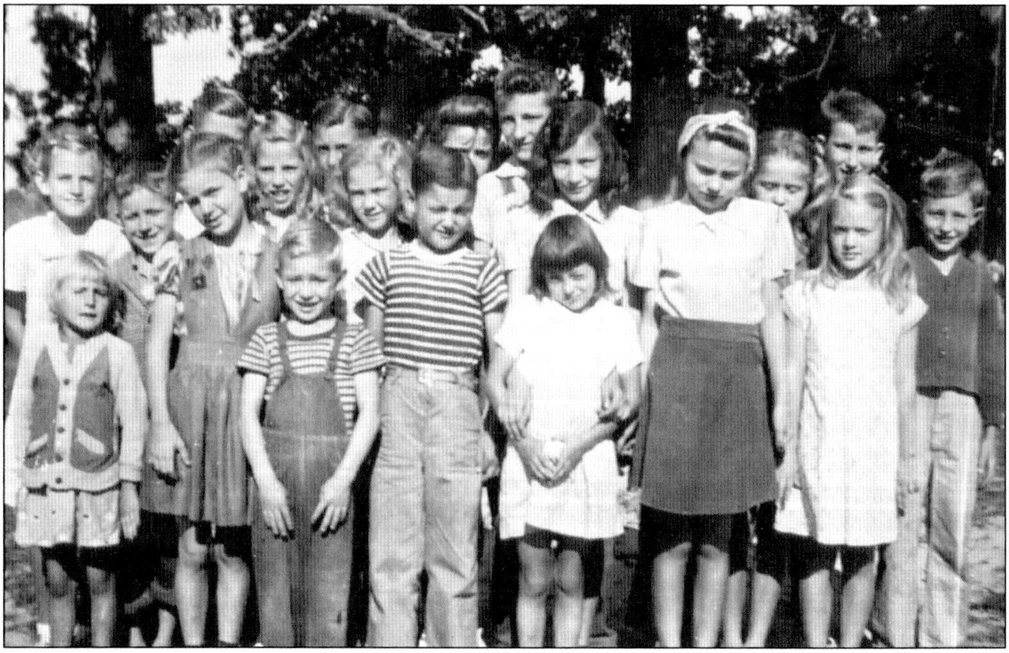

In the 1950s, these students posed at the Oak Hill School in Sonora, LaRue County. The only students identified are in the second row; the third child from the left is Mary Kathryn Pennington and her sister is the fifth child from the left, Yvonne Pennington. (Courtesy Mary Kathryn Pennington Puckett.)

These two girls in the back row, Laura Ann Cruse (left) and Patricia Ann Fields, pose in their LaRue County Hawks sweatshirts. Patricia's two little sisters in the front row, Shirley Dean (left) and Peggy Lynn Fields, couldn't resist being in the photograph. (Courtesy Patricia Fields Hornback.)

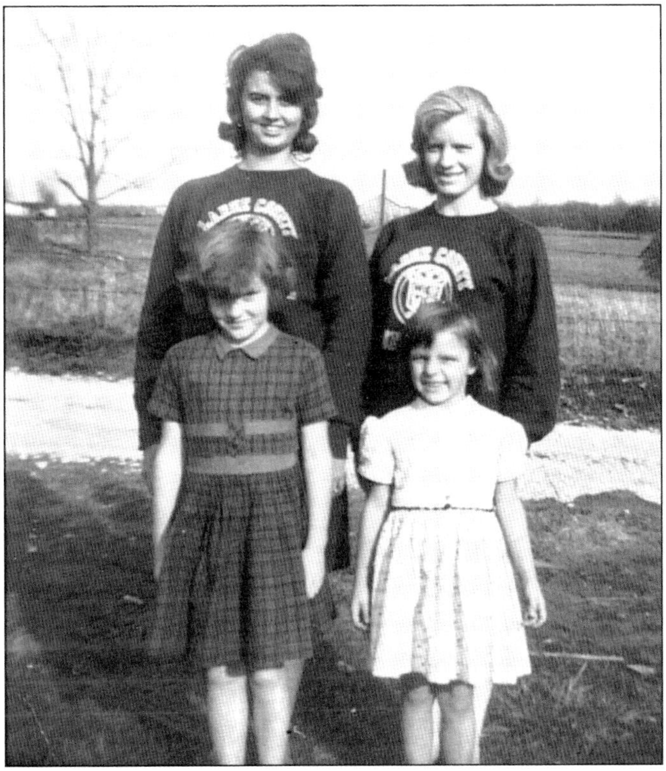

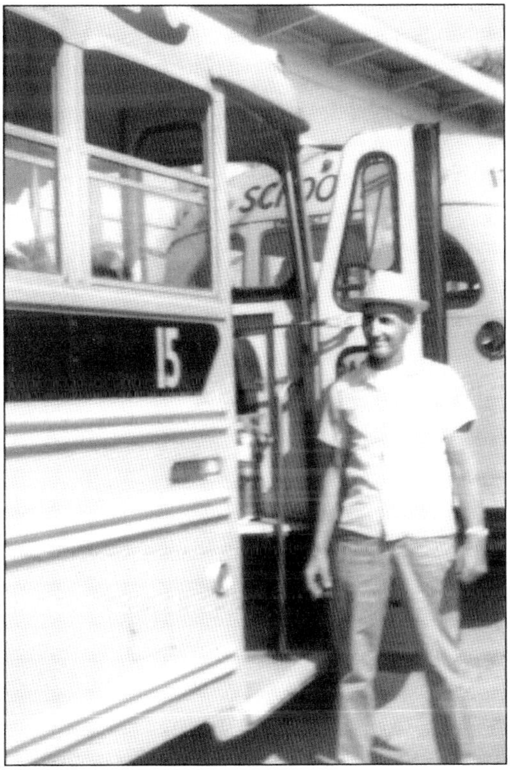

Archie Tucker drove the bus for LaRue County for several years. One of the first school buses in North America was designed and built on a Ford Model T chassis in 1913 for $700. This photograph was taken in 1963. (Courtesy Patricia Fields Hornback.)

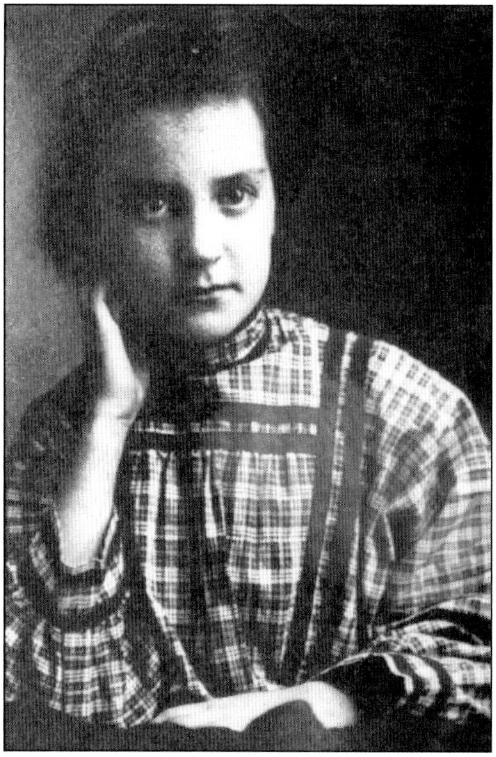

Susan Abell poses for her school photograph. Susan was born August 24, 1899. Susan attended Barren Run School. Modern conveniences of water and electricity had not yet been established in the 1890s and early 1900s. Older school boys were responsible for keeping the wood stoves filled with cut timber. Girls often retrieved water from the nearby creek to keep on hand in the classrooms. Sack lunches, made from home, would be carried in lunch pails or bags. (Courtesy Alva Martin Tharp.)

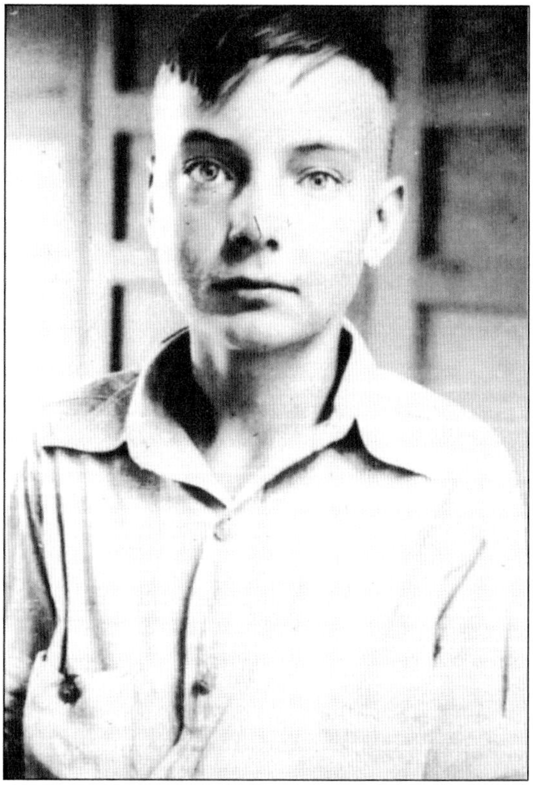

Alva Martin Tharp attended Barren Run School during the 1920s and 1930s. Some of the children's last names were Catlett, Routt, Hornback, Arnett, Thurman, Gusler, Middleton, Walters, Phelps, Corum, and Duckworth. (Courtesy Alva Martin Tharp.)

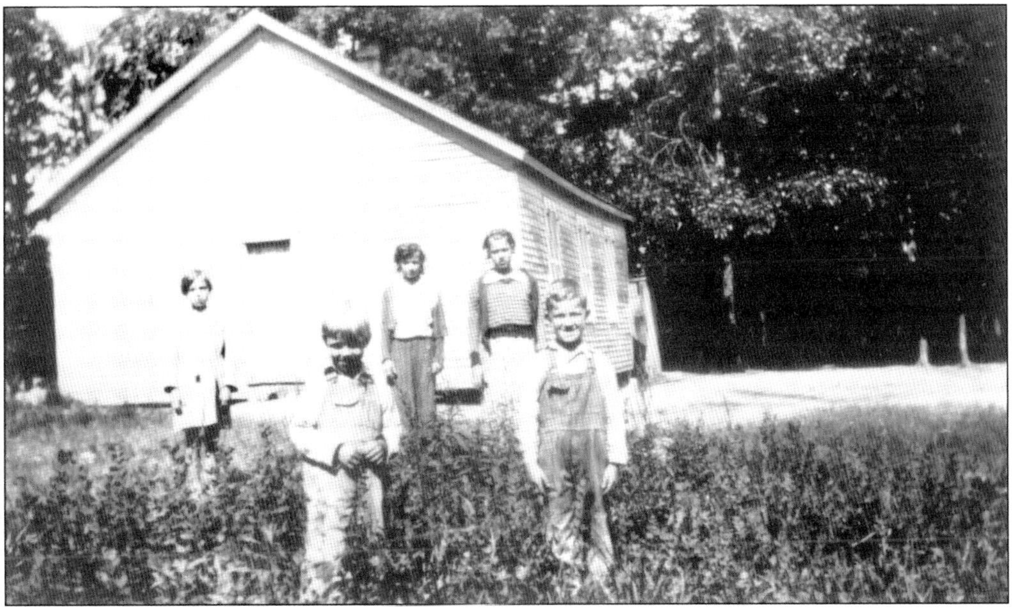

These children attended Knobs School in LaRue County in 1914. Photographed are the children of Arvin Edward and Elizabeth Madden Renfro. Other LaRue County School Districts in 1914 included Barren Run, Brooks, Talley, Siberia, Mount Tabor, Morrison, and Parker's Grove. (Courtesy Kathy Hensley Cooke.)

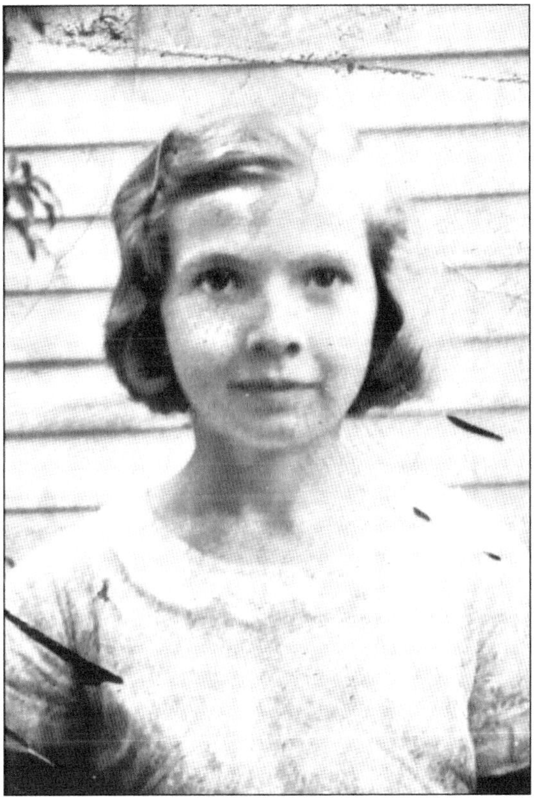

Beatrice Hornback, daughter of Ollie and Nannie Hodges Hornback, attended Oak Hill School in 1934. Oak Hill School was considered District 30 of about 43 districts in LaRue County at the time. (Courtesy Beatrice Hornback Gibson.)

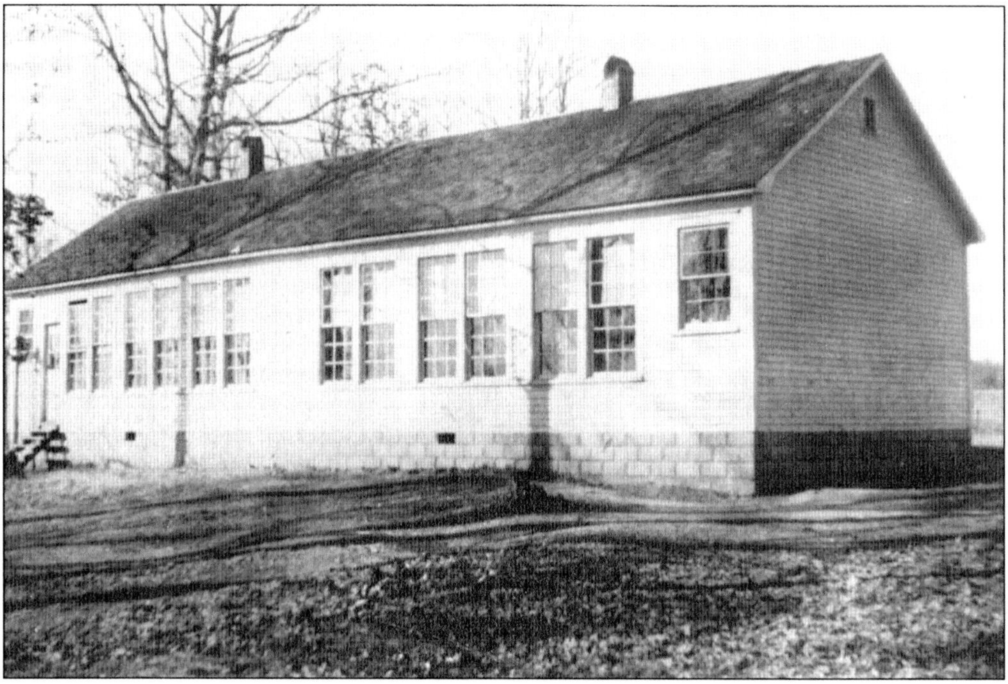

Barren Run School was located in Sonora, LaRue County. In 1895, Barren Run School was known as District 43 and was just north of Barren Run Baptist Church and just off of Tanner Road. (Courtesy Darlene Routt Bryan.)

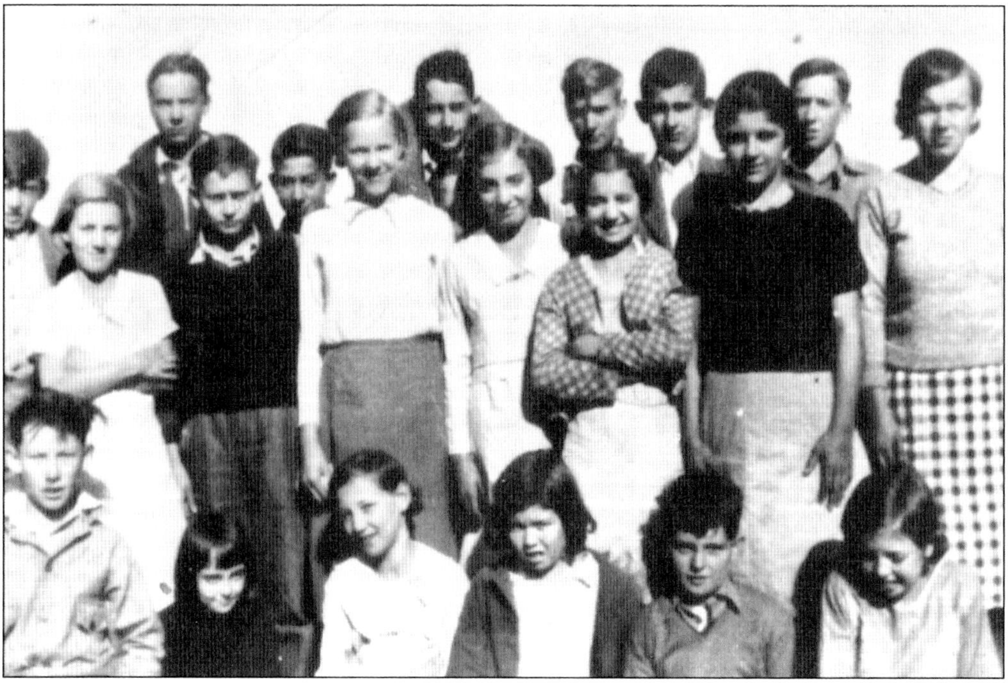

Alva Martin Tharp is pictured with his classmates at Barren Run School. Alva Martin is the first boy from the left in the third row. This school photograph was taken in the late 1930s. (Courtesy Alva Martin Tharp.)

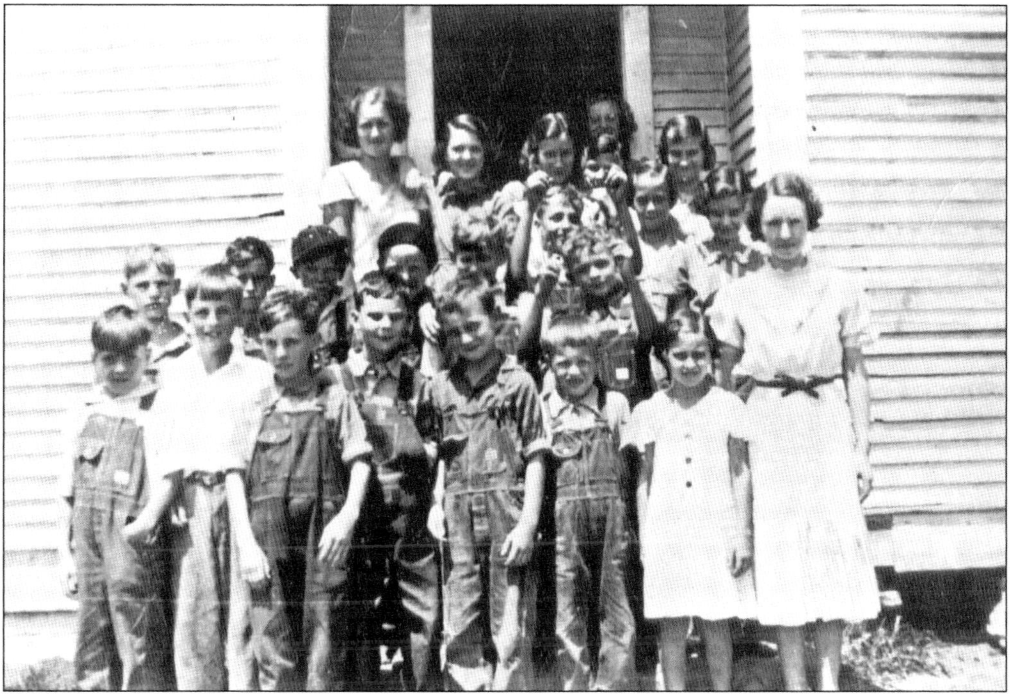

Barren Run School students were photographed around 1935. Dorothy Hornback, the daughter of Elzie and Jo Hornback, is the second person from the left in the fourth row. Sarah Margaret Hornback is on the far right in the fourth row. (Courtesy Sarah Margaret Hornback Massie.)

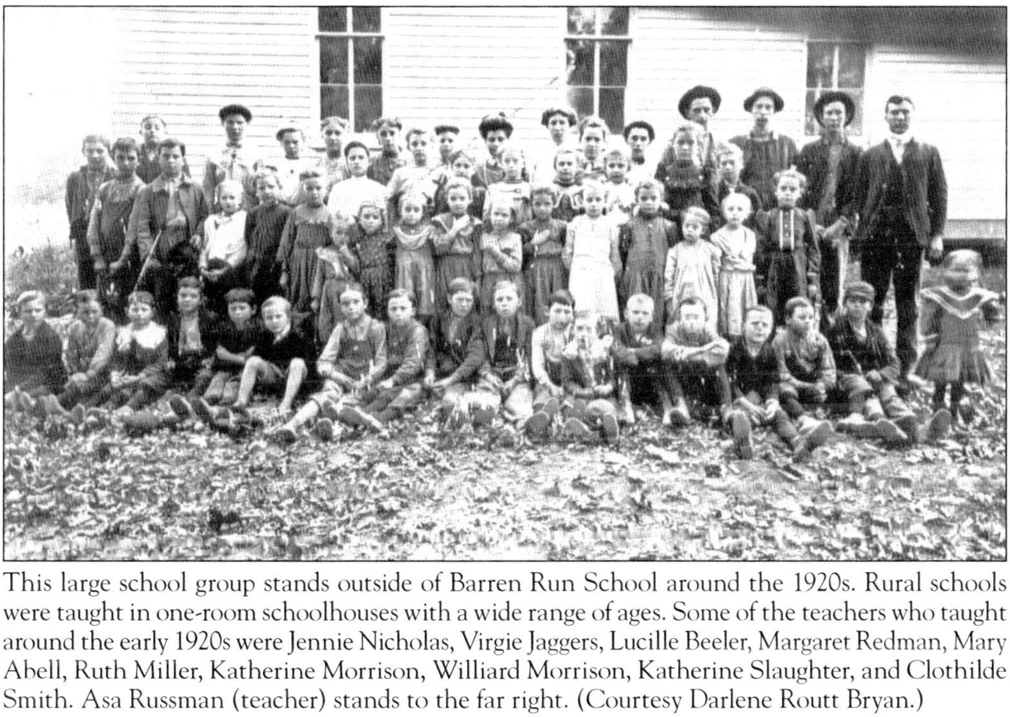

This large school group stands outside of Barren Run School around the 1920s. Rural schools were taught in one-room schoolhouses with a wide range of ages. Some of the teachers who taught around the early 1920s were Jennie Nicholas, Virgie Jaggers, Lucille Beeler, Margaret Redman, Mary Abell, Ruth Miller, Katherine Morrison, Williard Morrison, Katherine Slaughter, and Clothilde Smith. Asa Russman (teacher) stands to the far right. (Courtesy Darlene Routt Bryan.)

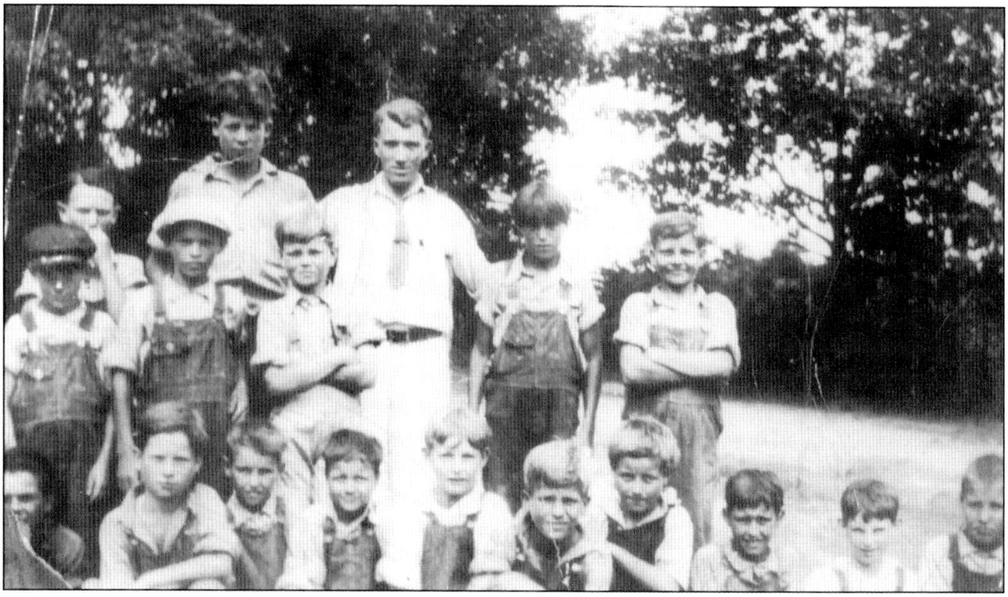

Knob School children pictured here from left to right in the 1930s are (first row) James "Blacky" Flanders, unidentified, Norman Brackett, unidentified, James "Buck" Miller, ? Cruse, unidentified, James Marshall Brackett, unidentified, and Goldman Cruse; (second row) unidentified, Wilburn Lee Brackett, unidentified, Harold Cruse (teacher), unidentified, and ? Hill; (third row) ? Cruse and ? Creal. Oak Hill Baptist Church once owned the schoolhouse until 1959 and held revival services there. (Courtesy Adeline Bush Chappell.)

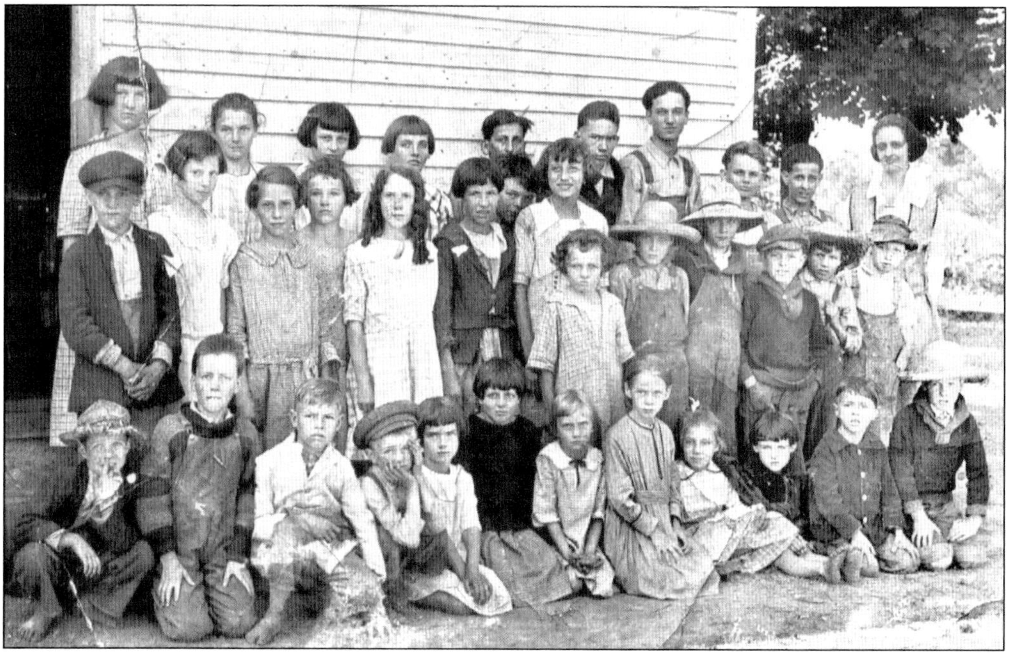

These students of Barren Run School pose together around 1925. Note the little ones in the first row with bare feet. Rural schoolchildren walked to school on beaten dirt paths. Some children would receive one pair of shoes a year or inherit older siblings' shoes when they outgrew theirs. (Courtesy Darlene Routt Bryan.)

Five

SERVING OUR COUNTRY

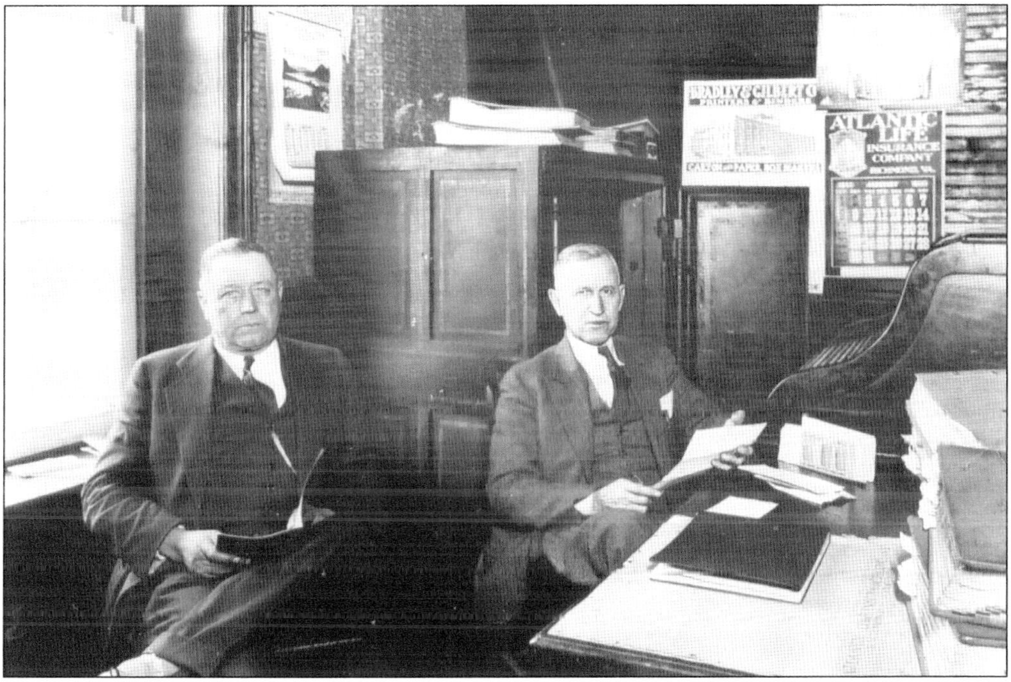

LaRue County sheriff Jim Ward sits alongside Vern Kenny, right, and they seem to be deeply involved in paperwork. Communication was difficult for police officers until radio broadcasting began in the 1930s. Note that the calendar in the background displays January 1933. (Courtesy Mary Kathryn Pennington Puckett.)

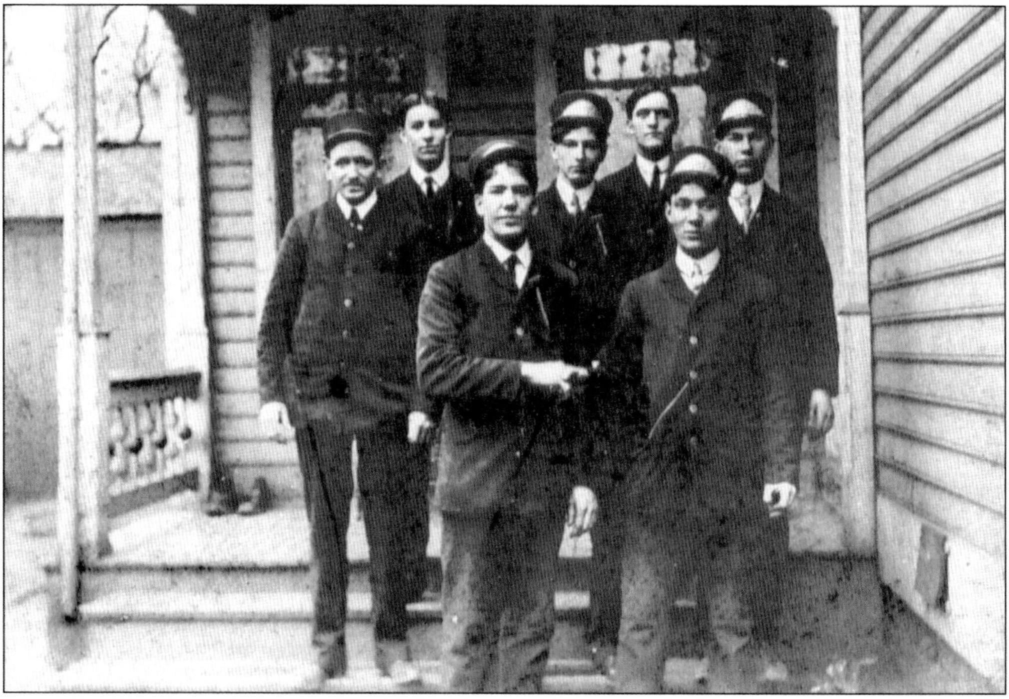

Boss Miller (left) shakes hands with David ?. This group is thought to be either the LaRue County's sheriff's department or maybe a local fire department. The photograph was taken around the 1920s. (Courtesy Mary Kathryn Pennington Puckett.)

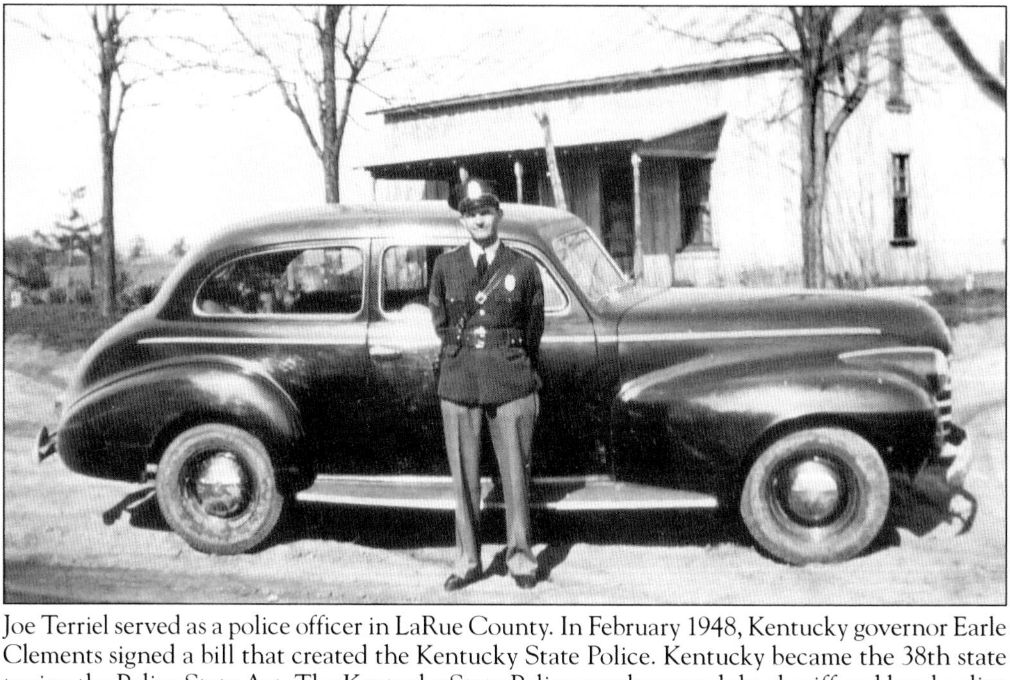

Joe Terriel served as a police officer in LaRue County. In February 1948, Kentucky governor Earle Clements signed a bill that created the Kentucky State Police. Kentucky became the 38th state to sign the Police State Act. The Kentucky State Police supplemented the sheriff and local police departments with statewide law enforcement, providing full power of arrest beyond Kentucky's cities and counties. (Courtesy Beatrice Hornback Gibson.)

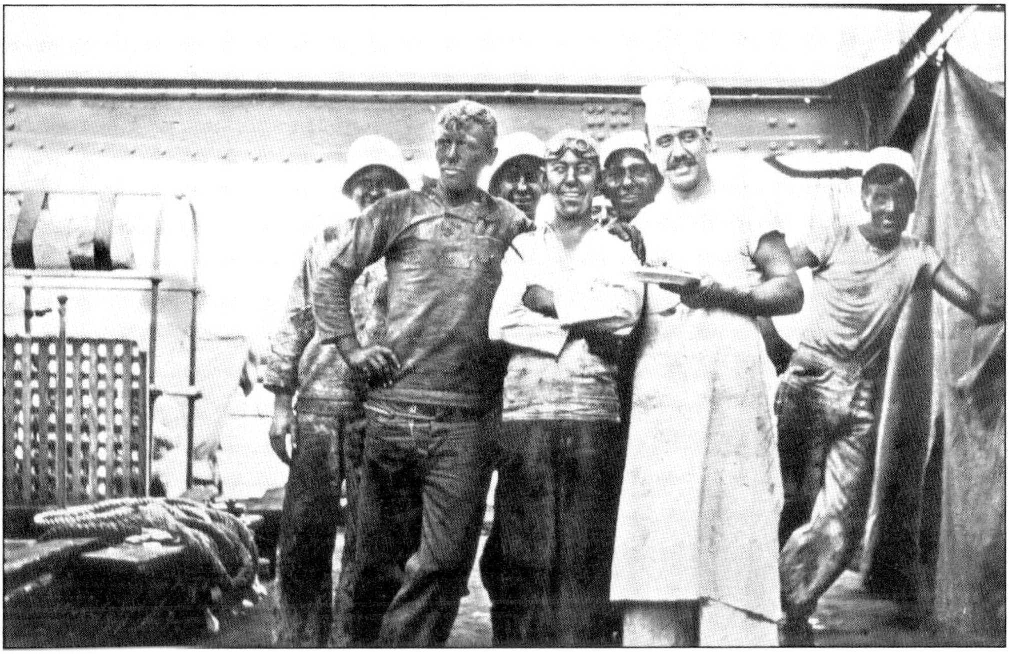

William Alva Abell, born in 1892, served in the U.S. Navy from April 14, 1910, until April 30, 1926. William served as chief commissary steward while serving in the navy. William holds a plate of food with a group of fire stokers aboard the ship. Fire stokers shoveled heaps of coal kept in a coal bunker into the furnace. They were responsible for getting merchant seaman and supplies from place to place and returning the seaman back to safety. (Courtesy Alva Martin Tharp.)

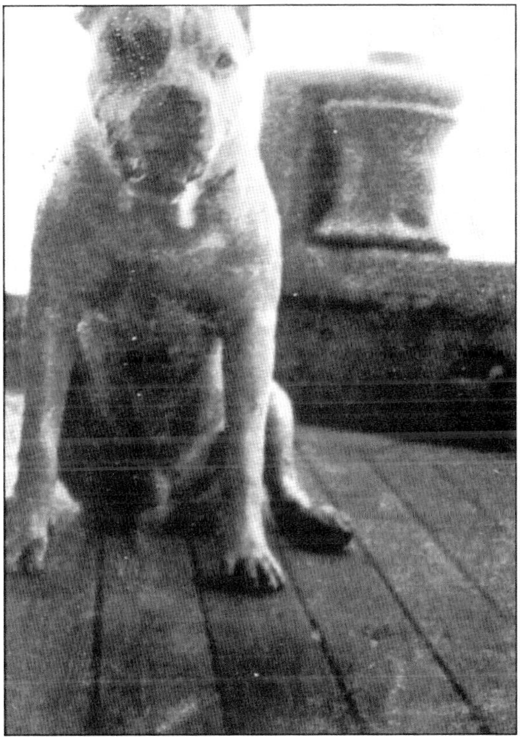

Many dogs served during World War I. France trained canines to search for wounded men; the British used canines as messengers. The Italians used dogs to deliver food, while Germany's 6,000 dogs rescued more than 4,000 wounded soldiers. From 1914 to 1918, more than 7,000 dogs were killed in action. (Courtesy Alva Martin Tharp.)

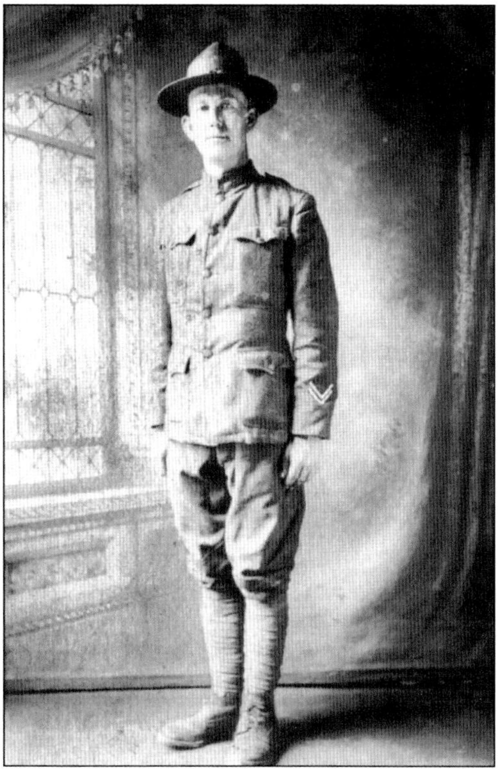

Shelton "Big" Routt, son of Malcolm and Artimicia Routt, was born December 20, 1886. This photograph was taken in the early 1900s while he served in World War I. During World War I, Colt produced 151,700 revolvers while Smith and Wesson produced 153,311. (Courtesy Darlene Routt Bryan.)

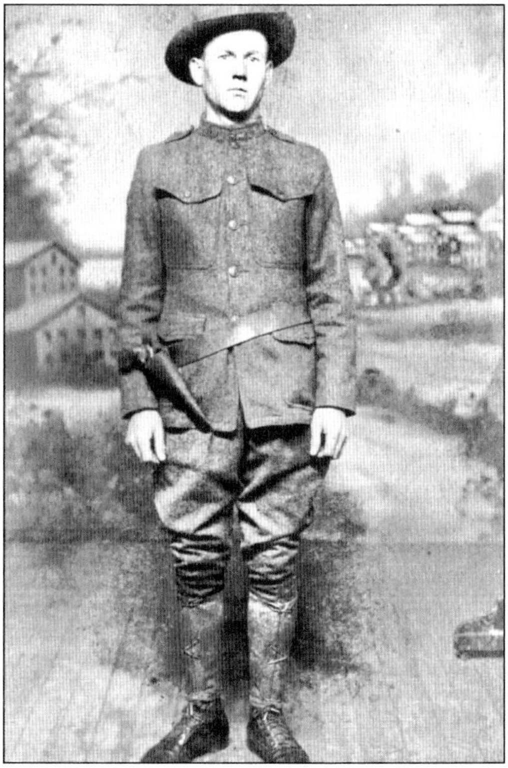

Clark Waller Routt, also a son of Malcolm and Artimicia Routt, served in World War I. Clark was born January 14, 1894. (Courtesy Darlene Routt Bryan.)

Homer Routt served in World War I. This photograph was taken of Homer in 1920. The Selective Service Act was passed on May 18, 1917, to register eligible men for service. Three registrations were performed starting on June 5, 1917, for men between the ages of 21 and 31. (Courtesy Darlene Routt Bryan.)

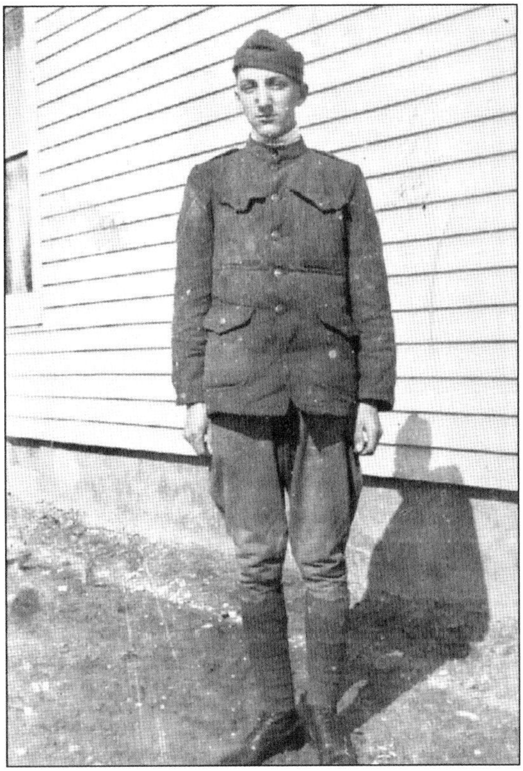

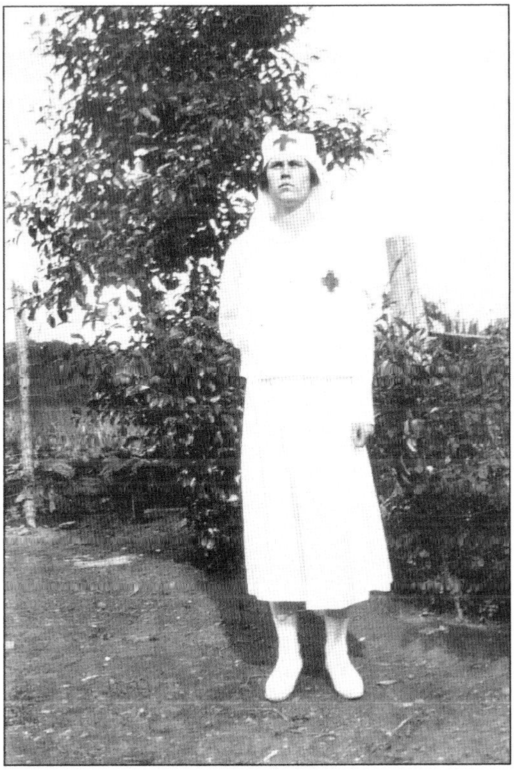

Ola Routt served as a nurse in World War I. The Red Cross provided women with opportunities to aid the war efforts as nurses. Nurses' duties would include rolling bandages, knitting socks, and serving in military hospitals. (Courtesy Darlene Routt Bryan.)

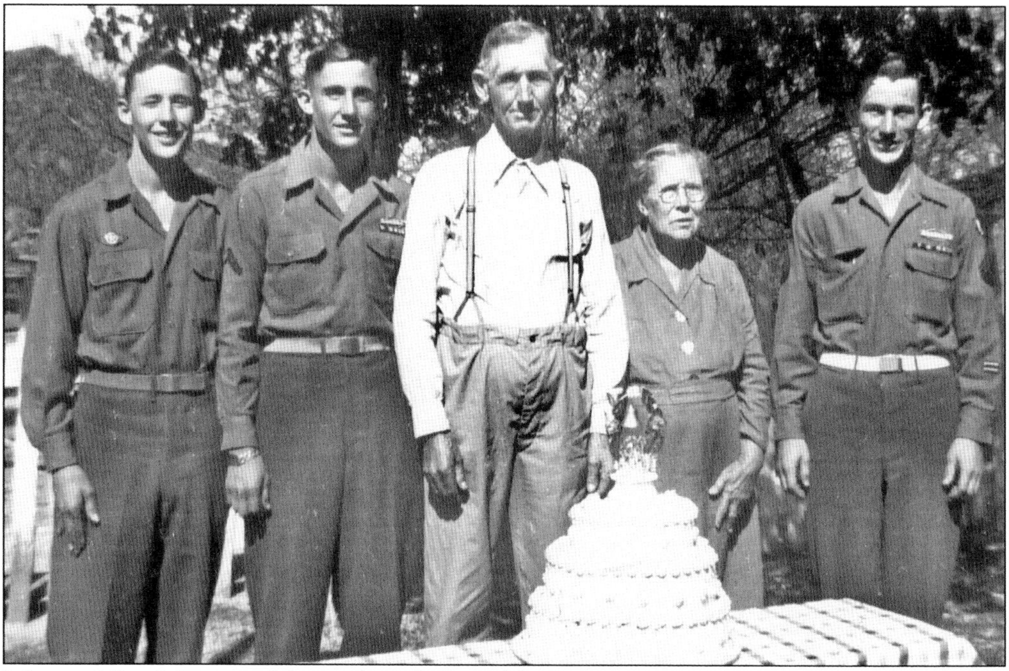

John and Sarah Routt celebrate their 50th wedding anniversary. The Routts were married in 1895. Photographed with the couple are three of their grandsons who all served in World War II. Pictured from left to right are Roy Rock Jr., Walter Daniel Rock, John W. Routt Sr., Sarah Walters Routt, and Chester Rock. The three brothers are sons of Roy and Ruby Rock. The photograph was taken in 1945. (Courtesy Darlene Routt Bryan.)

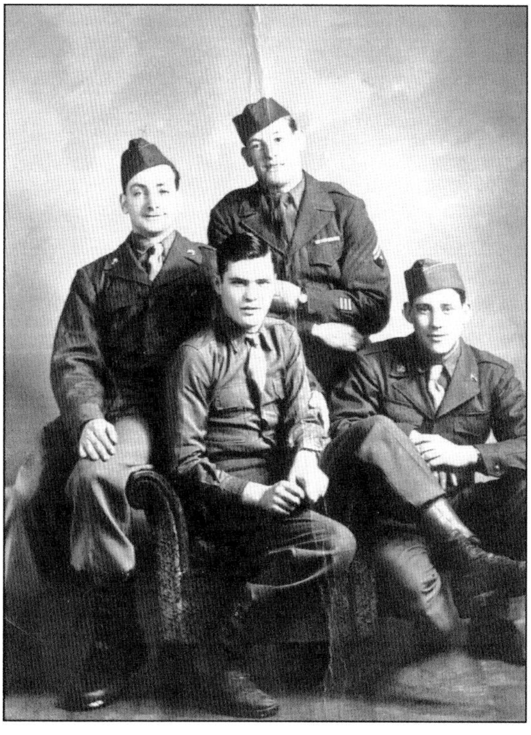

This group of military men served in World War II. The only man identified is Calvin Rock in the lower right corner. (Courtesy Darlene Routt Bryan.)

Gillie Tennison Gibson poses with her three sons: Arleigh Monroe (left), William Thomas (middle), and Leslie Bert. All three served in Germany during World War II. The family is from Buffalo, Kentucky. (Courtesy Beatrice Hornback Gibson.)

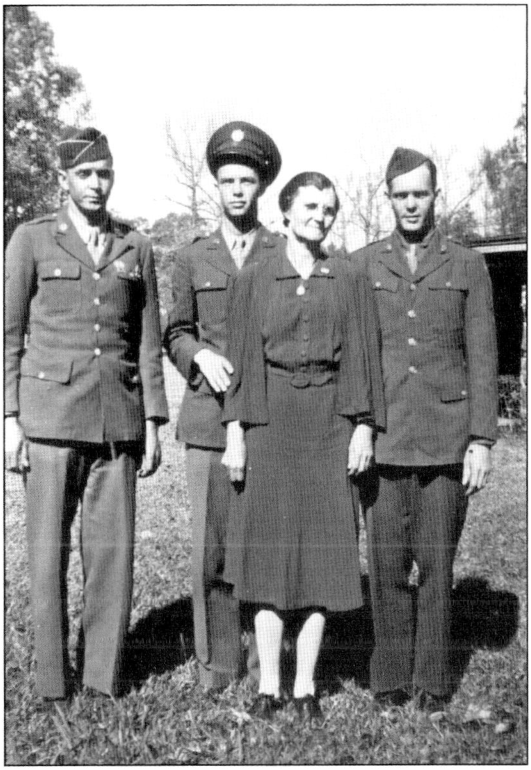

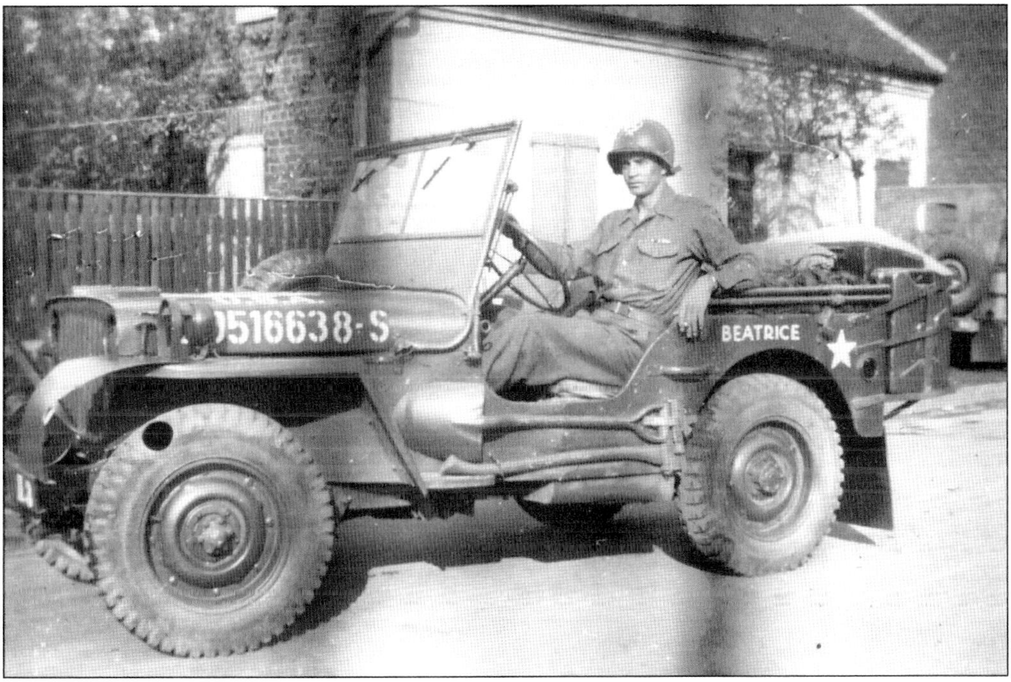

Arleigh Gibson served in the infantry in Germany, driving ammunition to the front line. This photograph was taken in the 1940s before crossing the Rhine. Arleigh had his girlfriend's name, Beatrice, inscribed on his Jeep. (Courtesy Beatrice Hornback Gibson.)

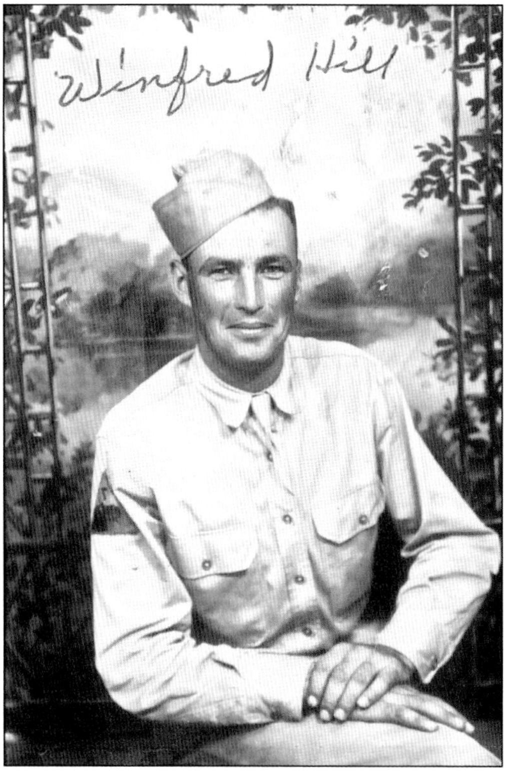

Winifred Hill served in the military during World War II. Note the patch located on his upper arm. This patch stands for the 7th Calvary Armor Recon Battalion. (Courtesy Gertrude Hill Conder.)

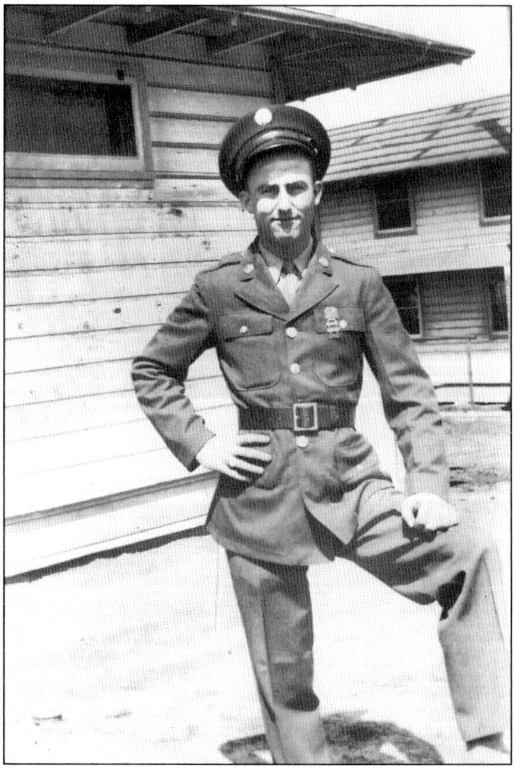

Eldred "Mug" Routt served in the U.S. Army during World War II. Eldred is the brother of June Routt. The U.S. Army had more ships than the navy. When the U.S. Army landed in North Africa, they had among their supplies three Coca-Cola bottling plants. (Courtesy June Routt.)

Union soldier John Lobb was born February 25, 1844; this tintype was taken of him in his Civil War uniform. John served in the 27th Regiment, Kentucky Infantry, Company E. John was the son of William Duncan and Sarah Willock Lobb. (Courtesy Darlene Routt Bryan.)

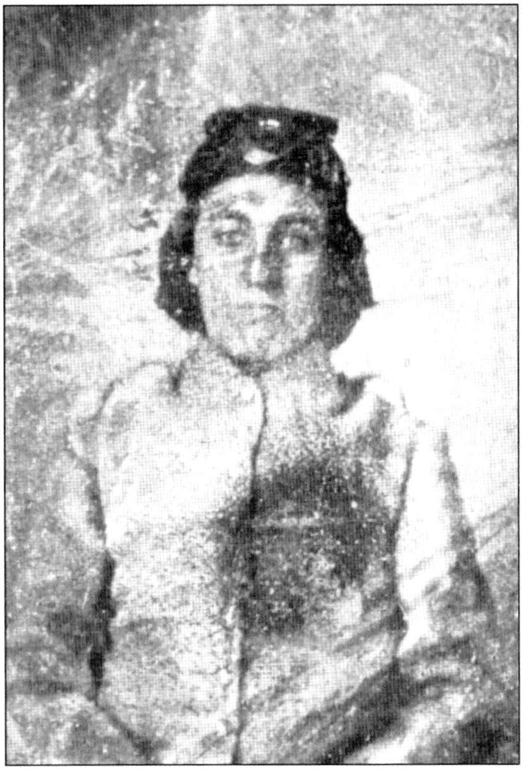

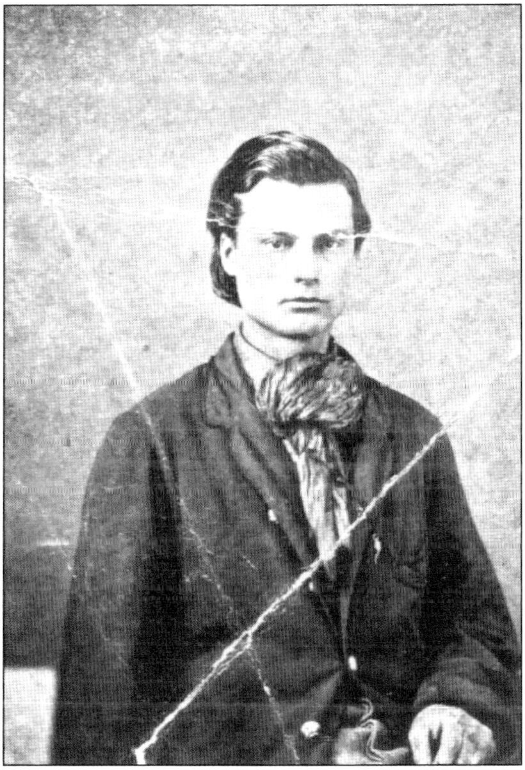

Confederate soldier Elijah Thomas Jackson was born February 14, 1843. This tintype was taken of Elijah in his Civil War uniform. Elijah was captured and held prisoner during part of his service, during which time he contracted tuberculosis. Elijah married Lydia Ann Bush of LaRue County on March 2, 1865, and they had four children. Elijah died July 15, 1877. (Courtesy William Leslie Hornback Jr.)

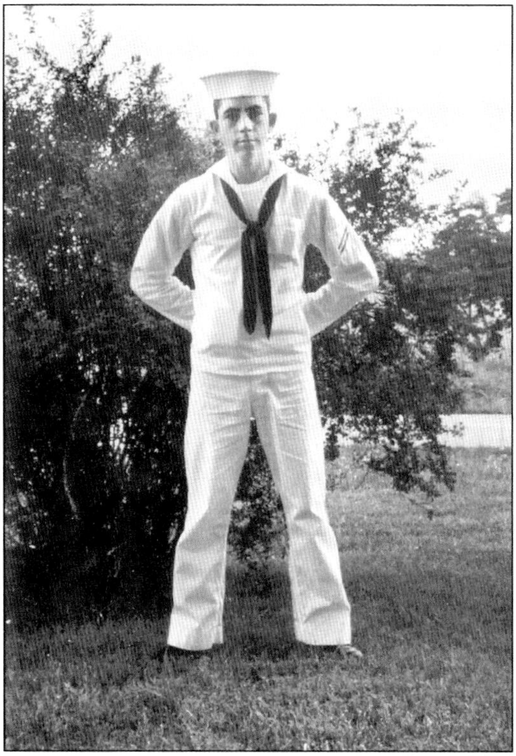

Paul T. Hornback, son of Wilburn and Opal Thompson Hornback, served in the U.S. Navy. Paul served a five-month deployment in Vietnam on the USS *Damato* as a boiler man. During the five months, the *Damato* sunk 20 enemy logic crafts, while 18 others were damaged. On nine different occasions, the *Damato* was under attack by enemy fire. Paul now resides in the Buffalo, Kentucky, area. (Courtesy Beatrice Hornback Gibson.)

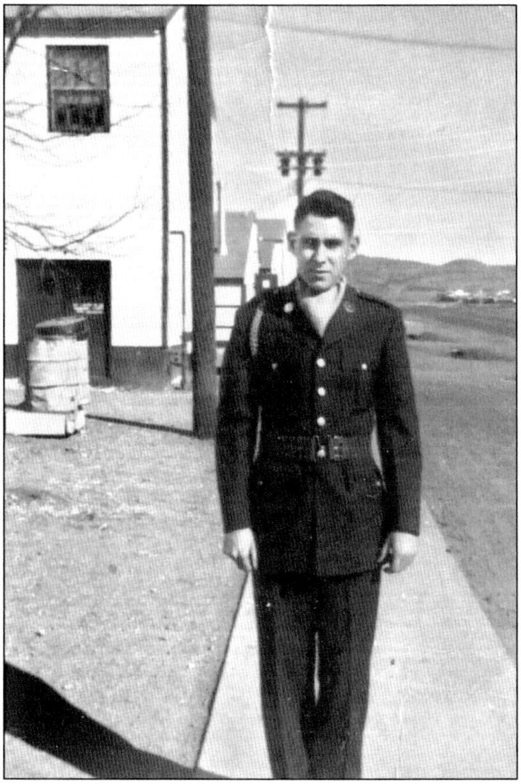

Martin M. Hornback, the son of Albert and Eva Leasor Hornback, was born November 10, 1942. Martin served in the U.S. Army and was stationed in Korea in the 1960s. Martin resides in the Oak Hill community in Sonora. (Courtesy Elizabeth Priddy Fields.)

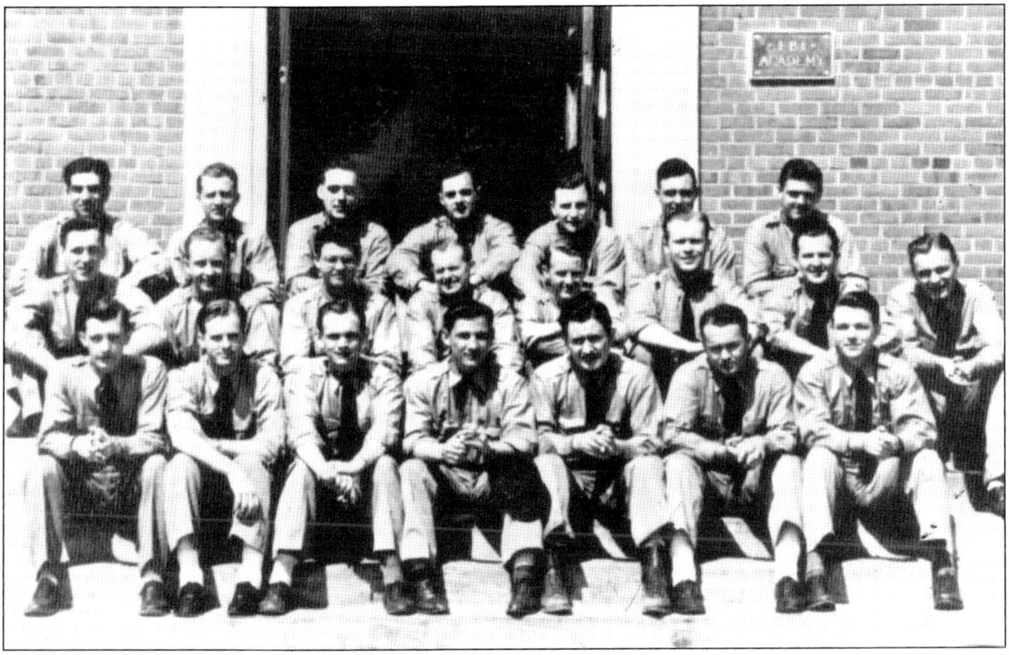

William Leslie Hornback Jr. served as an FBI agent for 35 years. This photograph was taken at the FBI Academy at Quantico Marine Corp Base in Virginia in the spring of 1943. William, or "Les," is shown with his class, smiling and with his hair all combed (first row, third from the left). He served from January 16, 1939, until December 24, 1974. After his retirement from the FBI, he spent several years as a private investigator and now lives in Louisville, Kentucky. (Courtesy William Leslie Hornback Jr.)

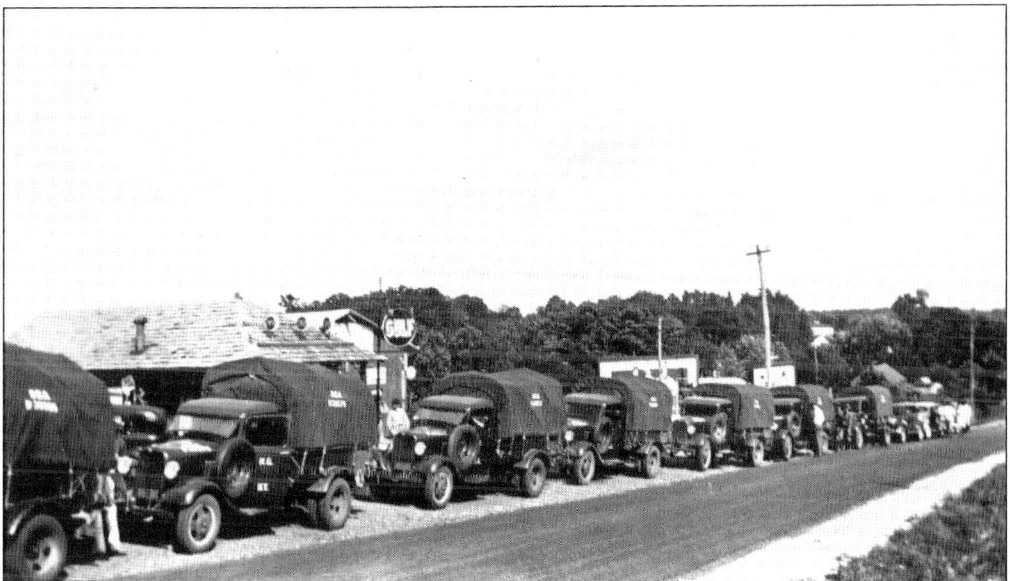

During World War II in the early 1940s, this convoy of army men stopped off in Buffalo, Kentucky, for a pit stop. (Courtesy Beatrice Hornback Gibson.)

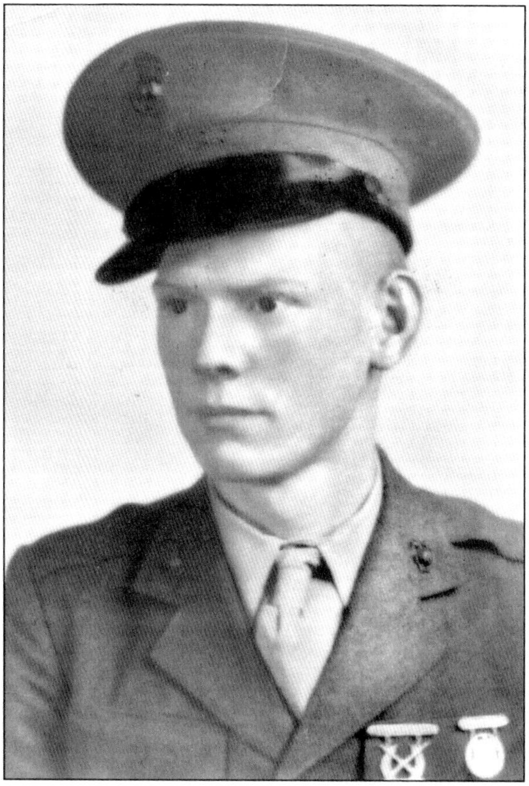

Calvin Lee Hornback was born September 21, 1925. He died May 15, 2001, in Las Vegas, Nevada, and was buried at Chloride, Arizona. Calvin served in the U.S. Marine Corps, 3rd Division. While in the marines, he served in the South Pacific and received an honorable discharge in 1945. (Courtesy William Leslie Hornback Jr.)

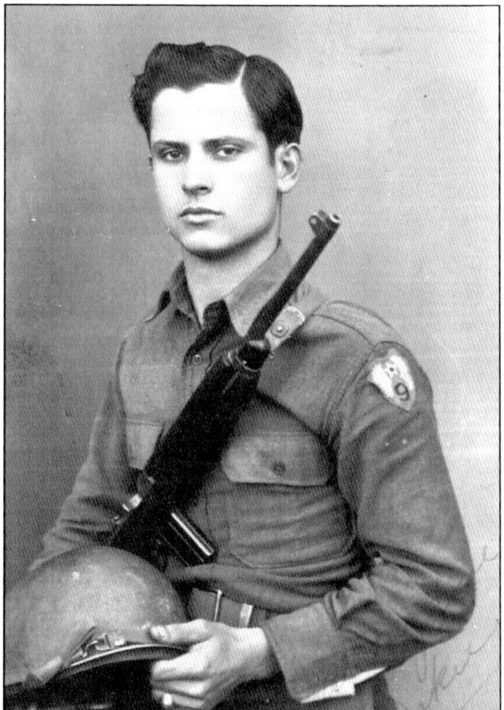

Jesse Clyde Hornback served in the FBI as his brother, Les, did. He started as a clerk in the Louisville office in 1942 and retired as a special agent in 1976, the only interruption being a tour of military duty during World War II in the European theater of the war. (Courtesy Beatrice Hornback Gibson.)

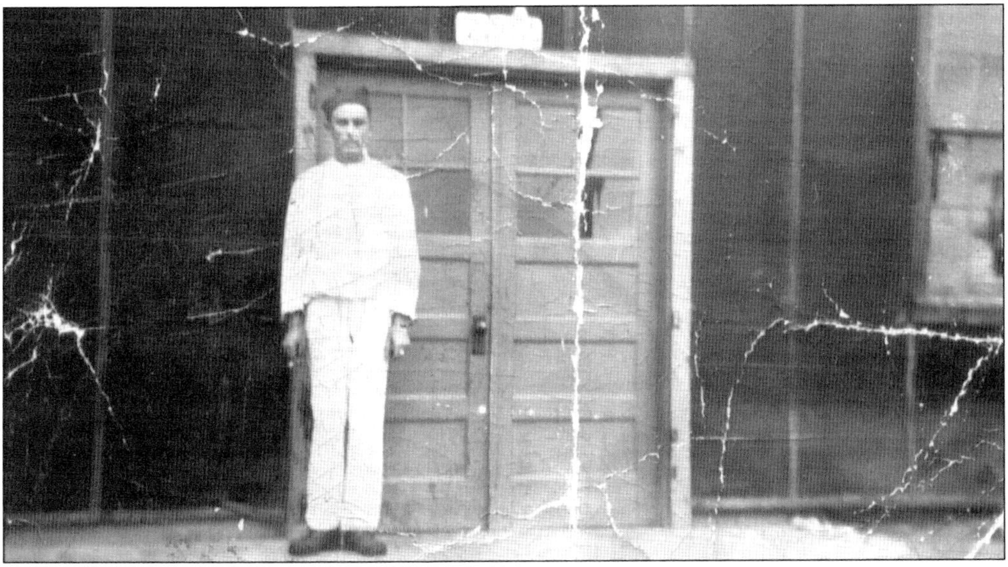

Steve Hornback was born December 9, 1909, in LaRue County. Steve served in the U.S. Army as an army cook. He entered service at Fort Benjamin in Harrison, Indiana, and served in the army from February 17, 1942, through September 27, 1945. While in the army, he received the Good Conduct Medal, World War II Victory Medal, Honorable Service Lapel Button World War II, American Campaign Medal, and Sharpshooter Badge with carbine bar. After serving in the army, Steve came home to LaRue County, where he rejoined his wife, Juanita, and their new son, Marion Lee Hornback. (Courtesy Shirley Hornback Miller.)

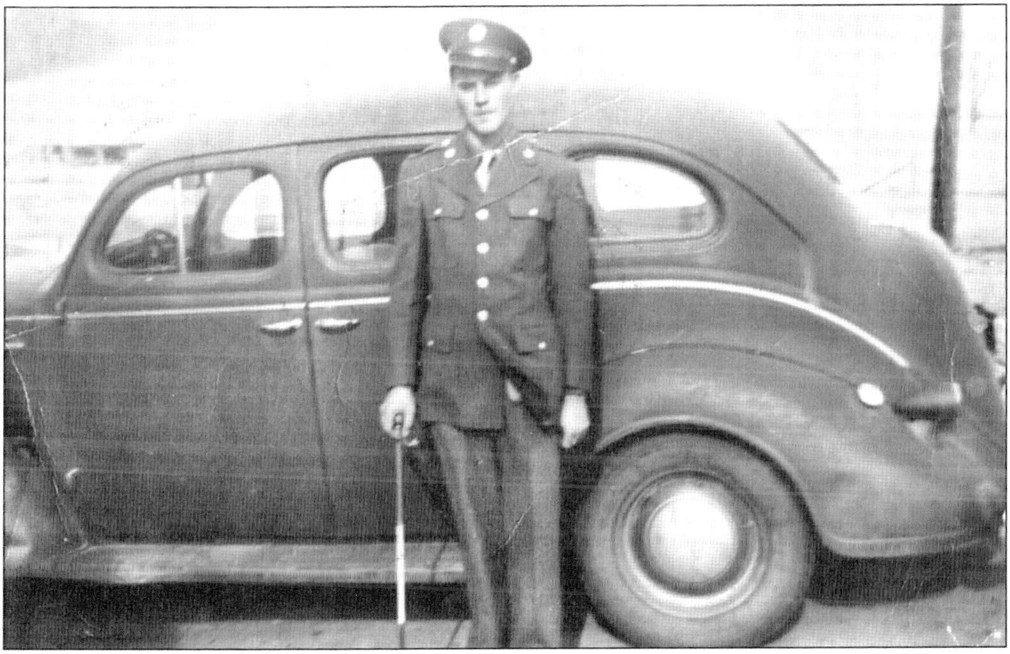

Elmer Lee Hornback, born in 1922, served in the U.S. Army like his brother, Steve. Elmer entered his service in Louisville, Kentucky, and served from December 1, 1942, until November 14, 1945. While in the army, Elmer received the World War II Victory Medal and Honorable Service Lapel Button. His place of separation was Camp Fannin, Texas. (Courtesy Clifford Hornback.)

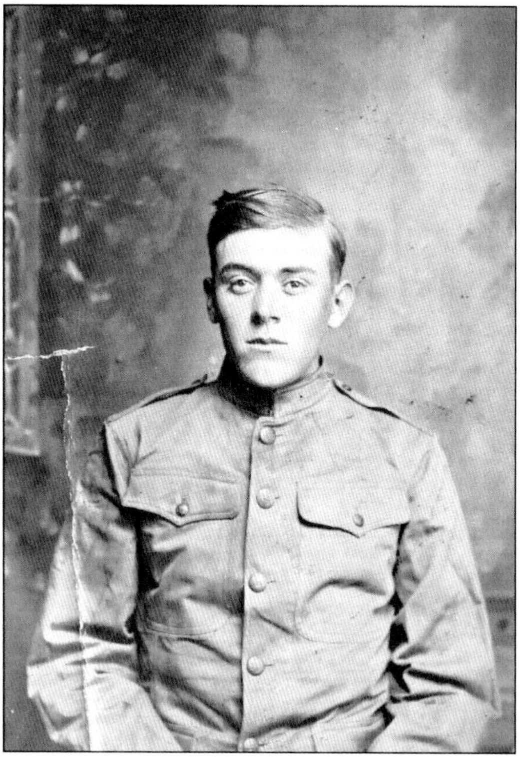

Henry L. Cruse served in the military in the 143rd Infantry, 36 Division, Company L. On the back of this photograph, his mother had written, "Here is his picture but not a good one. It was made the day he got out of the hospital after he had the measels [*sic*]." This photograph was in a private collection of Steve and Juanita Hornback's. (Courtesy Shirley Hornback Miller.)

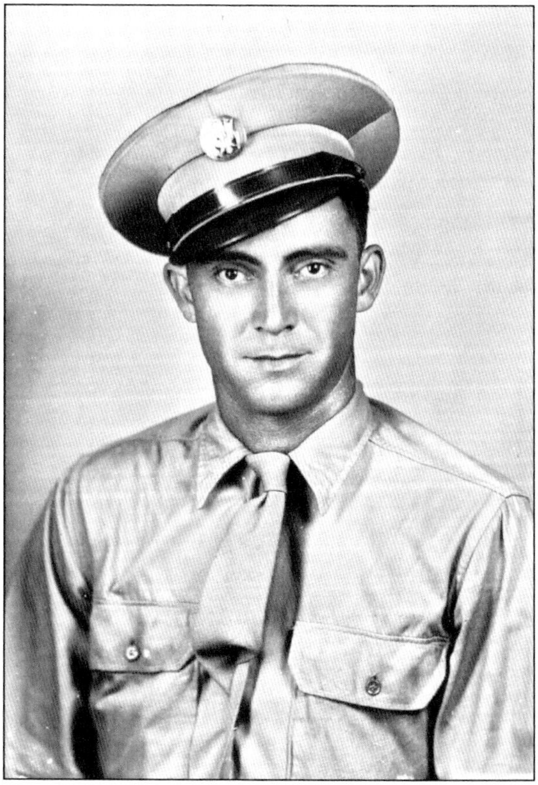

Wilburn "Webb" Hornback, son of Ollie and Nannie Hodges Hornback, served in the U.S. Army. Webb was born on June 24, 1918, and died November 1985. Webb had two sons, Gary and Paul. Webb is buried at Oak Hill Cemetery in Sonora. (Courtesy Beatrice Hornback Gibson.)

Six

Spiritual Moments

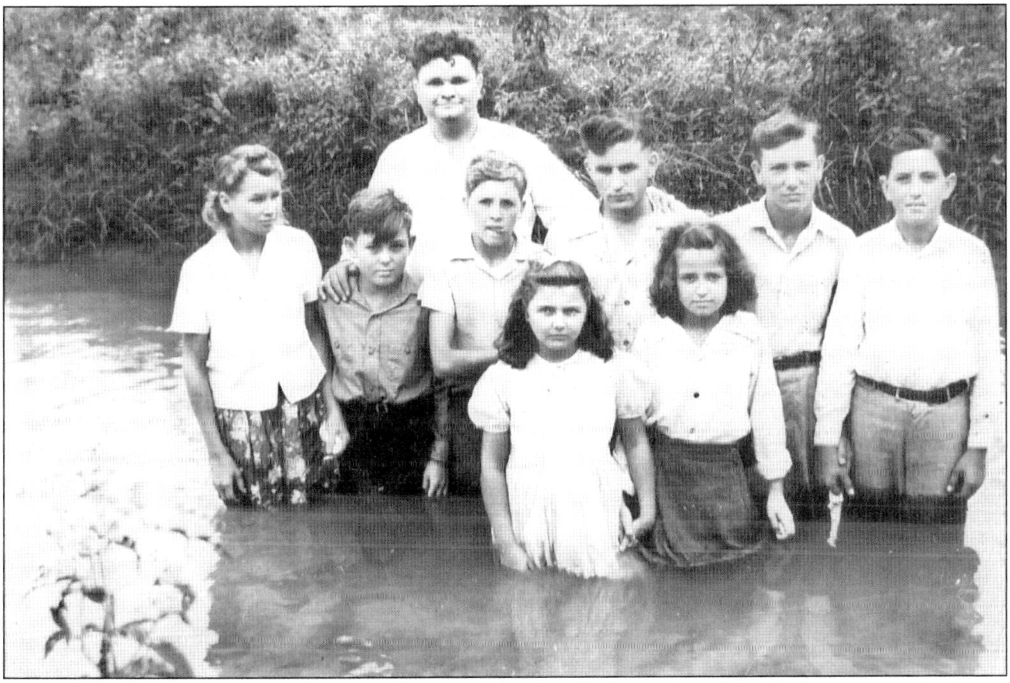

Br. Nobel Cottrell, a pastor at Oak Hill Baptist Church in Sonora, Kentucky, baptized a lot of new believers in his lifetime. Photographed from left to right were (first row) Melva Hornback and Barbara Thompson; (second row) ? Sloan, Durrett Gardner, Clarence Gardner Jr. ("Junior"), Carl Flanders, Donald Puckett, and Roy McCubbins with Br. Nobel Cottrell in the back awaiting their baptism. (Courtesy Mary Kathryn Pennington Puckett.)

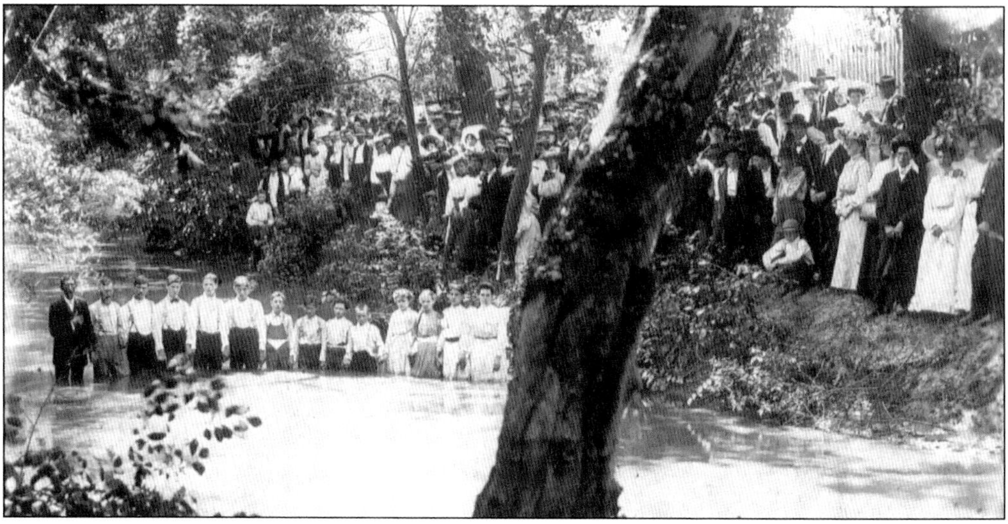

This 1890s picture of a baptism is the full view of the cover photograph. The gentleman standing next to the preacher is Will Reynolds. The young boy in the baptism line next to the woman is Doran Bowling. The man on the far side of the bank is Henry Lobb holding Buford Lobb. The woman next to him is his wife, Mary Lobb. The young boy sitting at the right of the photograph is Walter Wright. Also pictured is Johnny Lobb, who served in the Civil War. He is barely seen at the far right past the tree three rows up with a long white beard. This photograph might have been taken at Mather's Mill Bridge in LaRue County. (Courtesy Darlene Routt Bryan.)

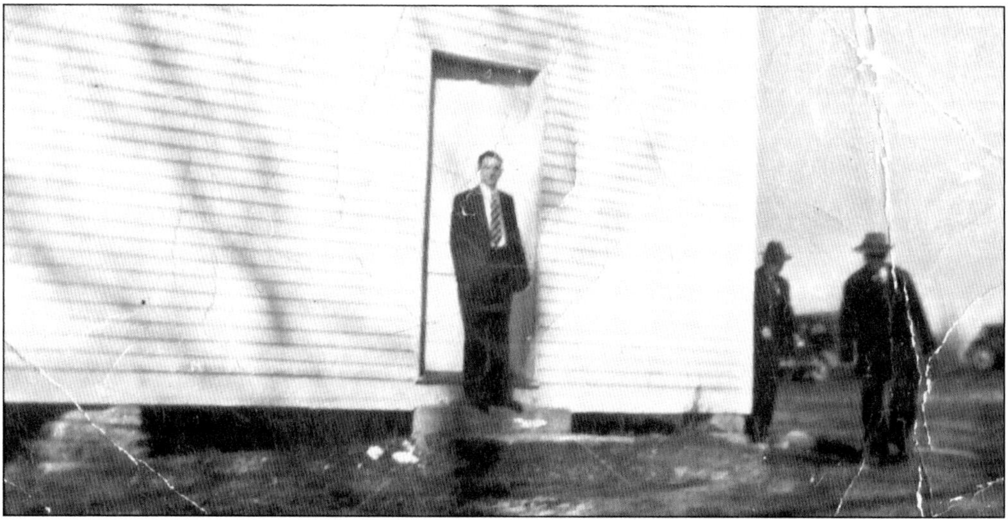

Lamont Hornback is seen coming out of the door of Oak Hill Baptist Church. On April 30, 1856, members from Three Forks Bacon Creek sent a petition to ask for their church letters to start a new church, Oak Hill. The charter members were Thomas and Lydia Hornback, Paul and Mary Tucker, Susan Tucker, Anderson and Susan Tucker, Nancy Brooks, William Brooks, William Brooks Sr., James Brooks, Mr. and Mrs. William Steel, Charles and America Brooks, Mr. and Mrs. James Ship, Dudley H. Brooks, Elizabeth Brooks, Nancy Tucker, Sally Kinked, Mary Brooks, Mr. and Mrs. Bob Hodges, Sam and Milly Tucker, Sally Brooks, Mr. and Mrs. William Hodges, Mr. and Mrs. Tom Wilder, Willy Goodman, Obediah Hodge, Elizabeth Hodge, and John Tucker. Martha Brooks was the first one to be baptized into the new church in April 1856. (Sarah Hornback Massie.)

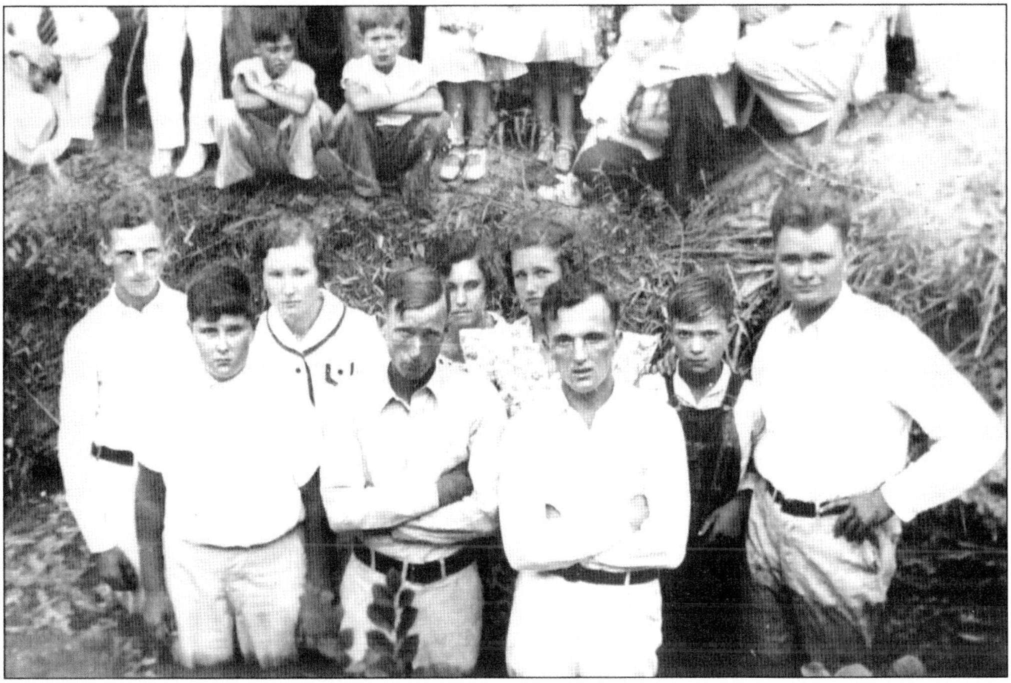

These members of Oak Hill Baptist Church await their baptism in 1937. Pictured from left to right are (first row) James McCubbin, Cod Burba, and Roy Lee Freeman; (second row) Charles Freeman, Louise Patterson, Thelma Thomas Brackett, Lenora Watkins, ? Hornback, and Rev. Nobel Cottrell. (Courtesy Adeline Bush Chappell.)

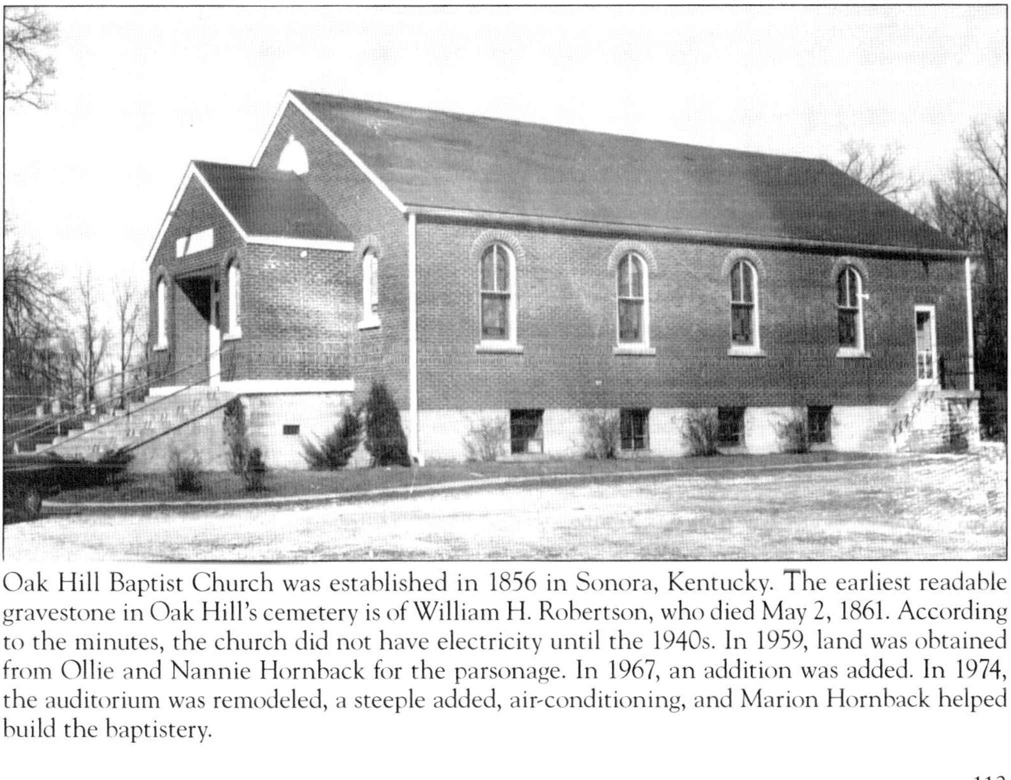

Oak Hill Baptist Church was established in 1856 in Sonora, Kentucky. The earliest readable gravestone in Oak Hill's cemetery is of William H. Robertson, who died May 2, 1861. According to the minutes, the church did not have electricity until the 1940s. In 1959, land was obtained from Ollie and Nannie Hornback for the parsonage. In 1967, an addition was added. In 1974, the auditorium was remodeled, a steeple added, air-conditioning, and Marion Hornback helped build the baptistery.

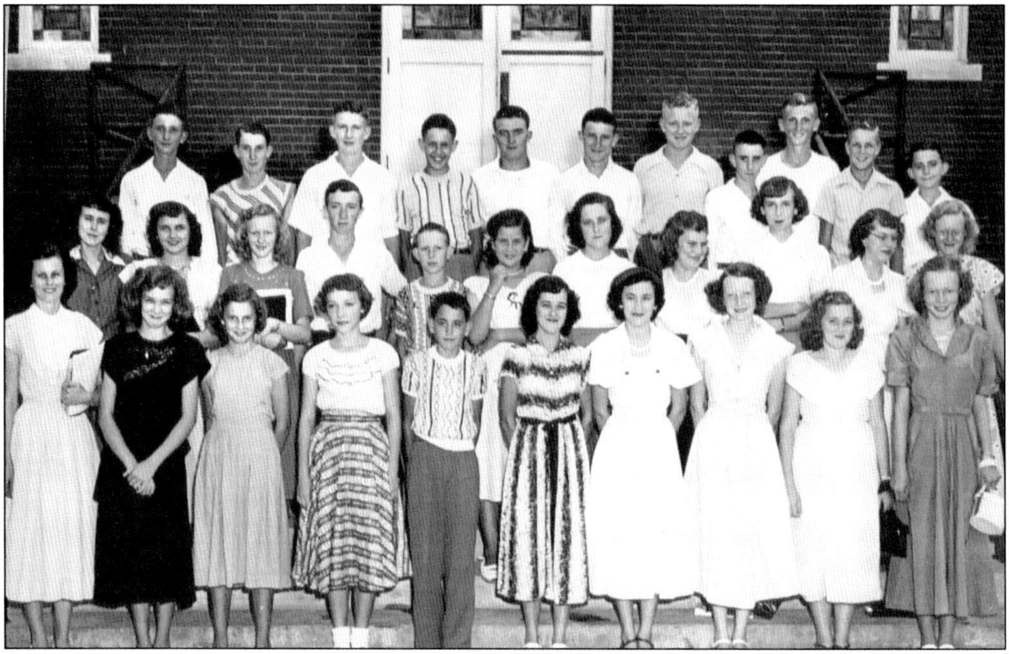

Myrtle Ward's Sunday school class at Oak Hill Baptist Church poses for their group picture. Once students attended her class, they did not want to leave. Myrtle Ward is pictured in the first row (far left) holding her Sunday school books. (Courtesy Mary Kathryn Pennington Puckett.)

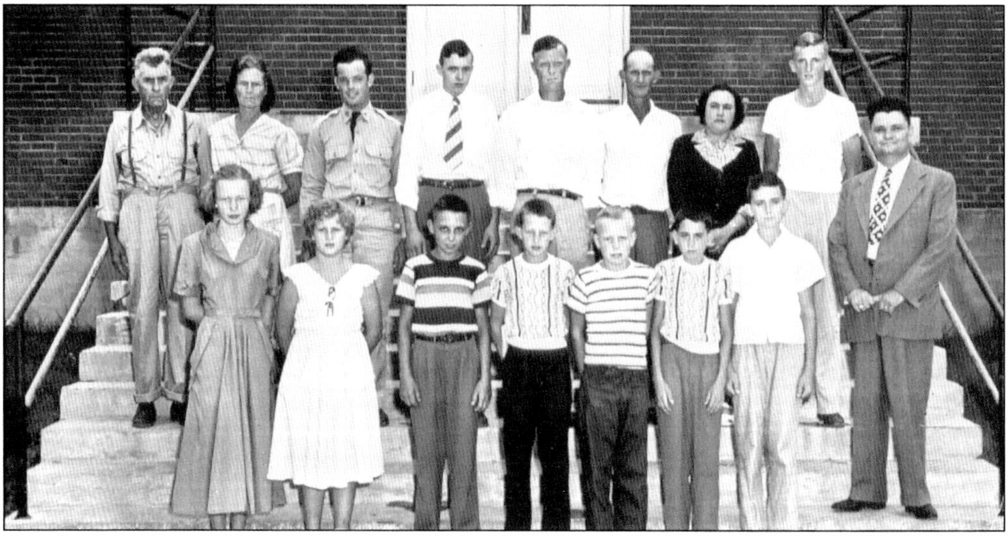

In 1947, this group awaits baptism on the front steps of Oak Hill Baptist Church. Br. Nobel Cottrell was the pastor from 1936 to 1954 then again in 1972. Several men were licensed to preach by Oak Hill Baptist Church. W. Judd Tucker was the first to be licensed on May 12, 1888; W. E. Walsh, October 1892; Joe Sallee, June 1912; Herbert Brooks, August 1941; Rush Hornback, June 1944; Vernon Talley, February 1951; Ferrill Gardner, February 1951; Jesse T. Hornback, November 1952; Toby Lewis, January 1961; Sonny Priddy, 1963; Gale Hornback, November 1965; Phillip Bradshaw, September 1977; Everett Priddy, August 1979; Mike Akridge, December 1978; Marion Lee Hornback, January 25, 1981; and Derek Cromwell, 1983. (Courtesy Mary Kathryn Pennington Puckett.)

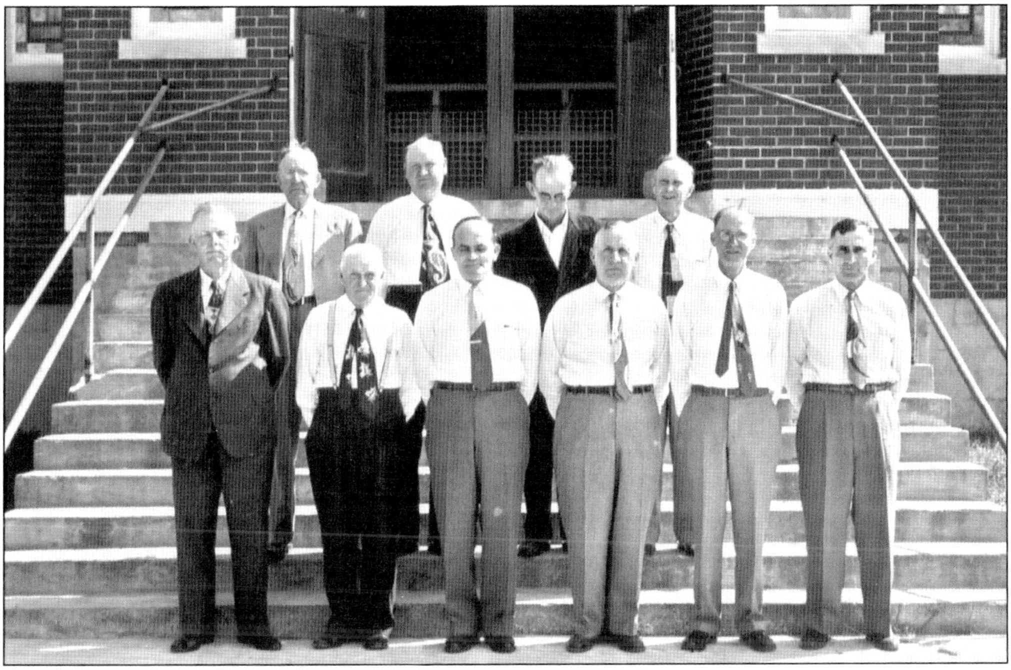

This men's Sunday school class at Oak Hill Baptist Church was photographed in the 1950s. From left to right, they are (first row) Oliver Tabb, Jimmy Hines, Gentry Hornback, Everett Cruse, Granville Cruse, and Ollie Hornback; (second row) Ira Ackridge, Cecil Edwards, Raymond Roten, and Bill Shipp. (Courtesy Mary Kathryn Pennington Puckett.)

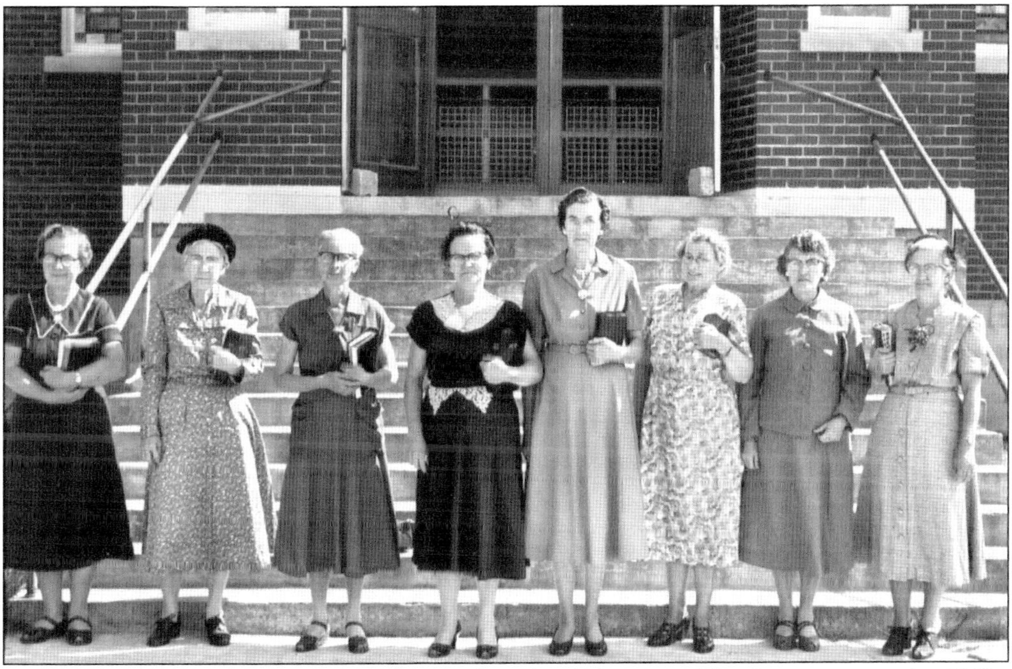

The Oak Hill Baptist Church women's Sunday school class posed for this picture in the 1950s. Shown from left to right are Mary Shipp, Annie Roten, Nannie Hornback, Stella Edwards, Ada Tabb, Clifford Cruse, Bessie Kessinger, and Susan Cruse. (Courtesy Evelyn Cruse.)

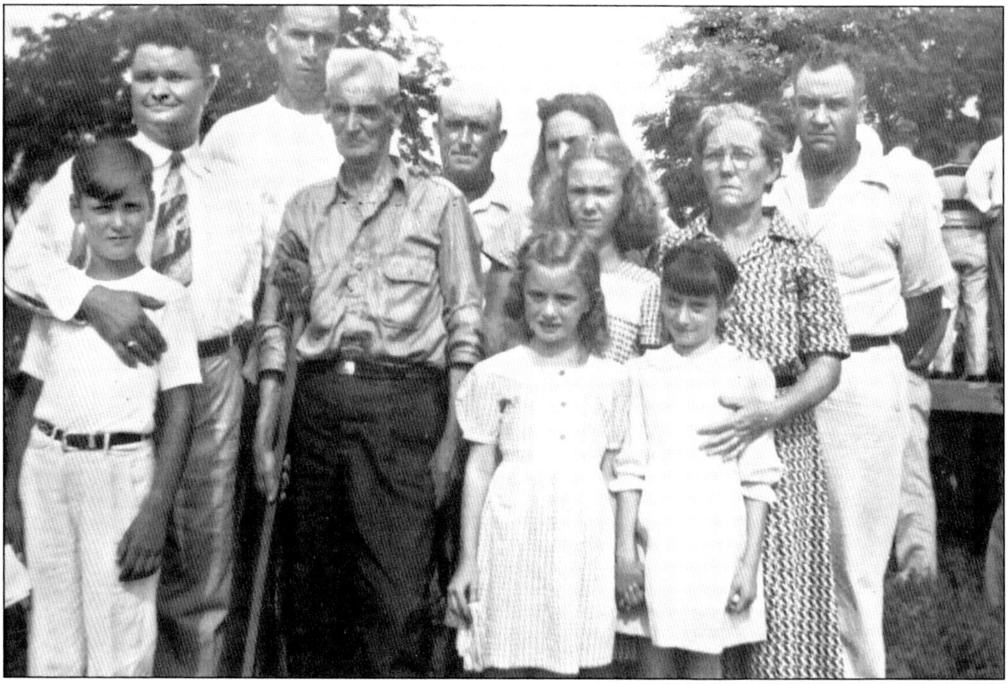

From left to right are (first row) Cleston Hornback, Doris Brooks, and Alice Faye Milby; (second row) Br. Nobel Cottrell, Perry McCandless, Georgina Puckett, and Robelia Puckett; (third row) Virgil Cox, Charlie Walsh, unidentified, and Ed Wheeler. (Courtesy Mary Kathryn Pennington Puckett.)

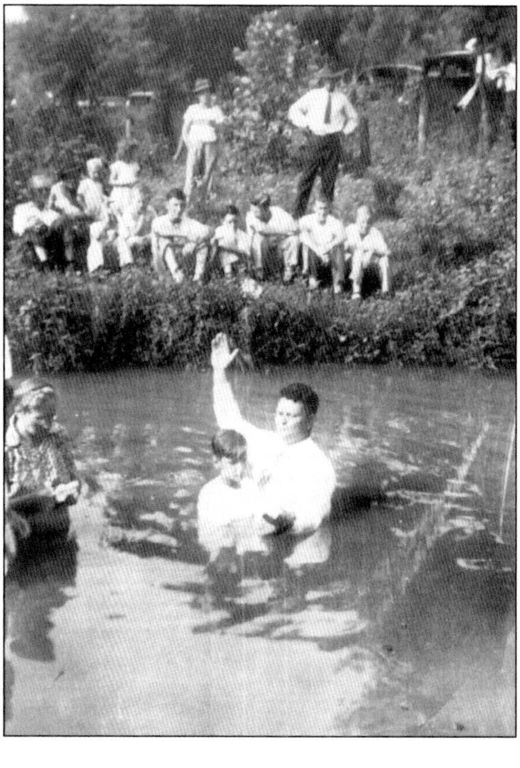

In this 1950s photograph, Br. Nobel Cottrell prepares to baptize Cleston Hornback as Robelia Puckett is on the left in the water. Baptisms were celebrated events; note the cars lining the road in the background. Once a person receives Christ as his savior, then the person may be baptized by being totally submerged under water. Before baptisteries were placed inside of churches, believers were baptized in creeks, rivers, or ponds. Sometimes livestock had to be run out of the water in order to baptize the person. (Courtesy Beatrice Hornback Gibson.)

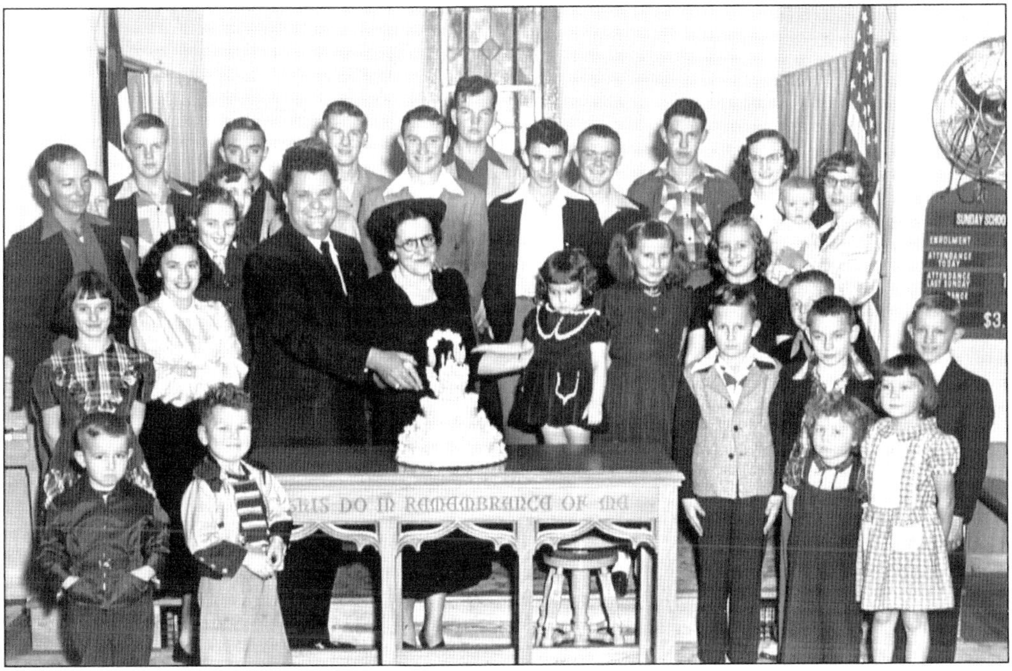

Rev. Nobel and Lilly Cottrell celebrate their wedding anniversary with members of Oak Hill Church in Sonora. Some of the people celebrating were Donald (third row, far left) and Mary Kathryn Puckett (fourth row, far right holding a baby), David Meers (fourth row, center), Gale Hornback (first row, far left), and Rose Nell Roten (second row, sixth from the left). (Courtesy Mary Kathryn Pennington Puckett.)

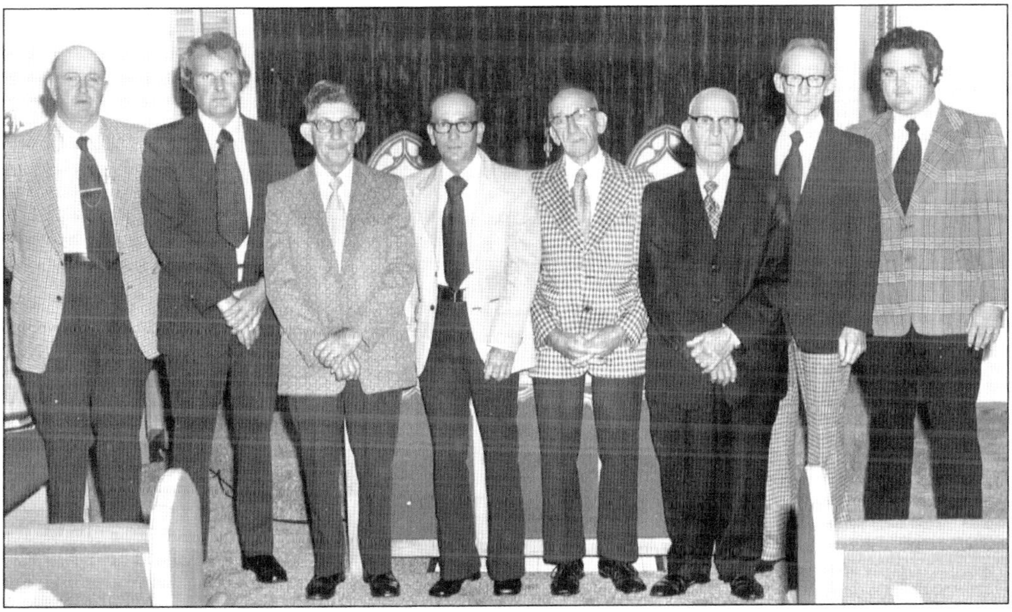

These deacons are photographed from left to right as follows: James McCubbins, Arlene Bennett, Johnny Talley, Donald Puckett, Virgil Pennington, Everett Cruse, Stanley Ward, and Br. James Watt. Brother Watt was the pastor from 1973 to 1976 at Oak Hill Baptist Church. (Courtesy Mary Kathryn Pennington Puckett.)

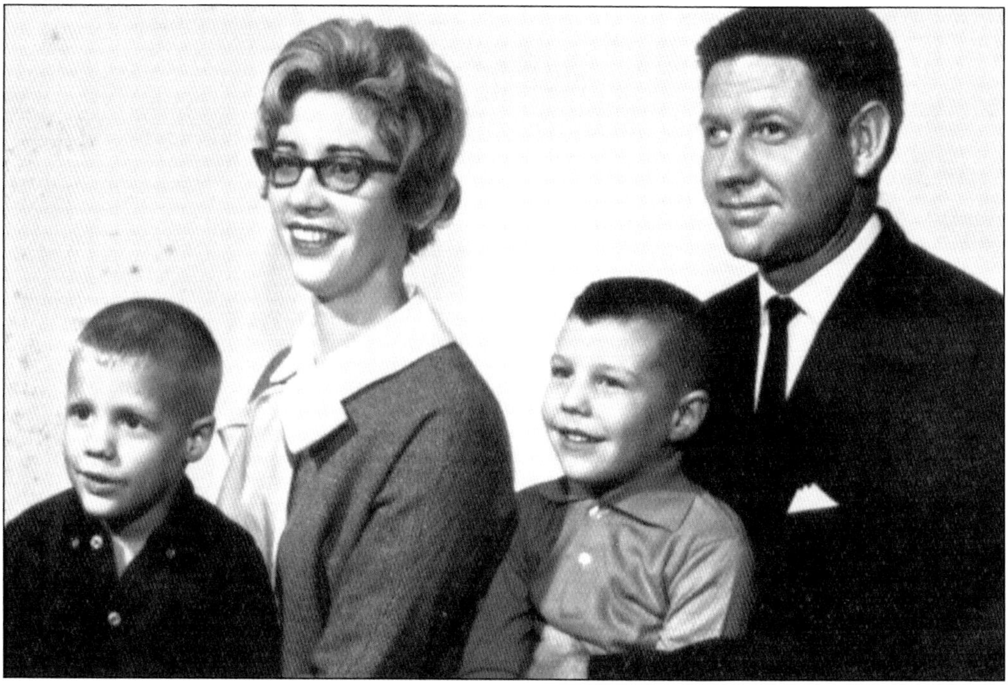

This family portrait was taken at Christmas 1964 of Br. James Spaulding, Barbara, and their two boys. Brother Spaulding was the pastor at Oak Hill Church from 1963 to 1965. (Courtesy Mary Kathryn Pennington Puckett.)

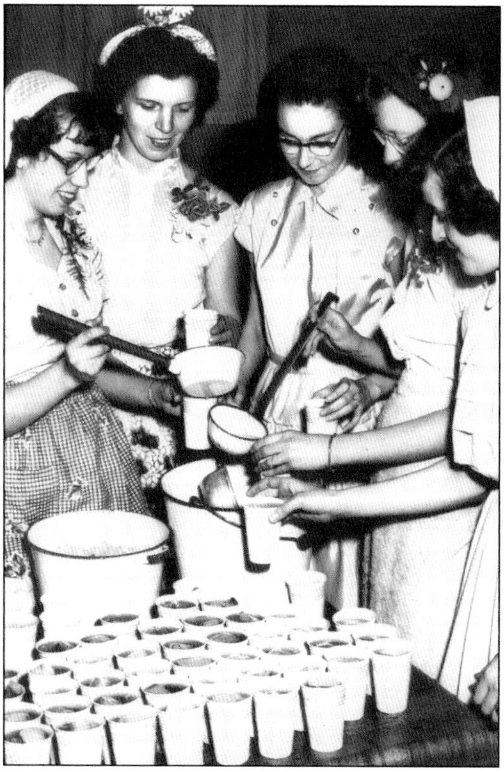

The women of Oak Hill Baptist Church prepare for a social event in the basement. From left to right, Mary Kathryn Pennington Puckett, Evelyn Kincaide Talley, Mary Edith Milby Bell, Louise McCandless Hargrove, and Verna Dean Hornback Cottrell pour drinks from a pail. (Courtesy Mary Kathryn Pennington Puckett.)

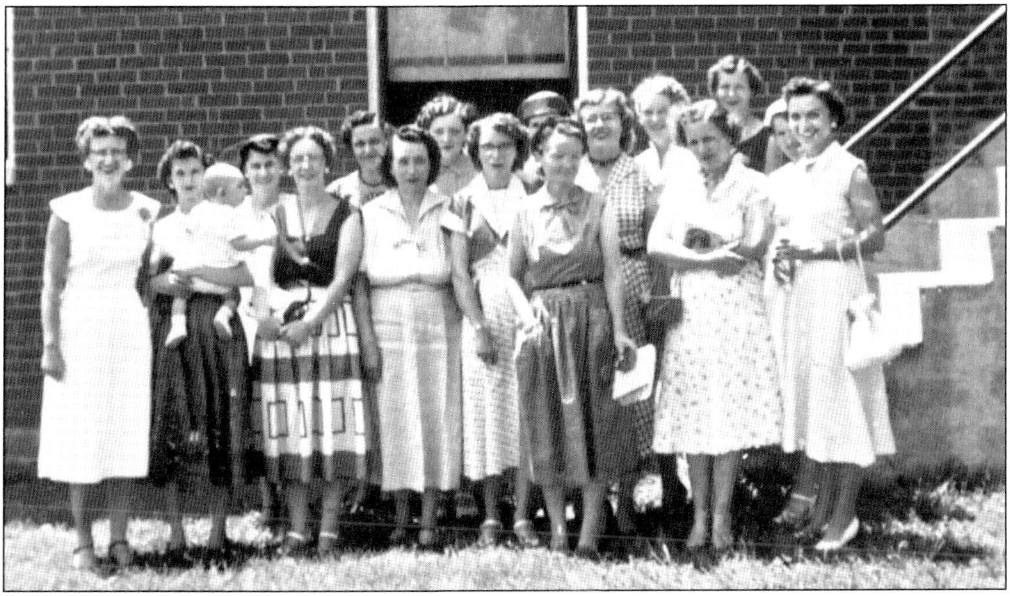

Mount Tabor Baptist Church was established in 1850 with Rev. Jesse P. Bryant as the first pastor. William Brown had named the church after a mountain in Galilee. The first person to be buried in the cemetery was a Revolutionary War soldier by the name of Peter Despain. In 1942, Mount Tabor United Baptist Church was renamed Mount Tabor Missionary Church. This 1956 photograph is the Mount Tabor Women's Sunday school class. Beatrice Gibson is on the far right with a purse on her arm. (Courtesy Beatrice Hornback Gibson.)

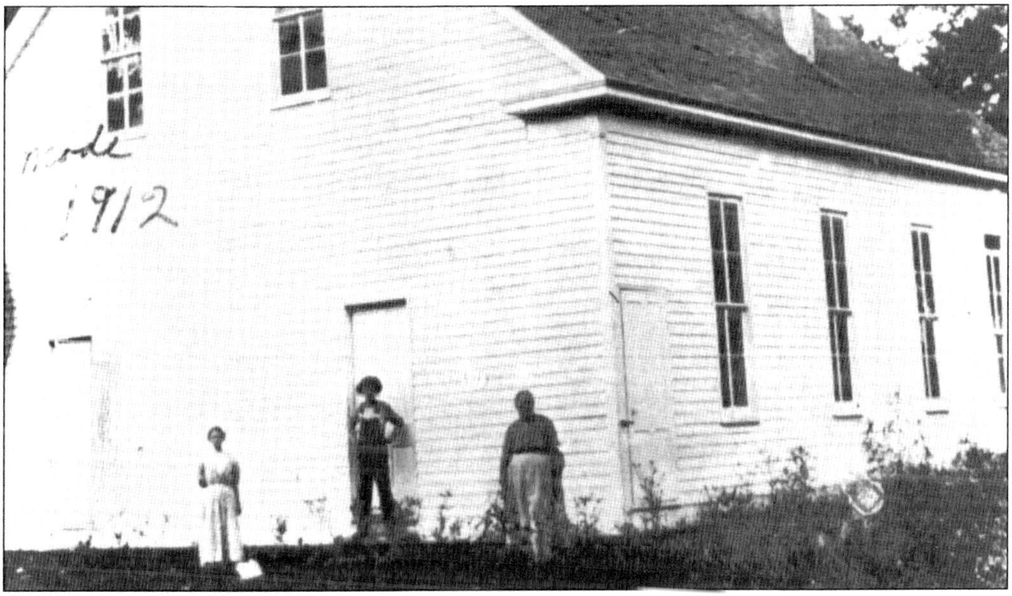

In 1912, Pearl Ann Hornback was 18, Herbert Cruse was 16, and Mollie Hornback was 78 when this photograph was taken of Barren Run Baptist Church. Established in 1850, the church had been used as a hospital during the Civil War by the Union army. The cemetery dates back to the 1840s, and several soldiers were buried there, including Andrew Hornback, Alfred Hornback, James Middleton, William Routt, Burr Sympson, Thomas Obrien, Thomas Phelps, Samuel Phelps, Henry Corum, and Napoleon Ireland. (Courtesy Darlene Routt Bryan.)

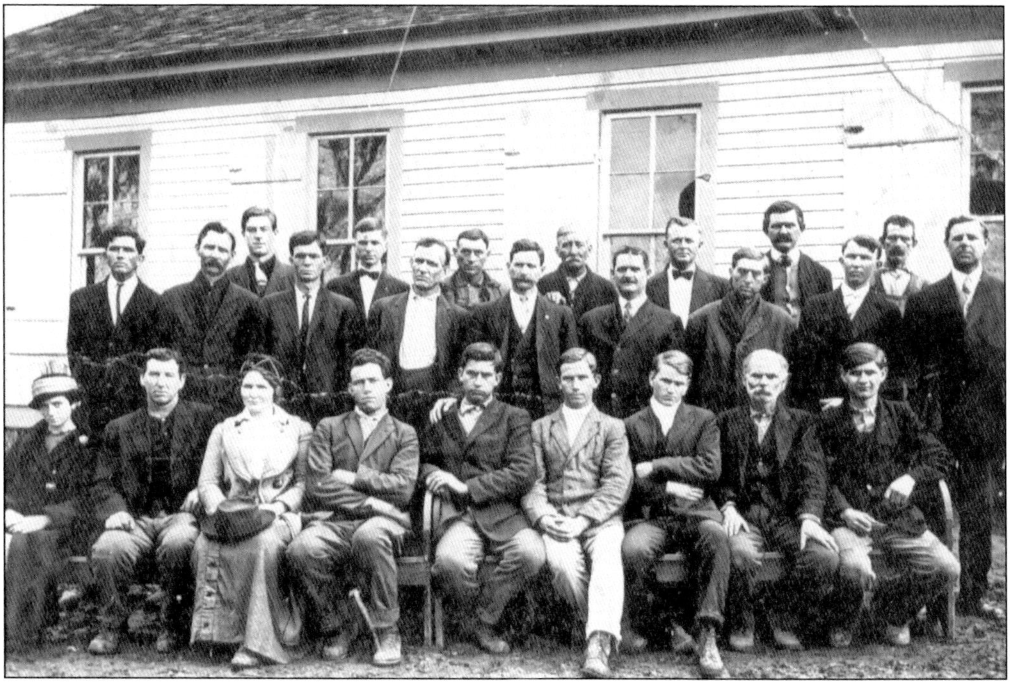

This photograph was taken in 1917 at Barren Run School after a revival. Among the surnames of those attending were Hornback, Massie, and Dixon. (Courtesy Jesse Massie.)

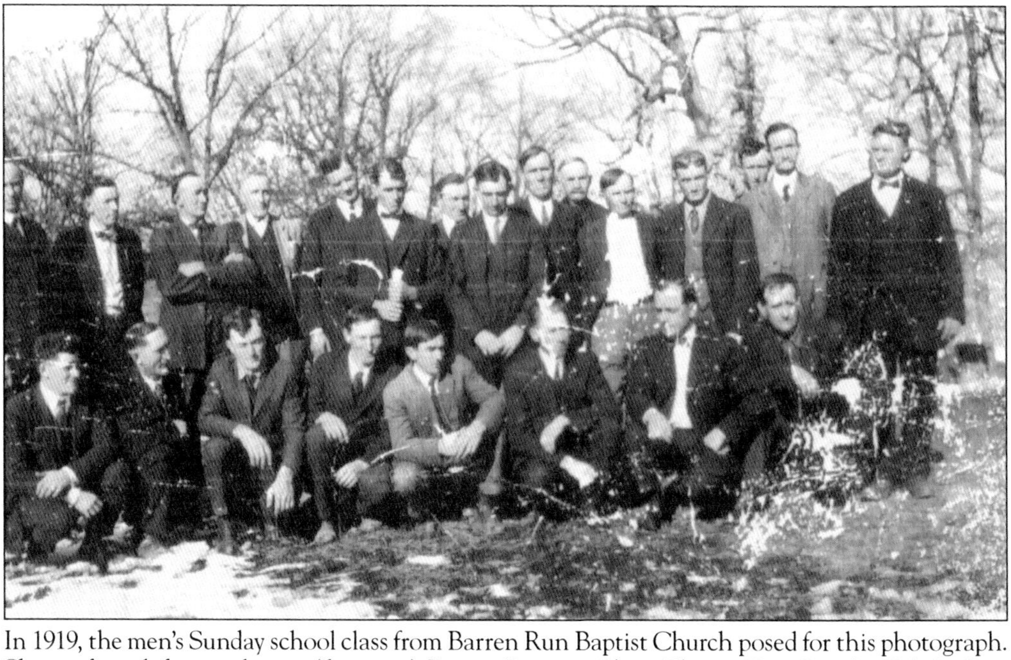

In 1919, the men's Sunday school class from Barren Run Baptist Church posed for this photograph. Shown from left to right are (first row) Dewey Bryant, Chris Tharp, Tom Brooks, Ed Catlett, Cap Routt, Tommy Walters, Erwin Duckworth, and David Earl Hornback; (second row) Wilburn Brashear, Roscoe Miller, Willie Ebb Tucker, Henry Blankenship, Less Williams, Willie Dixon, Earl Catlett, Beeler Routt, Tom Druen, Will Rock, Tom Thurman, Lee Routt, Jim Blankenship, Sam Howard, and Sherman Phippen. (Courtesy Alva Martin Tharp.)

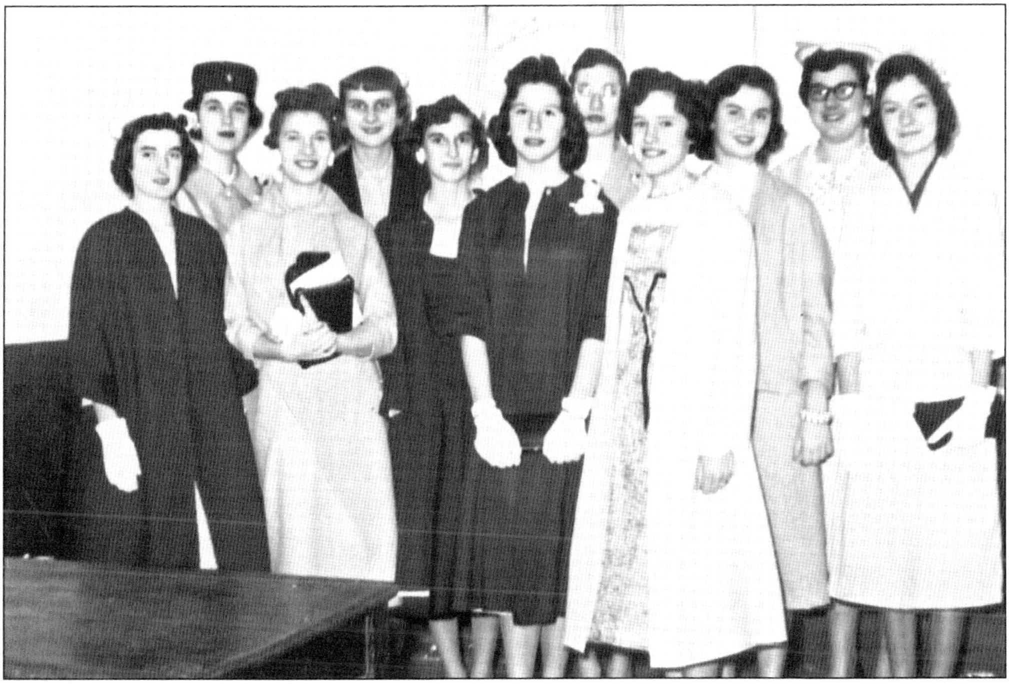

At the Easter Sunday meeting in 1958, the intermediate Sunday school class at Barren Run Baptist Church in Sonora paused for a group photograph. Shown from left to right are (first row) Carolyn Hawkins, Sarah Routt, Wanda Reynolds, Nada Routt, B. J. Rock, Joyce Nunn, and Judy Self; (second row) Jan Allison (teacher), Joyce Cruse, Darlene Routt, and Ann Hazlewood. (Courtesy Darlene Routt Bryan.)

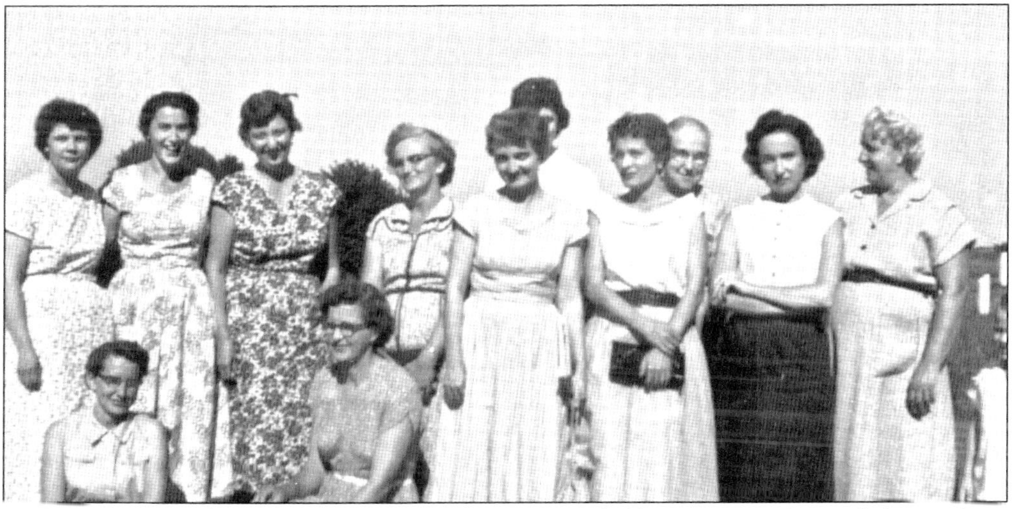

Each summer, teachers and workers pave the way for children's spiritual growth by teaching Christian songs and Bible verses. During the services, children pledge allegiance to the American flag, the Christian flag, and the Bible. Vacation Bible School teachers and workers at Barren Run Baptist Church posed for this photograph in 1957. Pictured from left to right are (first row) Fay Miller and Mable Wells; (second row) Evelyn Catlett, Elizabeth Brooks, Juanita Catlett, Edna Lee Routt, Maude Hawkins, Zelma Hazle, Betty Allison, Gevina Routt, and Glenn Routt; (third row) Jane Allison and Elsie Catlett. (Courtesy Darlene Routt Bryan.)

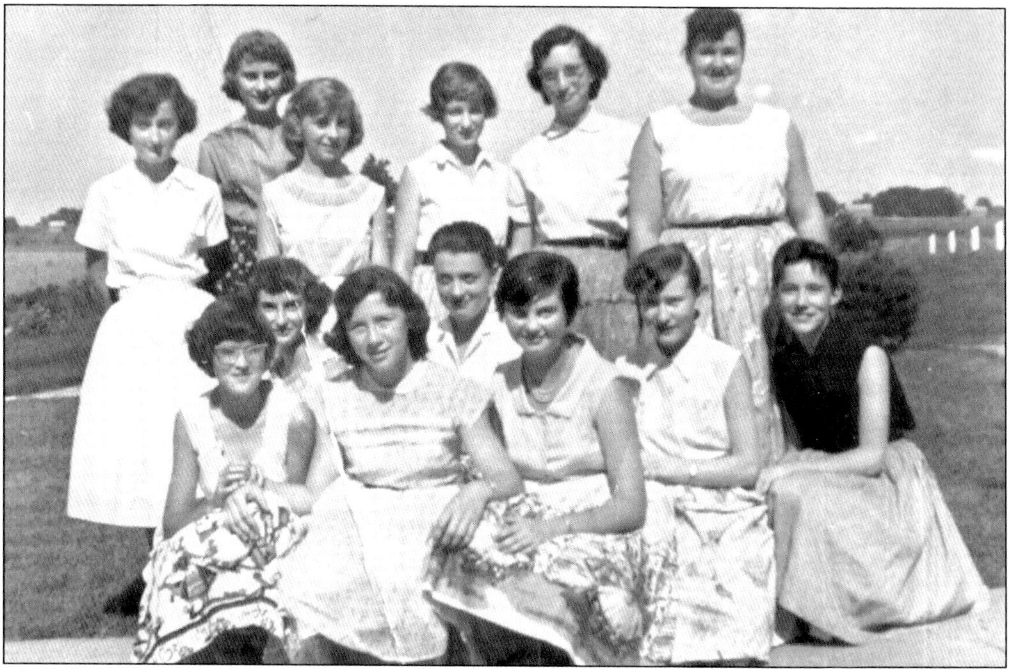

The intermediate class of girls from Barren Run Baptist Church was photographed in 1957. Shown from left to right are (first row, kneeling) Linda Wells, Wanda Reynolds, Nada Routt, Sue Ann Hawkins, Joyce Nunn, Betty Hornback, and B. J. Rock; (second row, standing) Carolyn Hawkins, Joyce Cruse, Shirley Eastridge, Marilyn Routt, Darlene Routt, and Ann Hazlewood. (Courtesy Darlene Routt Bryan.)

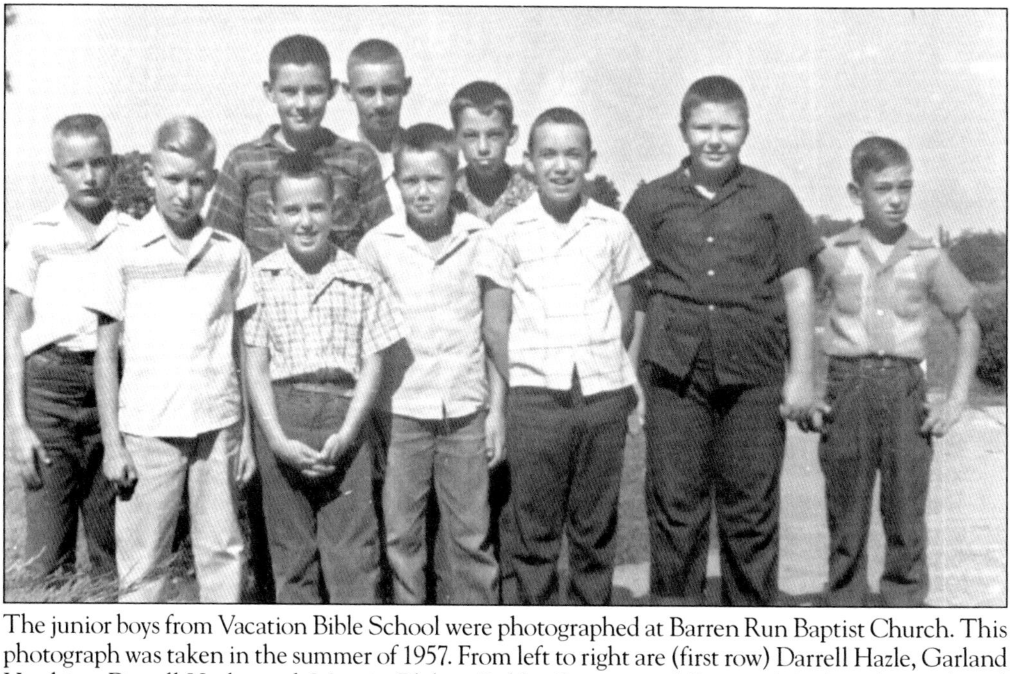

The junior boys from Vacation Bible School were photographed at Barren Run Baptist Church. This photograph was taken in the summer of 1957. From left to right are (first row) Darrell Hazle, Garland Hawkins, Darrell Hazlewood, Marvin Blakey, Bobby Cooper, and Damond Tucker; (second row) Jerry Miller, Wayne Rock, Eston Routt, and Clayton Rock. (Courtesy Darlene Routt Bryan.)

Seven

HOMESTEAD

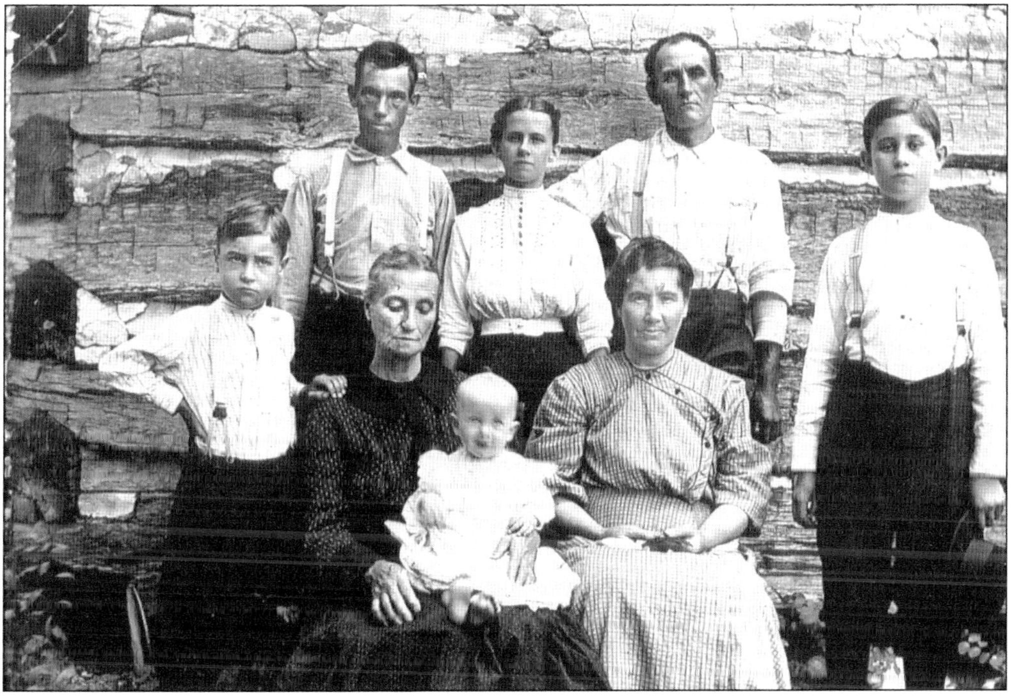

In 1885, the Bowlings posed in front of their cabin. Pictured from left to right are (first row) Raymond Lobb, Elizabeth Lobb Bowling, Leonard Bowling (baby), Mary Bowling Lobb, and Bufford Lobb; (second row) Cleveland Bowling, Mary Lou Tennyson Bowling, and Henry Lobb. Pres. Grover Cleveland had just been elected our 22nd president of the United States. Cleveland was the only president to serve two non-consecutive terms. (Courtesy Darlene Routt Bryan.)

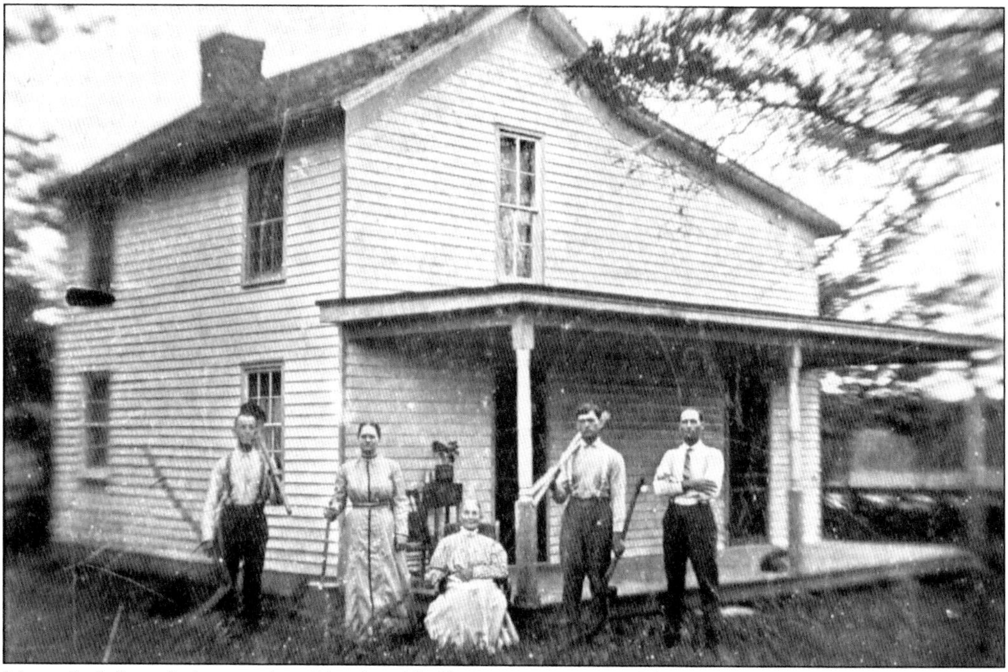

Identified from left to right, Charlie Abell, Marium M. Highbaugh Abell, Margaret Slaughter Abell, Lewis Abell, and James Abell stand by this house with work tools in their hands. This photograph was taken in the early 1900s. This house was built around 1890 by Nicholas Brashears for Steve Froman, from whom James Abell bought the house in 1895. Alva Martin and Anna Mae Tharp raised their children—Carolyn, Sue Ann, James Martin, Hester, and Molly— here in Sonora. The family ran a dairy farm. (Courtesy Alva Martin Tharp.)

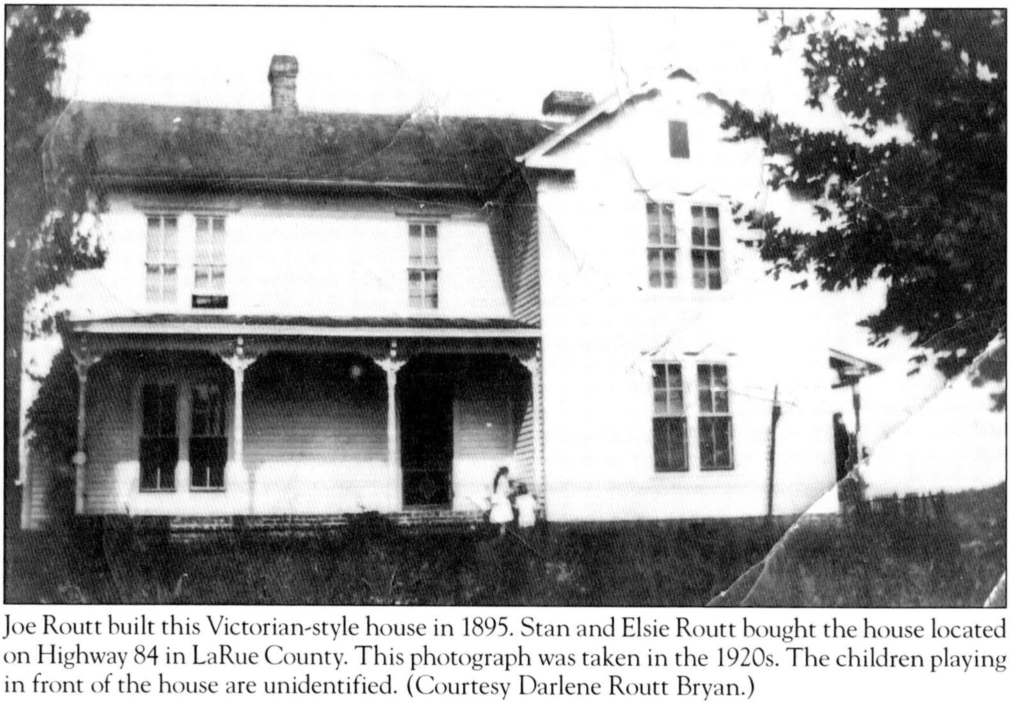

Joe Routt built this Victorian-style house in 1895. Stan and Elsie Routt bought the house located on Highway 84 in LaRue County. This photograph was taken in the 1920s. The children playing in front of the house are unidentified. (Courtesy Darlene Routt Bryan.)

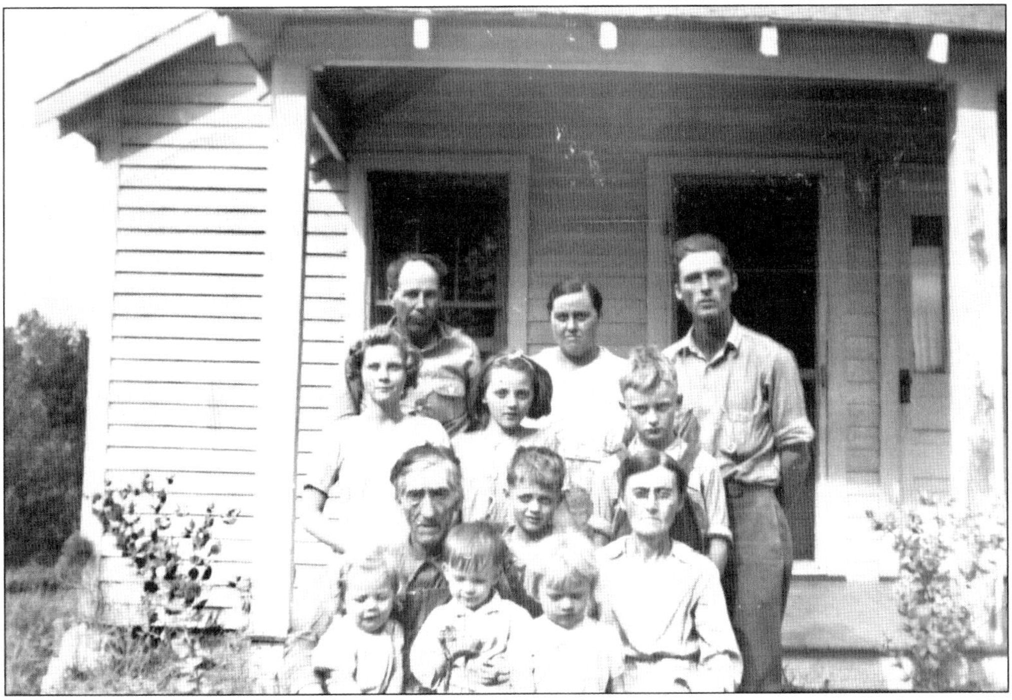

The Hornbacks gather together for this photograph taken around 1945. Shown from left to right are (first row) Harold Hornback, Randall Lee Sallee, and Daisy Hornback; (second row) John Wesley Hornback, Albert Ray Hornback, and Ella Lee Wheeler Hornback; (third row) Lucille Hornback, Kathleen Hornback, and Vernon Hornback; (fourth row) Ray Sallee, Blanch Hornback Sallee, and Herman Hornback. (Courtesy Clifford Hornback.)

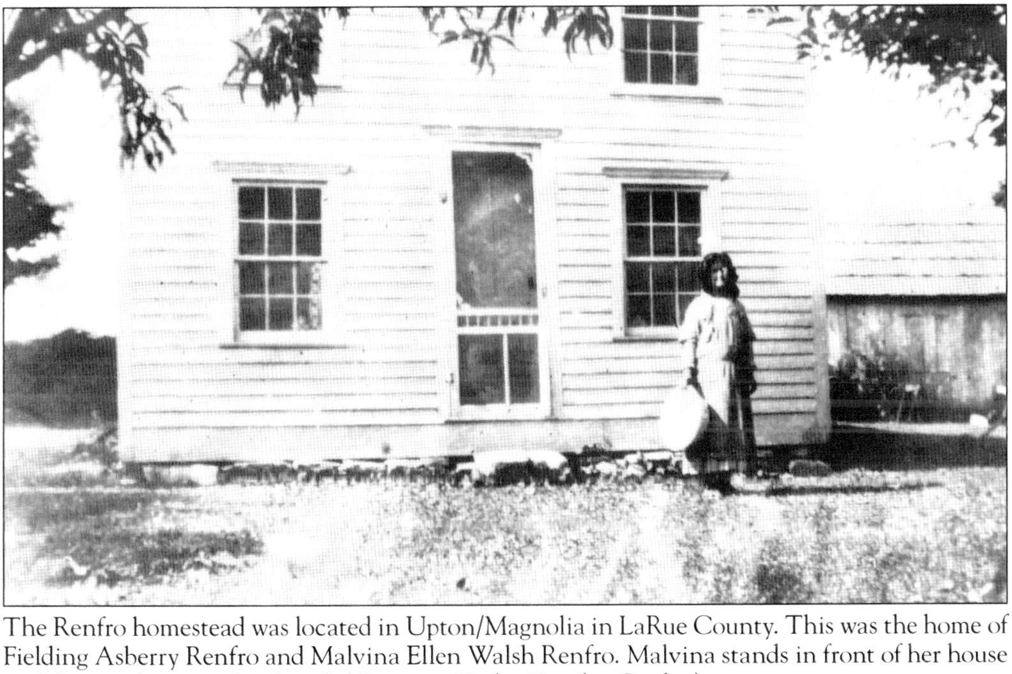

The Renfro homestead was located in Upton/Magnolia in LaRue County. This was the home of Fielding Asberry Renfro and Malvina Ellen Walsh Renfro. Malvina stands in front of her house with her wash pan in her hand. (Courtesy Kathy Hensley Cooke.)

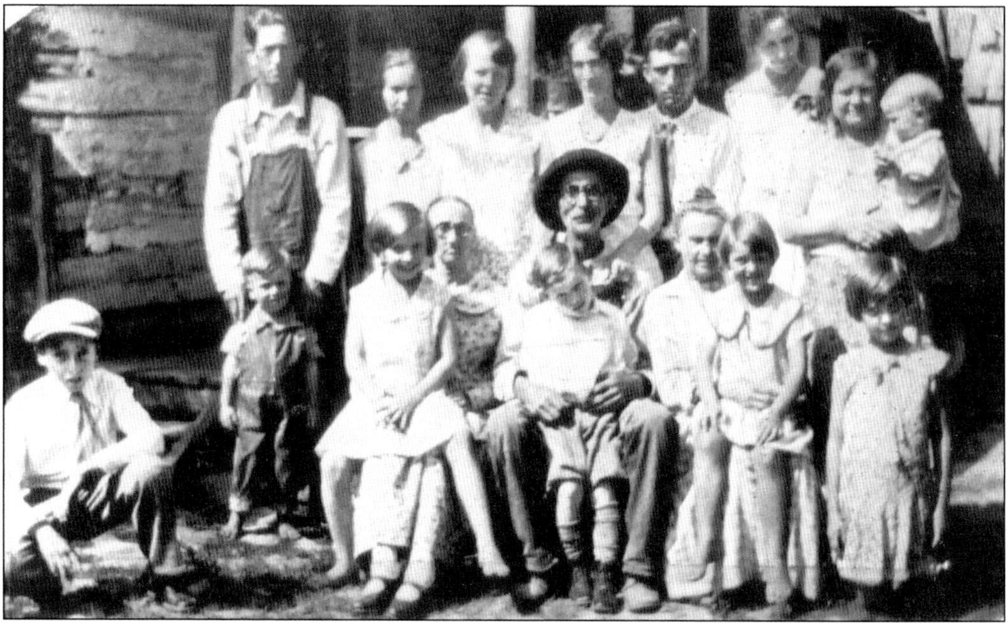

Benjamin Hornback and Martha "Mattie" Wheeler Hornback pose with their family in 1932. From left to right is (first row) Wilburn "Webb" Hornback, Beatrice Hornback in Melvina Hornback's lap, Calvin Hornback in Granddad Benjamin Hornback's lap, Dorothy Hornback in Mattie Hornback's lap, and Juanita Hornback; (second row) Elzie Hornback with son Delmar, Nannie Hodges Hornback, Jo Robinson Hornback, Ira Hornback Angel, Ollie Hornback, Eva Leasor Hornback, and Maude Pearl Jackson Hornback holding Wilma Jean Hornback. (Courtesy Patricia Fields Hornback.)

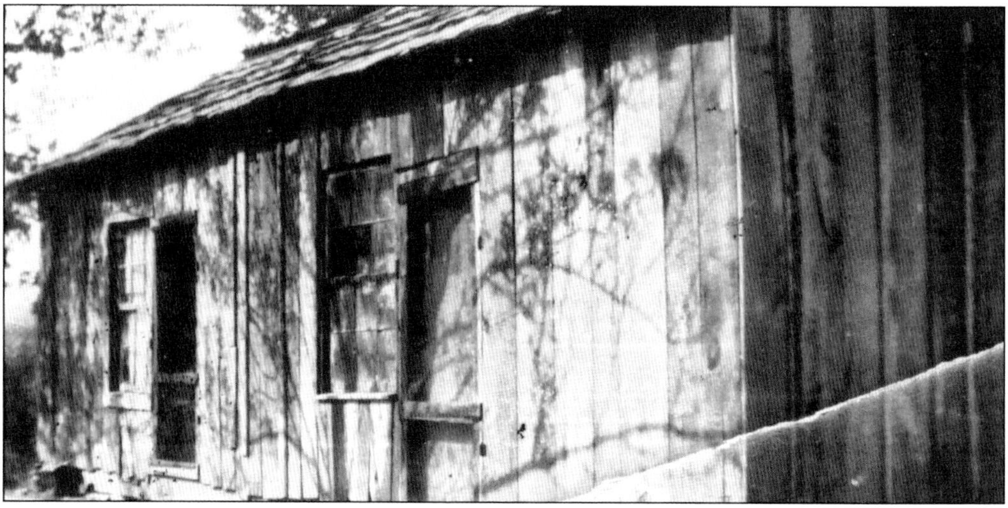

The Walsh homestead was located in Upton, Kentucky. Adgar Walsh and Margaret C. Yates Walsh made this house a home. They raised their family here. Adgar was born December 2, 1824, and died April 28, 1905. Margaret Yates Walsh was born November 24, 1835, and died August 12, 1920. When the couple was starting out in 1852, Harriet Beecher Stowe's novel *Uncle Tom's Cabin* was published regarding anti-slavery. In 1853, Franklin Pierce had become the 14th president of the United States, and in 1857, James Buchanan was inaugurated as the 15th president. (Courtesy Kathy Hensley Cooke.)

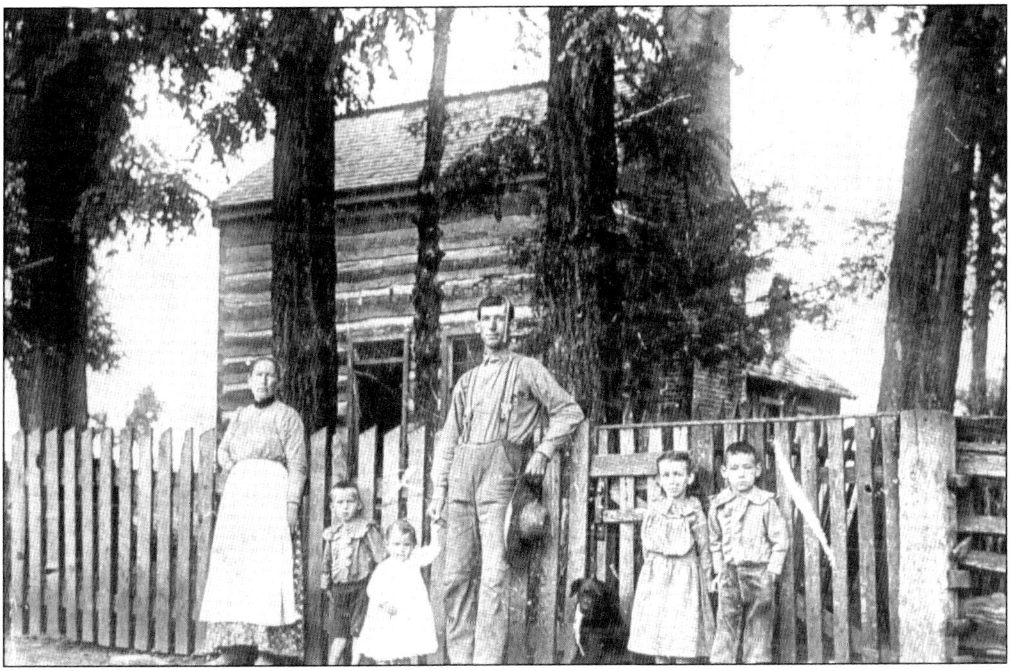

Listed from left to right, Sarah Bell Routt, Troy Routt, Ola Routt, John W. Routt, the family dog, Pearlie Routt, and Dink Routt were photographed at the Omar Routt place on Highway 84 between Sonora and Hodgenville, Kentucky, in 1895. According to the 1890 U.S. Census, the population was 62,947,714. In 1895, African American Frederick Douglass, leader and statesman, died on February 20. (Courtesy Darlene Routt Bryan.)

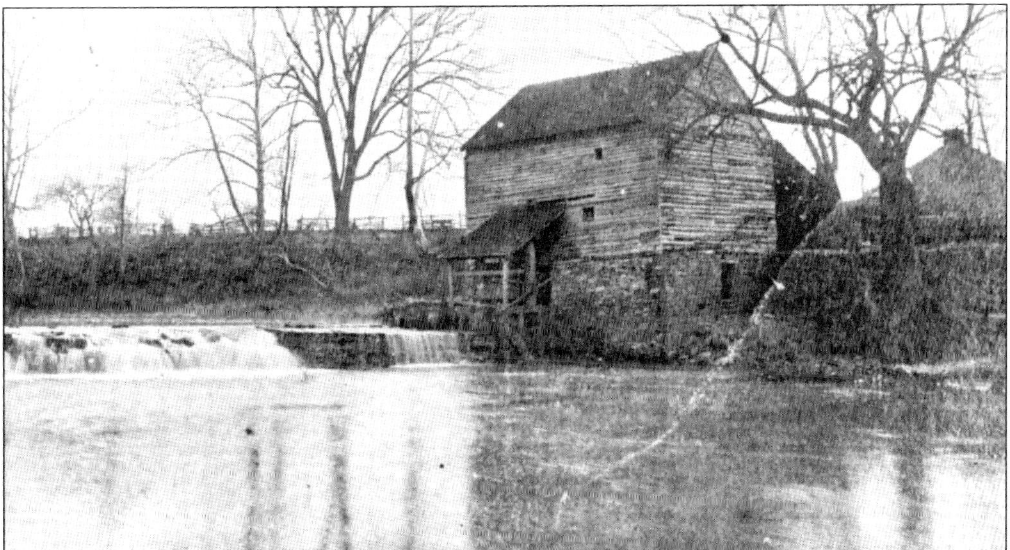

Mather's Mill Bridge is located at Junction 84 on Highway 357 overlooking Nolynn River. Around 1780, Philip Phillips, a Pennsylvania settler and surveyor, brought several settlers into the area with him. These settlers built one of the first settlements on the Nolynn River. On December 9, 1788, one of the original settlers received permission to build a mill on the Nolynn River. (Courtesy Darlene Routt Bryan.)